Sun of Righteousness,
ARISE!

Sun of Righteousness,
ARISE!

God's Future for Humanity and the Earth

JÜRGEN MOLTMANN

Translated by Margaret Kohl

Fortress Press
Minneapolis

SUN OF RIGHTEOUSNESS, ARISE!
God's Future for Humanity and the Earth

First Fortress Press edition 2010

Translated by Margaret Kohl from the German *Sein Name ist Gerechtigkeit: Neue Beiträge zur christlichen Gotteslehre*, published by Gütersloher Verlagshaus, Gütersloh, copyright © 2009.

Cover image: *The Sun* by Edvard Munch (1863-1944) © Scala / Art Resource, NY
Cover design: Paul Boehnke
Interior design: John Goodman (Incite Design Works)
Reproduction of art from *Book of the Dead* on page 130 by John Goodman (Incite Design Works).

Library of Congress Cataloging-in-Publication Data
Moltmann, Jürgen.
Sun of righteousness, arise! : God's future for humanity and the earth / by Jürgen Moltmann ; translated by Margaret Kohl.
  p. cm.
Presented as lectures at meetings of the Gesellschaft for Evangelische Theologie or as essays in the journal, Evangelische Theologie.
Includes index.
ISBN 978-0-8006-9658-0 (alk. paper)
1. Apologetics. 2. God (Christianity) 3. Church history. 4. Theology—History. I. Title.
BT1103.M58195 2010
236—dc22
                              2009042741

The paper used in this publication meets the minimum requirements of American National Standard for Information Sciences—Permanence of Paper for Printed Library Materials, ANSI Z329.48-1984.

Manufactured in the U.S.A.

14   13   12   11   10   1   2   3   4   5   6   7   8   9   10

To the Universidad Evangélica Nicaragüense
in Managua
And the Chung Yuan Christian University
in Chung-Li, Taiwan
in cordial friendship

Contents

PART THREE
GOD IS RIGHTEOUSNESS AND JUSTICE

PART FOUR
GOD IN NATURE

Preface

And this is the name by which he will be called:
The Lord is our righteousness.

The contributions published here came into being during the last ten years, being presented as lectures at meetings of the Gesellschaft für Evangelische Theologie or as essays in the journal *Evangelische Theologie*. They are intended to contribute not only to the specific Christian perception of God, but also to joy in the God of Jesus Christ. The One who lets the sun rise on the evil and the good is himself 'the sun of righteousness'—and this is the title I have given to one of the chapters in the present book.

The order of the contributions in the present book follows three fundamental Christian insights:

God is the God of Christ's resurrection.
God is the righteousness which creates justice and puts things to rights.
The traces and signs of God give the world meaning.

These insights lead us into the wide living spaces of the triune God.

I began to study theology sixty years ago. Theology was for me then, and is still, a fascinating, disturbing and wonderful discipline, an adventure of ideas, a progression into new spheres, and a beginning without end. This book is intended to bring out my experience that it is a profound joy to think about life and death, the future and the earth before God, and what that means theologically. But at the beginning and at the end is always God himself. God is our joy, God is our torment, God is our longing. It is God who draws us and sustains us. We are theologians for God's sake. Theology is a function of God's before it becomes a function of the church.

When I think back, I discover with some surprise that I have always understood Christian theology as a unity, irrespective of the persons who have thought it and maintained it. From Orthodoxy to the Pentecostal movement in Europe, Asia, Africa and America, all theologians belong to the whole of Christendom on earth and to the thousand-year-old *communio theologorum*. In Christ there is neither Jew nor Gentile, neither Greek nor barbarian, neither master nor servant, and neither man nor woman. All become one because the frontiers that divide them have been broken down. And the same is true in Christian theology. Everyone who has contributed something to the knowledge of God must be listened to and taken seriously. Christian theology reaches out beyond denominational frontiers and cultural barriers. Its discussions do not run parallel to confessional boundaries. I myself have never felt the need to defend my own confession towards anyone else, but have taken account of the other traditions with curiosity, and with admiration too, as being complementary to my own. I was ordained in the Reformed tradition and have served as pastor in its congregations, but this tradition is my starting point, not my boundary. To be evangelical in the true sense means thinking ecumenically, for the gospel of Christ—the 'evangel'—is ecumenical. To be Reformed means thinking in life's reforming processes, so as to conform to the gospel: *theologia semper reformanda*, not *semper idem*: theology must always be reformed, not always be the same. Perhaps I am also simply a relic left over from the ecumenical era, which is now supposed to give way to an era of confessional profiles. If that is the case, it is a good thing, for I believe that the only future for a divided Christendom before God, and hence on earth too, is a common future.

At a time when different religious communities are living together in a world threatened by violence, interfaith dialogue is necessary. But this dialogue cannot be carried on just 'for the sake of peace', although this is what is demanded by people for whom religion is a matter of indifference and who therefore maintain that 'one religion is as good as another' or that 'all religions are somehow or other related to God'. The dialogue must be pursued honestly, because of what it is about. But it can only be carried on honestly if it is a dialogue about the truth. Without truth there is no peace in which we can live. And part of honest dialogue is also confrontation, and the 'yes' and 'no.' For me, it is impossible to be tolerant towards satanism, the belief in the devil in the world religions, the religion of death, and the religion of nihilistic destructions. I have no desire for dialogue with religious anti-Semitism. So my concern in this book is to bring out what is *specific, strange and special about the Christian faith*. This by no means leads to a depreciation of other religions, but all the others have a right to discover what Christians believe and what they don't believe. The same is of course true for the others too. For me, what is distinctively Christian is the confession of Christ and belief in the resurrection. I don't know whether all religious people believe in the same God, but I am certain that the same God believes in all human beings, whether they are religious or not, because they are the beings he has created on his beloved earth.

So my concern in this book is also the *consistent Christianization* of the religious and philosophical traditions in Christianity and in theology. I am putting forward here an outline for an idea about the *last judgment* which has Christ at its centre and no longer takes its bearings from the Egyptian judgment of the dead. This is not a matter of speculations about a far-off future. It has to do with overcoming the deadly friend-enemy thinking of the Armageddon warriors and the Islamic terrorists here and now. The last judgment is the world's salvation, not its annihilation, just as Gretchen, we are told in Goethe's *Faust,* is *gerichtet—gerettet*: judged—saved. I am fully aware that here I am challenging, and putting up for discussion, ancient traditions in historic Christianity. In doing so I am developing further the victim-orientated doctrine of justification which I published earlier.[1]

In the last part of this book, the section on God in nature, I am trying to continue the conversation which I began in 2002 in the book *Science and Wisdom* (ET 2003)—the conversation between the sciences and theology. In the section on resurrection in nature, I have thought about the natural world in the perspective of Christ's resurrection, and the cosmic Christology which follows from that; while the chapter within this section, entitled 'The Resurrection of Nature: The New Creation of All Things', has to do with the signs and lights through which the natural world points to the indwelling presence of God's Spirit. This transcendent divine immanence is part of a *natural theology* which sees itself as a response and resonance to a *theology of nature*. Nature in the perspective of Christ's resurrection points to God in its language of natural signs. We come a step closer to the community of the sciences and cultural studies if we ask about the meaning of what we can scientifically know. Do we understand what we know? The *hermeneutics of nature* I am putting forward here could be a bridge between the sciences and theology, a bridge that can be crossed in both directions.

I am still continually surprised at the great number of dissertations which have been written in different countries, seminaries or faculties about my theology and its problems, for my real intention was only to gain clarity about my own problems. But it is what is concrete that is apparently the relevant thing, and experience-based theology appears to be universal theology. The response to my theological attempts of course gives me pleasure, the more so since I hope that through their study of my own reflections the authors have arrived at their own theological ways forward.

PART ONE

THE FUTURE OF CHRISTIANITY

In the winter semester of 1899/90, in Berlin, the great liberal Protestant Adolf von Harnack held his famous series of lectures, '*What Is Christianity*'. So I should like to begin by recalling what was called Christianity in the nineteenth century, especially in the German Empire. More particularly, we shall look at the 'culture Protestantism' which was a part of that, and which Harnack represented.

In the twentieth century, with the First World War, the age of catastrophes began. The war put an end to the 'Christian Century' and 'the Christian World' (to quote the names of two important Protestant journals). What we experienced afterwards was what, in 1927, Otto Dibelius called 'a century of the church'. In Germany this was the transition from the state church to the *Volkskirche*, the so-called people's church, which was supposed to serve everyone. Yet today the churches are minorities in multifaith and secular societies. But they are minorities in an ecumenical, worldwide community and with a universal mission. So my theses in this essay can be reduced to simple formulas:

1. The future of Christianity is the church;
2. The future of the church is the kingdom of God.

1

The Christian World

The nineteenth century truly was 'the Christian age', not just for Europe but for the rest of the world too. Christianity determined not only its churches but its 'world' as well, in public life, in politics and in culture. We call this worldwide complex 'Christianity', 'Christendom', '*cristianidad*', meaning by that not just 'the essence of Christianity', as we might also talk about the essence of Judaism or Buddhism in whatever cultural form they may take, but the form it takes in the world.

In the nineteenth century the Christian nations of Europe became great powers on a worldwide scale. For these nations, this century became the age of progress and expansion. Continually new scientific discoveries and technical inventions brought them a tremendous growth in power: from the locomotive to the motor car, from the sailing ship to the steamship, from the telegraph to the telephone, from classical physics to the relativity theory, and so forth. 'Knowledge is power', Francis Bacon had proclaimed at the beginning of modern times. The immense progress in knowledge during the nineteenth century gave the European nations the increased power with which they believed they could advance to universal domination. By means of education, from the primary school to the university, a nation's own people, and then the peoples of the world as well, could be led out of the night of superstition into the light of reason.

The Christian nations in Europe conquered their colonial empires in Africa and Asia and spread Europe's 'Christian civilization' with messianic missionary zeal. They all participated: Holland in Indonesia, Belgium in the Congo, Italy in Libya and Eritrea, and finally Germany too, in East Africa and 'the German Southwest' [Namibia]. The rest already belonged to the British Empire, which stretched from Calcutta to Cape Town and Cairo, as Cecil Rhodes boasted. In the United States, the transcontinental railroad carried settlers west; in Russia the Trans-Siberian Railway took the Cossacks as far as Vladivostock. By 1900 the time was not far off when the great Christian powers would carve up China too among themselves. Little was needed for the whole inhabited globe to become Christian.

Even then there was already an unspoken ecumenical community among the national Christian religions in Europe. We can see this from the domed buildings of the national churches, which followed the model of the Hagia Sophia in Byzantium and St Peter's in Rome: St Paul's in London, St Isaac's Cathedral in St Petersburg, the Sacré Coeur in Paris, and the Berlin Cathedral in Prussian Germany.

It is no wonder that these expansions of European Christianity into the world of the nations conduced to messianic notions about Christianity's end-time domination of the world, nor was it surprising that the unheard-of progress in science and technology should have led to a limitless secular faith in progress.

We call messianic notions about Christian lordship over the world *chiliastic* or *millenarian* if they use the image of 'the Thousand Years' Empire' in which, according to Revelation 20, Christ and those who are his will rule the world and judge the nations. We call them *messianic* if they already determine and enthuse the present here and now.[1]

These millenarian visions go back to 'the image of the monarchies' in Daniel 7, which counts as an early theopolitical picture of world history. The four bestial empires rise up one after another out of the sea of chaos, each being destroyed by the next. The last of them is the Roman Empire. But then God will send from heaven on to earth the humane kingdom of the Son of Man: 'His dominion is an everlasting dominion, which shall not pass away, and his kingdom one that shall not be destroyed' (7.14). 'And the kingdom and the dominion and the greatness of the kingdoms under the whole heaven shall be given to the people of the saints of the Most High; and their kingdom shall be an everlasting kingdom' (7.27). Although according to Daniel this divine kingdom of the Son of Man is an alternative to the violent empires of chaos in history, in the early political theology of Byzantium and later in Spain, it was held to be 'the fifth world empire' and put on a level with the others.[2] As heir to the preceding world empires of the Persians, Greeks and Romans, 'the Christian universal monarchy' is supposed to complete world history and will finally be victorious in the struggle for world domination. All the other empires will be annihilated by the 'stone of Daniel' (Dan. 2), or 'the fire of Daniel' (Dan. 7), until in the end all the nations will be 'one flock under one shepherd'. After the victorious struggle against the Moors, it was with this political theology that the Spanish court theologians justified the conquest of the Aztec, Mayan and Inca kingdoms in Latin America. That was the so-called messianism of the Iberian cultures.[3]

This was also 'the new world order' with which history and its conflicts were to be consummated in a universal empire of eternal peace. *Novus ordo saeclorum* is impressed on the seal of the United States and on every one-dollar note. This messianic solemnity is still inherent in the political culture of the United States today.[4] Every president invokes anew his messianic destiny for the world.

In the 'old world' of Europe, the emotional fervour of 'modern times' took over the corresponding messianic role in firing the sense of superiority and the will to bring history to its completion. The transition from the conflicts and crises of history into the perfected state of eternal peace was dated 'now' by the prophets of modernity such as Lessing and Kant, Hegel and Marx: what had once been merely awaited could now be realized. After the ancient world and the Middle Ages, modern times are now beginning. That is the end time. The end of history is now almost within our grasp, and it will be our era, 'the Christian era'. After the age of revolutions, the age of evolution is now beginning, and its progress will have no end. The kingdom of God is coming so close to us in the kingdom of Christ that without any apocalyptic catastrophes it can now already be made the greatest good of morality and the highest goal of cultural developments in all spheres of life. That is the moral and teleological form of the kingdom of God taught by liberal Protestantism from Immanuel Kant to Albrecht Ritschl.[5]

Throughout the whole era, the educated classes in Europe and New England cherished the dream of the moral improvement of humanity. My grandfather was the headmaster of a private school and the grand master of a Freemasons' Lodge in Hamburg. On his gravestone stands instead of some comforting verse from the Bible, Lessing's hopeful sentence from his essay 'On the Education of the Human Race' (1777, § 88): 'It will come, it will surely come, the time of perfecting , when man . . . will do the right just because it is the right.' But neither he nor most of the educated people of his time realized that this moral optimism had an ancient apocalyptic presupposition: that the good can only spread unhindered because in the Thousand Years' Empire 'Satan has been bound for a thousand years' (Rev. 20.2-4). For Christendom, Lessing and Kant had already proclaimed the 'transition from the historical faith of the church to the general faith in reason', a transition which was supposed to begin *now*, with the general Enlightenment.

For inward reasons of faith and for external sociological ones, Protestantism was the first of the Christian confessions in western Europe and the United States to enter into the modern world. For many people liberal Protestantism became the convincing cultural form of Christianity. After the old Byzantine symbiosis of throne and altar, after the feudalist and monarchist symbiosis of hierarchy and class society, among the progressive middle classes of the nineteenth century a new unity developed between personal belief and modern culture, a unity which Friedrich Schleiermacher insistently invoked in his introductory letters to Lücke.[6] Modern university foundations with theological faculties at their head, and private universities in the United States with divinity schools in their forefront, were directed towards the evangelization and education of humanity in their own country and of other nations as well. 'Hurrying towards Zion' was the clear future goal of these educational institutions.[7]

Sharp-eyed theologians were well aware of the distinction between this cultural Protestantism, with its joyful proclamation of progress, and Jesus' preaching about the kingdom of God, or the persecuted Christianity of earliest times, for the very reason that they expected from this cultural Protestantism the approach to the future kingdom of God. I may give two examples:

1. Johannes Weiss was a New Testament scholar and the son-in-law of Albrecht Ritschl. In 1882 (revised edition 1900) he published a book which made a considerable stir called *Die Predigt Jesu vom Reich Gottes*.[8] As a historian he maintains that 'The kingdom of God is in Jesus' view an entirely supernatural entity which is in exclusive contrast to this world. That means that in the thinking of Jesus there can be no question of the kingdom of God's developing within this world'. But as 'a Christian belonging to his own time' he declared: 'The real difference between our modern Protestant world view and that of the first Christians is hence that we do not share the eschatological mood . . . We no longer pray "may grace come and the world pass away"; we live in the joyful confidence that this world will increasingly become the stage for "God's own humanity".'

2. This happy confidence in the world, then, was the mood of 1900. But fifty years earlier, for Richard Rothe, a Hegel pupil and the chairman of the Baden Protestant Association in Heidelberg, it was not just a mood. It was a firm conviction about the now

possible and necessary transition from the church to the kingdom of God on earth. Ultimately God wills the state, the perfected state, the moral theocracy, because he desires mature human beings. The pious churchgoer is a thing of the past, and is now replaced by the responsible Christian as an independent citizen in the realm of morality and culture. For in the progress of world history Christ himself is striding ahead. He is in the process of relinquishing his provisional way of life in the form of the church, and of acquiring his final, moral and political kingdom. Once that has been achieved, the church will have made itself superfluous, since it was a necessary but provisional educational institution. That is perfect millenarianism in modern secular form.[9] Only in Christ's consummating kingdom does the Christian spirit abandon the form its life has taken in the church, and become the 'soul' of the worldwide political commonwealth, which will then for its part become 'the body of Christ'.

The Primal European Catastrophe and the End of Modern Christendom

The age of progress and expansion which began in the West with the industrial and the democratic revolution ended in 1914 in what George Steiner rightly called the 'primal European catastrophe' of the First World War. Afterwards nothing was the same. The age of catastrophes began. Verdun and Stalingrad, Auschwitz and Gulag Archipelago are names typifying the unimaginable crimes against humanity which marked the twentieth century. In them the progressive, modern, Christian world destroyed itself.

Without any justified or even detectable reasons for the war, the great Christian powers in Europe, which were just about to divide up the rest of the world between themselves, fell upon each other. It was a war of annihilation without any victory aims. A true symbol for this was the battle of Verdun in 1916.[10] The German idea was that it was to be 'a battle of attrition'. After six months there were more than 600,000 dead and almost no gains or losses of territory. In Ypres the Germans began the poison-gas war and profited nothing by it. It was only the intervention of the United States in 1917 which decided the war between the great European powers. In Germany the patriotic enthusiasm for the war developed into the pure nihilism with which Hitler continued and completed the task of destroying Europe in the Second World War. In the Soviet Union, Stalin exterminated whole classes and peoples through hard labour and hunger in the Gulag Archipelago. I need not describe any further what 'the age of catastrophes' brought on us in the twentieth century, because we may hope that with the end of the East-West conflict in 1989 this catastrophic age has also become a thing of the past.

What happened in 1914? The English foreign secretary Edward Grey found the apt word when he said: 'The lamps are going out all over Europe, and we shall not see them lit again in our lifetime.' At the same time the lights of progress toward a better world, and the blessings to be conferred on the world through colonization, went out too. 'The Christian world' collapsed and 'the Christian era' ended. This was not indeed what Oswald Spengler called in 1922 'the downfall of the West',[11] but what followed was nonetheless 'an end to the modern world', as Romano Guardini wrote after the Second World War.

A depressing sign of the self-inflicted end was the religious enthusiasm for the war which in August 1914 seized not only students but even the most famous German professors. On 4 October 1914 a 'Call to the Civilized World' appeared, signed by ninety-three of the best-known professors, among them Adolf von Harnack, Max Planck, Gustav Röntgen, and twelve Catholic and Protestant theologians. The call ended as follows:

> You who know us, who hitherto together with us have cherished the supreme possession of mankind, to you we appeal: believe us when we say that we shall fight this fight to the

finish as a civilized nation, for which the legacy of a Goethe, a Beethoven, a Kant is as sacred as its own hearth and acre.[12]

With this, for the men who had signed the declaration, their own 'civilized nation' replaced the shared civilized world, and their 'own hearth' took the place of humanity. A little later the German 'Ideas of 1914' were published, signed by more than 250 German intellectuals.[13] They were against the ideas of the French Revolution, and were therefore also against the principles of Kant, with his idea of world citizenship, a league of nations, and eternal peace. These ideas were replaced by Hegel's notion of the national spirit and his justification of the national state on the grounds of world history. German *Kultur* was to be elevated above French *civilisation*, and German 'idealism' over the English shop-keeper mentality. After the war this was bitterly regretted by Ernst Troeltsch, an important representative of *Kulturprotestantismus*.

2

The Rebirth of the Church

The great event of the twentieth century was the end of Christendom, the Christian era and the Christian nations, and the beginning of the church's rebirth as an independent and resisting community, a community with a universal mission and an all-embracing hope for the kingdom of God as the future of the world. As far as the Protestant church in Germany was concerned, I may name three factors.

1. In 1919 the constitution of the Weimar democracy put a legal end to the state church, and with that also ended the position of the princely rulers as head of the church in their domains. The Protestant regional churches still certainly remained public corporations, but they were obliged to give themselves their own, synodal and episcopal constitutions. They lost their role as the public religion of a Christian society, and could again cast back to their own proper form of existence as gathered community. This meant that the state became religiously speaking neutral, and society secular. The national Christian religions disappeared from the western European countries, giving way first to mixed denominational societies and today to multifaith ones. Nowadays all the churches, not just the Protestant ones, are becoming minorities in modern, partly secular, partly multifaith, societies.

A notable phenomenon is that during the same period the ecumenical movement came into being, and made the national and the minority churches members of a worldwide Christian community. Every church in its own society represented not just itself but 'the whole of Christendom on earth'—and that means a third of the human race, today about two billion out of six billion people. So in their own particular societies the churches have universal tasks and interests. For many Christians, in situations of conflict ecumenical solidarity is more important than national loyalty. I am a Christian first of all, and only after that a German. That is why after the Second World War the Protestant church in Germany renamed itself. It is no longer 'The German Protestant Church' (*Die Deutsche Evangelische Kirche*); it is now 'The Protestant Church in Germany' (*Die Evangelische Kirche in Deutschland*). Germany is the place where it is situated, but not its key signature or its primary designation.

2. In 1924 Adolf von Harnack published his last great book, which he called *Marcion. Das Evangelium vom fremden Gott* ('Marcion, the Gospel of the Alien God').[1] His thesis ran: 'To condemn the Old Testament in the second century was a mistake which the major church rightly rejected; to retain it in the sixteenth century was a fate which the Reformation was not yet able to escape; but still to conserve it in the nineteenth century as a canonical document in Protestantism is the outcome of religious and ecclesiastical paralysis' (1960 German ed., p. 217). With this outrageous thesis he was merely enforcing what Schleiermacher had said about Judaism in his book *The Christian Faith* and what he himself had described as 'the essence of Christianity'.[2] It is not by chance that it was in the degree to which the Protestant church became independent and resistant that the Old Testament was rediscovered, and a new relationship to Judaism began.[3] Of course the search for a positive relationship to the Jews was part of the period after Auschwitz, but the discovery of the presence of the Old Testament in the gospel of Christ was also a way of combating the paganization of Christianity and its dissolution into a religion

of society. And not least, it contributed to the rediscovery of the Christian faith's horizon of hope.[4]

3. The disintegration in the First World War of the Protestant culture Christianity we have described was perceived early on, and in its wake Karl Barth and the friends of dialectical theology began to develop a specifically 'church dogmatics'. Now theology was no longer to be the scholarly enquiry into the Christian religion, and Protestant theology was no longer to be a Protestant cultural discipline; it was to be quite consciously a 'church study': theology is a function of the church.[5] Later Barth said several times that the reason why he turned away from the liberal theology of his teachers was his shock over their avowed support for the warlike policy of the emperor William II. But that was certainly not the only reason for his turn from Christian culture to the church of Christ. Later on it was much more emphatically the way the so-called German Christians brought the Protestant church into line with National Socialism, and the rise of the resisting Confessing Church, in which he himself played a definitive part. However, after the Second World War, Barth's 'churchification' of theology led in Germany to the church's self-chosen retreat from the public forums of contemporary society. This was contrary to Barth's intention. But it left public life to other forces, as can be seen from the recent debates about instruction in ethics as alternative to religion in the schools of the new states of the Federal Republic (that is, those formerly belonging to East Germany, the GDR).

Summing up, it may be said that following the end of culture Christianity we find:
1. the rebirth of an independent church in the contexts of its ecumenical breadth;
2. a new theology of the church;
3. the rediscovery of the Old Testament as a living force, and the

search for new community with the synagogue;
4. a new turn to the future.

Three Paradigms for the Church

What form will the church find for itself in modern society, as a way of fulfilling its mandate for the time?

I believe that for the church the new millennium will be a millennium of the Holy Spirit. And I believe that not on the basis of ancient apocalyptic prophecies,[6] but because of present experience among the congregations. Today we are experiencing more than ever before the fellowship and manifold energies of God's life-giving Spirit. In saying that I am not simply lauding the successes of the worldwide Pentecostal movement, which has meanwhile become the second largest group in Christendom. I mean rather a transformation in the fundamental paradigm of the church. We see this transformation both in the young churches of the Third World and in the old churches in Europe. What are the different paradigms for the church?

The Hierarchical Paradigm

The first paradigm, in the Graeco-Roman world, was the hierarchy, the 'holy rule' under the monarchy of God the Father. From the time of Ignatius of Antioch, who is numbered among the apostolic fathers, the 'monarchical' episcopate which we can still see today in the Roman Catholic Church held sway: *one God—one bishop—one community or church.* In the political world, one ruler on earth corresponds to the one God in heaven, and in similar correspondence to the one God in heaven is the one bishop and high priest of humanity, as God's representative in religion. We find here a uni-linear structure of authority from God the Father by way of 'the Holy Father', to every priest who acts as 'father' to his congregation. This order consists of ordained 'spiritual pastors', that is bearers of the Spirit, to whom the 'ordinary' people in the church, 'the laity', are subordinate. If the church is identified in a one-sided way with the hierarchy and its functions, then the task of 'the laity' can only be to say 'Amen' to the liturgical, dogmatic and moral instructions of the hierarchy. This is in pure form a church for looking after people; it is not a self-confident church *of* God's people. It is the priest who 'represents' Christ to the people. He is Christ in person; the congregation is the recipient of the church's gifts of grace. A visible sign of this distinction between priests and laity was the separation at the Eucharistic communion: wine for the priest—bread for the people. It was the struggle about the cup for the laity which once provoked the Hussite Reformation. Another visible sign of distinction is the ordination of men only, not women. West European laicism is a product of Roman-Catholic hierarchism. It is widespread in the Catholic countries of France, Spain, Portugal and Italy. Laicist religious freedom is a negative freedom *from* religion, and laicist reason is an emphatically atheistic reason.

It was only after the Second Vatican Council that for the first time the image of the whole 'people of God' was added to the hierarchical image of 'the mystical body of Christ' which was organized from the head down.[7] According to this image, priests and laity belong together to the people of God. They are distinguished through their different tasks and functions. With its declaration about the general priesthood of all believers, Vatican II took an important step beyond the hierarchical paradigm, but it was only half a step, for the consecrated priesthood has still a special status, and is distinguished from the general priesthood.[8]

Today, in order to link hierarchy and community, the vertical and the horizontal, people like to talk in Catholic theology about a *communio hierarchica*. Practically speaking, this can only mean that the life of the church will be furthered by a mixture between elected congregational bodies, synods and councils and the hierarchy. The problematical areas are obvious: 1. the relationship between laity and clergy, 2. the relationship between women and men, 3. the relationship of local churches to the (Roman) universal church.

Reciprocity will take the place of the one-sided authoritarian structure. In the Western world, the Roman Catholic Church is today
undergoing what the then Cardinal Ratzinger called a remarkable
'congregationalization'. We see it happening before our eyes: a
parish—a particular area where a single pastorate is responsible for
the religious care of the people living there—is becoming a congregation which is making itself the determining subject of its own
history. More and more cross-connections within the community
are being introduced into the vertical structure of authority and
obedience. Some of the internal problems of the Roman Catholic
Church are coming to the surface in this paradigm change, for it
calls in question the previous authoritarian and unified form of the
universal church.

The Christocentric Paradigm

After the Reformation, the Protestant churches introduced a different paradigm as a way of interpreting the nature and unity of
the church: the christocentric paradigm. Christ, the incarnate Son
of God, is the head of his body and effects the unity of his church.
What unity? As 'the only begotten Son of God' he is at the same
time 'the firstborn among many brothers and sisters' (Rom. 8.29).
So his brotherhood with many brings them together into a community which is understood as the community of Christ.[9] 'The
Christian Church is the congregation of the brethren [and sisters]
in which Jesus Christ acts presently as the Lord in Word and sacrament through the Holy Spirit.' That is the definition in Thesis III
of the Barmen Theological Declaration of the Confessing Church,
which was drawn up in 1934.[10] Fellowship with Christ makes
the church a brotherly and sisterly community of equals, which
is what Gal. 3.28 already said it should be: 'here there is neither
Jew nor Greek, neither slave nor free, there is neither male nor
female, for you are all one in Christ Jesus.' All are God's children
through faith in Christ (3.26). All are priests and kings equally.
And so the general (better: the shared) priesthood of all believers

dissolves the division between priests and laity. In the Protestant church there is no 'laity'. Everyone is a bearer of the Spirit and hence a 'spiritual'. Of course, practically speaking the distinction between trained theologians and people without any theological training has taken the place of the priestly hierarchy; but according to the Reformation paradigm, every Christian belonging to the people of God is a theologian.[11] The people of God is a general community of theologians. The unity of the church is established through the brotherhood of Christ, not through a patriarchal hierarchy. Consequently the church is a community of free and equal men and women, joined with each other in an open, inviting friendship. All are joint heirs of God's coming kingdom, and are therefore a community of hope for the future of the world.

The unity represented by way of a hierarchy is replaced by the covenant. The community united in the brotherhood of Christ is a covenanted community, as Israel once was on Sinai. The covenant with God is also a covenant of confederates. The political analogies for this paradigm for the church are not the monarchy or the aristocracy, but democracy, and earlier the confederation of free farmers and the conciliar constitution of the free cities. The general priesthood of all believers thrusts toward a political community in which the human dignity and human rights of all are observed. In western Europe, the presbyterial-synodal principle of the Protestant churches pushed for the democratization of politics, and the social orders of Reformed congregations have inspired the social legislation of modern European democracies. To establish communities 'of the people, by the people, for the people' (to quote Abraham Lincoln) is a consistent part of the christocentric faith. Today we also find exactly these forms of life in the base communities of the Roman Catholic Church in Latin America.

The Charismatic Paradigm

Today the charismatic fellowship of the Holy Spirit is perceived, experienced and practised in many congregations and churches. I

mean that in the way that Paul describes the 'charismatic congregation' in 1 Cor. 12–14, not in a modern denominational sense.[12]
In a congregation which perceives its diverse gifts and tasks—its
'charismata'—all are accepted just as they are, and their individual talents and powers are used to build up the congregation and
spread God's kingdom. No one has a higher or lower position than
anyone else with what he or she can contribute to the community.
'When you come together, each one has a hymn, a lesson, a revelation, a tongue, or an interpretation. Let all things be done for
building up', says Paul in 1 Cor. 14.26 (NRSV). 'There are a variety
of gifts but the same Spirit' (1 Cor. 12.4). So there can't be any
fear of pluralism, which is alleged to split up the church; there can
only be trust in the one divine Spirit. God's life-giving Spirit is the
inexhaustible wellspring of a plurality of original powers and forms
of life, for it gives everyone what is his or hers.[13] In view of the
protean variety of human gifts and tasks, unity cannot be found in
any single gift or mandate, but only in the one source of them all.

> There are varieties of gifts, but *the same Spirit.*
> There are varieties of service but *the same Lord.*
> There are varieties of powers, but it is *the same God*
> who inspires them all in every one (1 Cor. 12.4–6).

If I understand this correctly, here Paul is putting forward a
trinitarian argument for unity in diversity and diversity in unity,
for 'one Spirit, one Lord and one God' are the names he uses for
the trinitarian persons. They act together in all the diverse 'gifts,
services and powers', and in this way make up the charismatic
community.

This is not a premodern eulogy of a uniform unity, nor is it a
postmodern glorification of diversity. The hierarchical church distinguished between priests and laity. The christocentric church made
all free and equal as brothers and sisters. But in the charismatic congregations which are growing up, everyone is taken seriously as an

expert. Everyone is an expert in his or her own life and personal calling, and all are experts in their original gifts and powers on behalf of the community and its mission. Their all-equalizing brotherliness is fanned out through the power of the divine Spirit which confers community in diversity.

When they take this diversity and variety seriously, people experience fellowship with God not as 'the power above them' or as 'the ground beneath them' but as the bond between them. Consequently the Holy Spirit has been described from time immemorial in terms of sociality.[14] It binds different people together and distinguishes between people who are thus bound. When as a result privileges and disparagements disappear, a community of respect and love comes into being, respect for the liberty of other people and affection for them. For this we ought to introduce the term 'open friendship'.[15] Communities of this kind are possible. Three hundred years ago, in the age of feudalism and absolutism, the Moravian Brethren came together as a lived alternative. Similar cooperative alternative life styles are possible, even in the competitive societies of the market economy, with their winners and losers. In these the presence of God's Spirit is experienced as the all-enlivening atmosphere in which social free spaces are opened up for the development of personal and shared humanity. In the charismatic congregations Christians at last 'come of age'. They leave behind their self-imposed immaturity and have the courage to live their own faith for themselves, and to follow their own consciences. They no longer see themselves as servants or children but as God's mature friends.

The Trinitarian Link between the Three Paradigms for the Church Today

After the *hierarchical church* of God the Father, Christianity came to know the *brotherly church* of God the Son. Today we are experiencing the *charismatic church* of God the Spirit. We do not experience all at once everything that essentially belongs together.

But the church will be united neither solely through the monarchy of the Father, nor solely through the brotherhood of the Son, nor solely through the power of the Spirit, but only through the *trinitarian unity* of the Father and the Son and the Holy Spirit. This is what Cyprian's much quoted saying tells us: the church is 'a people brought into unity from the unity of the Father, the Son and the Holy Spirit' (*Lumen Gentium* 4).

Like the Christian faith itself, the community of the church is a trinitarian experience of God. The reciprocal interpenetration of the ways of activity and the living spaces of the three divine persons constitutes the church's unity in its fullness.[16] The classic text is Jesus' high priestly prayer in John 17.21:

> That they may all be one,
> even as thou, Father, art in me and I in thee,
> that they also may be in us,
> so that the world may believe that thou hast sent me.

The community of believers corresponds to the mutual indwelling of the Father in the Son and of the Son in the Father: 'even as'. This correspondence is the *first dimension* of this petition of Jesus', in which he prays for the unity of those who are his. In the ecumenical movement our presupposition is that this prayer of Jesus has already been heard, and did not just remain 'a pious hope', so that the churches which visibly are still separated are in this already 'one'. The *second dimension* is equally important. The unity of the church is meant not only to 'correspond' to the unity of the triune God; it is also supposed to find its living space 'in' him. This might be called the mystical dimension of the unity: the unity of the triune God is an open, inviting unity. It is the spiritual living space in which the church exists. God is not just a personal counterpart. He is also the 'broad place in which there is no more cramping'.

The triune God is the church's divine living space, and the church is God's living space on earth (John 14.23). This mutual

indwelling of human beings in God and God in human beings
(1 John 3.16) is already the beginning, here on earth and now in
history, of the fulfilment of the Bible's final hope for God:

> Behold the dwelling of God is among mortals.
> He will dwell with them,
> and they shall be his people. (Rev. 21.3)

And that already brings us to the future of the church in the
kingdom of God.

3

Hope for the Kingdom of God

Sociologically speaking, in our multifaith society the church is one religious community among others. But that is not the way it sees itself. It sees itself as a minority with a universal mission, and as a community with a comprehensive hope for the peoples of the world and for this earth. The future of the church is more than the church; the future of Christianity is more than Christianity. The church answers for God's universal future. Jews and Christians are the people of God's coming kingdom, which was proclaimed through Israel's prophets and embodied in person through Jesus Christ. 'The church represents the seed and the beginning of this kingdom on earth' (Vatican II, Constitution on the Church, *Lumen Gentium*, I.5). So Christianity sees itself as 'the messianic people' (*populus messianicus*, ibid II, 9).

As regards their *gathering* into a community, Christians see themselves as brothers and sisters and as friends, but where their sending into the world is concerned they are all their own experts in their own lives, and in their callings and work in society. What do they work for? They will work to see the emergence in society and politics, in economic life and culture, of correspondences and anticipations of the kingdom of God and his righteousness which they expect in the world; and they will try to get rid of the contradictions and hindrances. If the expected kingdom of God is a unity of righteousness and peace, as Israel's psalms and Jesus' Sermon on the Mount say it is, then in their professions and the work they do Christians will stand up for a more just and more peaceful world. Papal encyclicals and Protestant memoranda may be helpful here, but it is not bishops and theologians who have the responsibility; it is Christian people worldwide. But what future for the world is envisaged and conceived of in that symbol of hope 'the kingdom of God'?

Some people have understood it to mean the universal and total theocracy. But that is one-sided and does not fit in with the experience of God in the community of Christ. Nor is it in line with Israel's experiences with the covenant. What Israel associated with the experience of the divine covenant on Sinai was a mutual happening: 'I will be *your* God and you shall be *my* people.' But behind this covenant experience with God there was a still deeper experience of him: 'I will dwell in the midst of the Israelites.' Israel's experience of God is therefore always the experience of the God who *indwells* Israel, whether it be in the Ark of the Covenant, or in the temple, or in the Torah. This indwelling of the Eternal One in history, and of the Infinite One in the finite, is called Shekinah.[1] In his indwelling in Israel the eternal God becomes for the Israelites the companion on the way, and then also the companion in suffering. He participates in their exiles; their sufferings are his sufferings too. Consequently Israel's hope is directed towards the universal, cosmic indwelling of God in a creation which through this indwelling will be newly created and then eternal. The experience of God in the community of Christ goes a step further and perceives that 'The Word became flesh and *dwelt* among us'. With Christ, God's indwelling takes on a body, a face and a name. 'In him the whole fullness of deity dwells bodily', says Col. 2.9. The kingdom of God is the perfected *perichoretic* unity of God and world.

The God in whom Christians believe is not just the power of their faith. He is also the creator of the cosmos. Through his Wisdom and his Spirit, the creator has already entered into his creation and no longer merely stands over against it. According to Israel's Wisdom literature, the Wisdom with which God created the world can also be viewed as God's word or his reason. At all events what is meant is the immanent presence of God in the world in all things, their movements and orders. Through his Wisdom the creator has founded his creation firmly in righteousness. Through his Spirit the creator already communicates himself to his creation: 'Lord thou art the lover of life and thy immortal spirit is in all things', we read in the Wisdom of Solomon (12.1). Calvin saw it in the same way: 'For thy Spirit is everywhere present, and sustains, nourishes and enlivens all things. That he should pour out his power in all things, thereby giving all things their being, life and movement, this is manifestly divine' (*Inst.* 1, 13, 14).

From the very beginning, belief in the indwelling presence of Christ did not confine it to the church, for people saw in Christ not only personal salvation, and not even just human salvation, but also the divine Wisdom through which all things exist. The Word which 'became flesh and dwelt among us' is the Word 'through which all things were made' (John 1.3). Consequently Christ is also understood as the secret of the world, and not just as the secret of the church. So whoever reverences Christ reverences all created things in him, and discovers him in all created things. 'Cleave a piece of wood and I am there. Lift up a stone and you will find me', we read in the Gospel of Thomas, Logion 77.

Through the presence of his Wisdom and his Spirit the creator impels his creation towards its goal: it is destined to become the temple of his indwelling glory, as the prophet Isaiah saw in his call vision: 'The whole earth is full of his glory' (6.3). All things are created, sustained and further developed so that they may become the shared house of all created being, the eternal house of God. Biblically this is brought out in the image of God's cosmic temple. When God comes to 'dwell' in his creation and to rest in this dwelling, then all things will participate in his eternal livingness, just as he will share in their finitude. The divine and the human, the heavenly and the earthly will interpenetrate each other without intermingling. God in all things and all things in God: that is what is meant biblically by the kingdom of God. When at the end Christ hands over 'the kingdom' to the Father, then 'God will be all in all' (1 Cor. 15.28).

If this is the church's all-embracing hope for the kingdom of God, then its universal mission is to prepare the way for this future. Christianity prepares for it now by already drawing everything into its worship of God, and by respecting everything, each in its own right, in 'reverence for life'. It is modern narrow-mindedness to relate the church only to the world of human beings; it has always been cosmos-orientated too, and is so still. If the church sees itself as the beginning and germ of the new creation, then the present ecological crisis is not just a crisis of modern civilization. It is the church's crisis in this civilization as well. The suffering of weaker creatures is the church's suffering too. 'If one member suffers, all suffer together.' What suffers is not just 'our natural environment'; it is God's environment as well. The modern nihilistic destruction of nature is nothing other than practised atheism. The perpetrators are excommunicating themselves from the community of creation.

In the face of this danger, a new cosmic spirituality is developing in many groups and churches today, a spirituality in which we reverence God's hidden presence in all living things and hope for their future in the kingdom of God. The Hildegard of Bingen renaissance is a sign of this, and Ernesto Cardenal's great 'Cosmic Canticle' fulfils what modern men and women are looking for in this new spirituality, which is growing up at the edge of the ecological abysses.

In closing, we can also apply these ideas about indwelling to humanity and the blue planet Earth. The species human being is only a latecomer on earth compared with other living things, and has apparently not yet found its place and its role for the community of earth dwellers and the geosystem. 'Every ant knows the formula for its ant heap, every bee knows the formula for its beehive. Only the human being does not know his formula', wrote Dostoievsky. Apparently we are not yet at home on this earth. We feel like strangers or guests on a beautiful star. Religions orientated towards the next world have increased this sense of alienation. 'The alien', '*homo viator*', 'the homeless human being': these were themes in existentialist poetry in western Europe. Making a virtue of necessity, modern philosophical anthropology has lauded the openness to the world of these deficient human beings, their self-transcendence and their spiritual culture.[2] But the disrupted relationship between modern human beings and nature, the earth and other living things on earth, has remained what it was. The depredations of nature with which we are today making the earth uninhabitable are ultimately based on this disrupted relationship to nature in modern times: in the German tradition, modern anthropology goes back to Johann Gottfried Herder who, writing about the origin of language in 1770, said:

> Nature was [man's] severest stepmother, while being the most loving mother of every insect. She gave every insect whatever it required, and in whatever measure: senses transformed into notions, and notions into instincts: organs for such language as was needed and organs for understanding that language. In the human being everything is in the greatest imbalance.[3]

If for human beings 'Mother Nature' is nothing but a severe stepmother, then human beings are evidently orphans on this earth, and have lost their motherly home. Why should they treat their stepmother well when she has treated them so badly? If human beings are nature's malformations, then they will do everything they can to recreate themselves and to construct a better world, a kind of artificial nature, as if in a great spaceship. And it is just this which the modern world is on the way to do.

But we can also ask about a humanity which has a home on this earth, and we can make the geosystem our home, the home in which we want to stay. The earth can exist without human beings and did so for millions of years, but the human race cannot exist without the earth and the other living things. So human beings are dependent on the earth, but the earth is not dependent on human beings. The simple conclusion from this realization is that human civilization has to be integrated into the ecosystem of the earth, not, conversely, that the earth must be subjugated to the human system of domination. Of course there is no 'back to nature'. The so-called primitive peoples are not an ideal either. But the integrations which they discovered in their natural environment in the course of thousands of years can very well be translated into the future of a postindustrial world. In the long run we cannot get along *against* nature but only with nature. When we ask about the habitability of the earth for us human beings, or when we look for a home in nature, we are also asking about the role of human beings for the geosystem. Perhaps one day human civilization will be able to develop something like the brain of this geo-organism. If we want to find a home on a habitable earth, and to come to rest there, the human and the natural will one day interpenetrate each other in the same way as do the spiritual and the physical. Psychosomatic 'wholes' and economic-ecological 'wholes' will then correspond and interpenetrate each other.

When the eternal God comes to dwell on the earth, 'on earth as in heaven', then this earth is to become God's temple. The restless God of history will arrive at his rest. That is the great biblical, Jewish and Christian, vision for the earth's future.

By virtue of this expectation, we human beings will already keep the organism of the earth and the earthly community of the living holy here and now, and will encounter them with reverence before God. We are not nature's 'lords and possessors', but perhaps one day we shall become priests who represent God to the earth and the earth before God, so that we may sense God in all things, and in all things perceive the reflection of his glory.

PART TWO

THE GOD OF RESURRECTION: CHRIST'S RESURRECTION— THE RESURRECTION OF THE BODY— THE RESURRECTION OF NATURE

4

In the End the Beginning

In what situation do we talk today about the resurrection and the life? Let us look first at the historical situation and afterwards at the theological one.

The Legacy of Our Time: Progress and Catastrophe

Every interpretation of texts that have been passed down to us—and this is especially true of interpretation of the gospel of Christ—is related to the geographical context, the temporal *kairos*, and the community in which people are living. At the beginning of the twenty-first century the situation in Europe and the Western world is determined by the two preceding eras: the era of beginnings and progress in the nineteenth century, and the era of annihilations and end in the twentieth. These eras are not measured in terms of years. Their paradigms, their experiences and their attitudes to life overlap, and are still present today. The nineteenth century saw the building up of the Western world in industrialized Europe and in the colonial empires of the great powers. The twentieth century saw the European nations destroy themselves in two world wars. In the twenty-first century we have inherited both these eras: the spirit of scientific and technological progress, and the potential for destruction which can plunge humanity and the earth into the abyss. What hopes and what fears are we taking with us as we move on, or as we go on our way just as before?

At the beginning of the twenty-first century we are linking up with the age of progress, and with our globalizations are taking it further to the ends of the earth. At the same time we know that we are building these globalizations of progress on the abysses of the annihilations we saw and experienced in the twentieth century. Ever since the invention of the atomic and hydrogen bombs, humanity as a whole has become mortal. Huge arsenals of missiles and bombs are poised for 'the final solution' of the question about humanity. There will be no human life after the nuclear winter. Regardless industrialization at the expense of nature, the irreversibility of man-made global warming, and the inability to retract the contamination of the earth, the oceans and the atmosphere— these things have made mortal and destructible the organism of the earth in which, and from which, human beings live.

We cannot prolong the era of beginnings and progress without seeing in front of our eyes the era of annihilations and end. There are no longer any beginnings without a recollection of the end to which they can lead. But nor is there an end in the face of which we are forced to drown in resignation and fatalism, without the wish and attempt to begin something new. If there is to be a new age which can create a positive link between the experiences of that age of beginning and this age of the end, it would have to be an age of *a beginning in the end*: in the end—the new beginning. The symbol for this is not unending progress. It is the *resurrection into life* in the midst of the world of possible universal death. A beginning out of the end is a beginning in which the possible end is always present.

The Christian message in this situation can be reduced to a simple formula: by virtue of his resurrection, Christ's end in the catastrophe on Golgotha became the true beginning of his new life for us. His raising from the dead shows the divine power of beginning in the end. That is the rebirth of life and the force of freedom. The nineteenth century believed in Jesus' message about the kingdom of God and by way of that wanted to realize humanity's dreams. In the twentieth century people experienced plunges into the abyss of annihilation, the universal Good Friday. Today the essential thing is to believe in the power of the resurrection, and to prepare the way for the kingdom of God in the context of today's apocalyptic horizons.

Resurrection:
The Acknowledgment of Christ and Belief in God

The situation of Christian theology can be described in a simple, banal-sounding but momentous comment: without the event which the first Christians called 'God's raising of Jesus from the dead' there would be no New Testament, no church, no Christianity—and no knowledge about Jesus of Nazareth. Without Jesus' resurrection we should know about him—nothing at all. So belief in the God who raised Jesus from the dead is essential to faith in Jesus Christ.[1] Paul put it as follows, about thirty years after Jesus' death: 'If Christ has not been raised … your faith is in vain' (1 Cor. 15.14). For Paul and for early Christianity as we know it, God's raising of Jesus was the foundation for their faith in Jesus, the Christ, the Lord.

Paul links belief in God and the confession of Christ at this point, the point of the resurrection: 'For if you confess with your lips that Jesus is Lord and believe in your heart that God raised him from the dead, you will be saved' (Rom. 10.9). The acknowledgment of Christ and belief in the God who raised him from the dead interpret each other mutually. Without this acknowledgment of Christ there is no belief in this God, and without belief in this God there is no acknowledgment of Christ. Anyone who makes a separation here loses sight of both. To quote Ernst Bloch, a witness who cannot be suspected of apologetics: 'Even Jesus was victorious in competition with the mysteries not as the messiah of the weary and heavy-laden, but as "the first-fruits of the dead"; and to be "the resurrection and the life" was his very character'.[2]

Nineteenth-century liberal theology searched for 'the historical Jesus' in order to find in him the primal image of the true human being, the man of God, the person with the perfect and unbroken 'God-consciousness'. It tried to maintain the original teaching of Jesus over against the doctrine of the church.[3] It pushed out the raising of Jesus from the dead, and came to terms with death as the natural end of human beings.[4] The historical Jesus became 'historical' through his death, in the way that all human beings are subjected to transience through their deaths, and with their deaths become people who are past and gone. All that is left of them is a passing remembrance.

But when people searched for the historical Jesus what they found was not the primal image of universal, true humanity, and it was not the teacher of an elevated morality either. They found a devout Jew, who lived in the Judaism of his time, and exercised his ministry only within the borders of Israel.[5] Jesus returned to Judaism again, as it were, and left the Gentile church and the Christian world.

The raising of Jesus from the dead does not just link Jesus with God. It also links God with Jesus and what happens to him. He is the God whom Jesus exclusively called 'Abba', dear Father; and for whom Paul found the formula: 'the Father of our Lord Jesus Christ'. The bond with Jesus distinguishes God from the gods of the Gentiles. It also distinguishes God from monotheism in a general sense.[6] The God who raised Jesus from the dead is 'the God of Israel', and yet as the God of Jesus Christ he is more than the God of Israel alone. 'Here there is neither Jew nor Greek, there is neither slave nor free, here there is neither male nor female', declared Paul in Gal. 3.28, 'for you are all one in Christ Jesus'. The God of Jesus Christ is universal, because the raising of Jesus from the dead does away with the frontier dividing Jews from Gentiles, masters from servants, men from women, indeed even the living from the dead. So the risen Christ is no longer just a Jew either. He is also the beginner and leader of the new humanity. Paul calls him 'the new Adam'. That does not put an end to God's covenant with Israel, but it takes that covenant up into the new hope, as Paul says: 'all Israel will be saved' (Rom. 11.26). For Christianity the consequence is that Israel's history of promise is made present in the Christian 'Old Testament', and that there is a forward-looking gaze towards the universal, cosmic redemption.

If we read the stories about the resurrection with the echo of the Psalms in our ears, we arrive at the idea that the raising of Jesus from the dead has to do with a *divine resurrection,* or rising up. The whole Psalter is shot through by the cry to God: 'Arise, O God, judge the earth' (Ps. 82.8; 108.5); 'Be exalted, O God, above the heavens, Let thy glory be over all the earth (Ps. 57.5, 11; 21.13); 'Bestir thyself and awake for my cause' (Ps. 35.23; 44.23); 'Arise, O God' (Ps. 17.13; 35.23; 44.26; 74.22); 'When God arises to establish judgment to save all the oppressed of the earth' (Ps. 76.9); 'Arise, O Lord; O God, lift up thy hand; forget not the afflicted'(Ps. 10.12). Hasn't the cry that God will arise, bestir himself and judge been answered through the raising of the wretched and crucified Jesus, as the beginning for everyone? With the raising of Jesus, God's own 'arising' has begun, and will bring about justice for all the wretched and for the whole earth. With the raising of Jesus, God himself has arisen, to fulfil his promises to all those he has created.

The hope for the resurrection of the dead is not an answer to the human yearning for immortality; it is a response to the hunger for righteousness and justice.

5

The Raising of Jesus

The raising of the *crucified* Christ says that a new beginning has been set with his end on the cross, and with that for the world. The raising of the *dead* Christ says that in him the order of this mortal world has been broken through. Through his death on the cross, Christ has been taken from the living; through his resurrection he has been taken from the dead. The male disciples run away in great terror from the helpless death of their Messiah on Golgotha. The women who have followed him as his disciples endure the horror of his death on the cross, but in their shock over his rising from the dead they run away from his empty tomb. By virtue of Christ's resurrection the Christian hope springs up at this double zero point: out of the disciples' crucified hope for the future, and out of the women's shaken belief in death.

The Disciples' Crucified Hope for the Future

The Gospels testify fully to the disciples' flight from the scene of their master's crucifixion, to Judas's betrayal, and to Peter's denial. The key lies in the Gethsemane story. Christ's prayer to be spared is not heard by the God whom he here addresses as 'Abba, dear Father' (Mark 14.36). Judas 'betrays' him to the Romans (Mark 14.44), which probably means that he handed him over to the occupying power. Peter, who was the first to confess Christ (Mark

8.29), and who was called a rock, denies him three times (Mark 14.66–72); and the disciples 'all forsook him and fled' (Mark 14.50). Jesus dies on the cross 'forsaken' by his God and by his friends. Betrayed, denied, forsaken: this was not just a case of human weakness and faithlessness. These were rather reactions to appalling disappointments. 'Blessed is the kingdom of our father David that is coming! Hosanna in the highest!' the people shout in jubilation as Jesus enters Jerusalem (Mark 11.10). 'We had hoped that he was the one to redeem Israel', lament the disciples on the way to Emmaus, after they had run away (Luke 24.21). This hope that the Messiah would restore a free kingdom of David and do away with Roman rule came to nothing because of the unexpected weakness of Jesus in his passion—a cruel disappointment for all the people who had left everything, acknowledged him, and followed him. So their hope switches over to disillusionment, their love to hate, their acknowledgment to denial, and their discipleship to flight. They betray, deny and forsake the one by whom they feel themselves betrayed, forsaken and denied. Jesus' helpless death on the cross is the end of their hope.

The Women's Shaken Belief in Death

In contrast to the fleeing disciples, the women remained faithful to the dying Jesus and 'looked on from afar'. They still looked Jesus in the eye, so they are named as 'eye witnesses' (Mark 15.40). Apparently they were not unfamiliar with death and grief. Jesus' death did not put an end to their love. Mary Magdalene, Mary the mother of James, and Salome went to the grave of their friend and master once the Sabbath was past. They found the tomb empty, and heard the angel saying: 'He has risen, he is not here; see the place where they laid him' (Mark 16.6). It was only at that moment that they 'fled' from the tomb. They were seized by 'trembling and astonishment ... for they were afraid' (Mark 16.8).[1] This is no Easter jubilation over the resurrection. It is icy terror over the empty tomb and the absence of Jesus. Like birth, death is part of finite life. So confidence in natural life includes confidence in death. What fills the women with bottomless terror at Jesus' tomb, according to Mark (who stresses this particularly), is the shattering of the earthly order of life and death. The ground of this order is trembling under their feet. This tomb is empty and death is no longer certain. This *mysterium resurrectionis* was later felt and celebrated as something wonderful. But originally, and essentially, it was a shattering *mysterium tremendum*. The first Easter accounts did not evoke faith, on the contrary: 'they did not believe' (Mark 16.11, 13).

The Appearances of the Risen Christ

Every analysis of the Easter accounts given by the disciples in Galilee and the women in Jerusalem brings out the unique new being in which the crucified and dead Jesus 'appeared' to them.[2] The reports exclude with scrupulous care a reanimated corpse or a mysterious return of the dead Jesus. But his bodiliness in his appearances is stressed with equal care, so that a metempsychosis is excluded as well. The disciples and the women did not of their own accord recognize Jesus either physically or spiritually in the new being of the resurrection. From the very beginning they used the eschatological symbol of 'raising' and 'resurrection' for the event between his death on the cross and his burial, and for the 'appearances' of his new existence. There are four Gospels which tell the life of Jesus, and numerous theological interpretations of his death, but that he was raised from the dead was from the very beginning *the* primal fact of Christian faith.[3] And here, already embodied in this expression, is a tremendous reinterpretation of Israel's eschatological hope for resurrection. According to that hope, all the dead will be raised simultaneously at the end of days (1 Cor. 15.52; John 11.24). But according to earliest Christian conviction, Jesus is raised '*from* the dead', ahead of all the others.[4] This is not meant in the sense of an individual exception to the general and simultaneous raising of the dead, but as its beginning, as Paul stresses in 1 Corinthians 15. In terms of time, with the resurrection of Jesus from the dead the last days have already begun. These are the final days of this world of sin, violence and death, and at the same time they are the first days of the new world of righteousness and justice, peace and eternal life (Rom. 13.12).

This brings us to the unique character of the *appearances* of the risen Christ. According to the accounts, there were a great many appearances to many of his disciples, men and women both. In his first letter to the Corinthians, written in 55 or 56 c.e., Paul talks about Cephas, the twelve, then five hundred brethren at once, and lastly about him, Paul, himself (1 Cor. 15.8). Acts 9 tells of Paul's conversion experience. Following the model of the prophetic calls in the Old Testament, it describes a vision of a blinding light from heaven, and an audition: 'I am Jesus whom you are persecuting' (9.3, 5). Since the disciples had fled to Galilee, and Saul had persecuted the Christians, Christ's appearances were not derived from the faith of the disciples; their faith was derived from the appearances. According to Mark, the risen Christ had first of all to disperse their fear and call them to believe.

The expressions 'Christ appeared' and 'Christ was seen' are revelation formulas, following Old Testament usage. They are intended to say: God revealed Christ, and Christ comes forward in the light of God's glory (Isa. 40.5). The activity emanates from the one who lets himself be seen; the seeing human being 'suffers' this divine appearance passively.

Paul links the christophanies with the word *apokalypsis*, and by doing so he gives them a particular meaning: Christ appears in the daybreak colours of God's new day. This world time of God's hiddenness is not able to endure the new world of God's universal presence. Human perception of the appearances of the risen Christ is not a perception analogous to anything comparable in this world; nor is it a supernatural perception of heavenly things;

it is a dialectical perception of the living God in contradiction to the conditions of this transitory world of death. If the risen Christ appears in the advance radiance of God's coming glory, then what follows from the appearances for the people concerned is the call to service for the coming One in this transient world. All the appearances of the risen Christ were incidentally appearances in the light of day, not dream apparitions in the night.

We can detect three dimensions in the structure of the christophanies and the Easter 'seeing' of the people concerned:

1. It is a *prospective seeing*: they saw the crucified Christ as the eternally living One in the daybreak colours of God's coming glory.
2. It is a *retrospective seeing*: they recognized him as being Jesus the Nazarene from the marks of the nails, in the breaking of bread, from his peace greeting, and from his voice.
3. It is a *reflexive recognition*: in this seeing of Christ they experience themselves as Christ's apostles. It is a motivating perception of the risen Christ.

The *gospel* has the same structure: it makes the person and history of Jesus Christ present in 'the word of the cross' and in the advance radiance of his Parousia in the 'gospel of the kingdom', and calls to service for his kingdom in this world.

The *Eucharist* has the same structure: bread and wine are a *signum rememorativum passionis et mortis Christi*—a recollecting sign of Christ's passion and death. At the same time they are a *signum prognosticon*—a sign that looks forward to the coming glory; and in harmony with both the recollection and the gaze forward, they are a sign of God's present grace.

Christian faith also has the same structure: in Christ, it makes present the Christ who has come, and anticipates the Christ who will come, and between the times it makes new creations of human beings in Christ's presence.

What was the nature of Christ's appearances, as a subjective perception?

Theologically, the word often used is 'vision'. But these were not supernatural perceptions in which the five senses played no part. The women and the disciples didn't 'see in their hearts' or 'with their spiritual eyes'. They didn't have intuitions, while they were 'caught up out of this world', nor did they receive enlightenment in trances. The accounts tell us that it was with their normal five senses that they perceived the risen Christ, who in God is eternally alive and creates life: 'That which we have *heard*, which we have *seen* with our eyes, which we have *looked upon* and *touched* with our hands—the word of life' (1 John 1.1) . Why is the sensory aspect so strongly emphasized? It is strongly emphasized because it is a matter of the bodily raising of Christ and his living presence in the transfigured body. 'Because the life of the resurrected Lord involves the reality of a new creation, the resurrected Lord is in fact not perceptible as one object among others in this world', says Wolfhart Pannenberg.[5] But that does not permit us to speak of 'the extraordinary mode of experience, the vision', as he concludes. It rather indicates the beginning of a fundamental change in the conditions of possible experience. In the presence of the coming One, we see and experience reality differently from the way we experienced it in the conditions of death and transience. We see mortal life in the light of the life that is eternal; we experience history in the light of God's kingdom, and nature in the perspective of its future perfecting in the eternal creation.

The Touchable yet Untouched Body of Christ

In the story about Mary Magdalene in John 20, Jesus forbids her to touch him, but in the story about Thomas in the same chapter he invites Thomas to touch the wound in his side.[6] According to Luke 24.36–43, the risen Christ presented himself to the startled disciples, who think they are seeing a spirit, by saying: 'See my hands and my feet, that is I myself; handle me, and see; for a spirit has not flesh and bones as you see that I have.' He even took some 'broiled fish and ate it before them' (v. 42f). Did the risen Christ appear in his pre-Easter 'flesh and blood', or in his glorified Easter body (Phil. 3.21)? What is the relation between the transfigured Easter body of the risen Christ and the pre-Easter mortal body of Jesus?

Noli me tangere

In the first story in John 20, Mary Magdalene returns to the empty tomb. Her question is: Where is the dead Jesus? 'They have taken away my Lord, and I do not know where they have laid him' (20.13). She is standing in a garden which calls to mind the Garden of Eden at creation, or the Song of Songs. She sees two angels sitting in the empty tomb, which is reminiscent of the ark of the covenant (Ex. 37.6–9), the place of Israel's encounter with God. When she looks for Jesus' body, it is his pre-Easter body she is looking for. She only recognizes Jesus when he calls her by her familiar name. She turns to him and responds with the familiar title, 'Rabboni', Master. When she is about to touch him in the familiar way, he repulses her in the famous words: 'Do not touch me', explaining: 'I have not yet ascended to the Father' (v. 17). Jesus sends her to the disciples, 'my brethren', with the message of his ascent to the Father, and she tells them: 'I have seen the Lord.' So what did Mary see when she saw Jesus? Was it his pre-Easter body or his transfigured body? Did she see her Rabboni or her Lord? Evidently both, for she encountered Jesus while he was on the way and in transition from his earthly flesh and blood to his transfigured body. He is *no longer* a dead body, but he has *not yet* ascended to the Father. He is no longer part of mortality but he is not yet in glory either. That is why she moved from the pre-Easter address 'Rabboni' to the Easter acknowledgment, 'Lord'. She is supposed to find the presence of the risen Christ in the community of the brethren and sisters, as the community of the exalted Lord. So the first eye witness of Jesus' resurrection becomes its first apostle: 'I have seen the Lord' (20.18).

Caravaggio's Picture

The story about Thomas in John 20 is different. Thomas the Twin comes to the assembly of the disciples to whom the risen Christ has already appeared. They have seen him, indeed have received the Holy Spirit from him; but Thomas does not believe their testimony when they say: 'We have seen the Lord' (20.25). He doesn't dispute what they have seen but he himself is not convinced by their testimony. He wants to see the pre-Easter Jesus and the marks of his wounds for himself, and to touch him physically. He doesn't doubt, but he refuses to believe. When after eight days the risen Jesus appears in the group of the disciples, Jesus invites Thomas to touch his hand with his own finger, and to touch the wound in his side with his own hand (20.27). The places that he is told to touch are highly symbolic: 'Put your finger here and see my hands.' Can one 'see' with one's finger? Or does seeing with the eyes take the place of touching with the finger? If the 'seeing' is a revelatory formula, then we have to assent to the second solution of the puzzle. In early Christianity the 'wound in the side' from which blood and water flow is a symbol for the Eucharist and baptism. The risen Jesus promises Thomas faith: 'Do not be faithless but believing', and Thomas responds spontaneously: 'My Lord and my God' (20.28). Jesus does not confirm Thomas's touch but only his seeing: 'You have believed because you have seen me.'

Did Thomas touch the pre-Easter body of Jesus 'with his hands', as 1 John 1.1 says, or was this just a possibility offered him by the risen Jesus, which he did not take advantage of? Caravaggio painted his famous controversial picture with Thomas's finger in the open wound in Christ's side. But according to John 20, Thomas contented himself with his seeing of the Jesus who had appeared to him, for the passage doesn't read: because you have touched me you have believed. However, Jesus did offer him this possibility, so he must have appeared to him in his pre-Easter body of flesh and blood.

I do not believe that a transfigured Easter body took the place of Jesus' mortal pre-Easter body of 'flesh and blood', so that we have to make a distinction between the two. It must be the same pre-Easter, crucified, dead and buried body of Jesus which has been raised, has ascended to God and is transfigured in the glory of God. Without the identity with Jesus' bodily existence, his resurrection cannot be conceived.

Touching and Seeing

The body of Christ in heaven, or with the Father, is no other body than the body of Jesus the Nazarene, born of Mary and crucified under Pontius Pilate. Resurrection and transfiguration means the one *in* the other, unmingled, even undivided, not in temporal succession but simultaneous in eternity. It is the same body, the whole body, the identical body which is transfigured through its raising to God. The story of the transfiguration on the mountain (Mark 9.1–8) gives visual form to the transfiguration of the pre-Easter Jesus: 'And they no longer saw any one but Jesus only.' Like resurrection, transfiguration is a transformation into a different mode of being, the identity of the person thereby being preserved. '*This* perishable nature will put on the imperishable, and *this* mortal nature immortality' is the way Paul puts it in 1 Cor. 15.53.

There may be another reason too why the risen Christ was seen but not touched. Touching is a tactile sense and means bodily contact, mainly with the fingers and hand, but with other sensitive cutaneous nerves as well. The tactile sense is the foundation of all the other senses and counts as the sense of proximity. Seeing with the eyes, in contrast, counts as the remote sense of distance. It cannot function without its medium, light. In immediate vicinity the speed of light conveys almost simultaneity, just as does immediate touch, but it preserves distance. We cannot recognize anything without a certain distance. As we have emphasized, the seeing of the risen Christ is based on his appearance. His appearance is his revelation through God. But what is *the medium between appearing and seeing*?

According to the accounts, it is the divine radiance. God himself dwells in an inaccessible light (1 John 1.5). According to the Gospel of John, Jesus is 'the light of the world'. 'In him was life, and the life was the light of men' (John 1.4). Believers 'walk in the light as he is in the light' (1 John 1.7). If Christ, 'being raised from the dead', appears in the radiance of God's coming appearance, I assume that the light which allows him to be seen is what a German hymn calls 'the dawning glory of eternity'[7] and what Charles Wesley (echoing Luke 1.78) describes as the 'dayspring from on high'.[8] Can we see this with our natural eyes? If it is the light that shone on the first day of creation (Gen. 1.3), we can see it. If it is the light of the first day of the new creation of all things, it is as blinding and overwhelming as it was for Paul (Gal. 1.16; Acts 9.3), for then it is a seeing for the first time, a perception of something qualitatively new, and not a recognition. 'What no eye has seen, nor ear heard, nor the heart of man conceived, what God has prepared for those who love him, God has revealed to us through the Spirit' (1 Cor. 2.9f).

If it is Jesus' mortal body that is transfigured, it can also be recognized with mortal eyes, which are enlightened through his appearance. According to Paul, the glory of God shines 'in the face of Jesus Christ' and 'in our hearts' (2 Cor. 4.6). What is meant here? According to John 20.20, the risen Jesus gives the disciples the Holy Spirit: 'Receive the Holy Spirit.' The appearances of the risen Christ and the outpouring of the Spirit, Easter faith and Pentecostal experience, belong together in a single movement. To recognize the living Christ and to experience in the Spirit the powers of rebirth to eternal livingness are one and the same. If this were not so, faith in Christ would be a dead thing, and experience of the Spirit would be without Christ. The Lucan distinction between Easter and Pentecost is meant symbolically. It is not a division between the two saving events. To believe in Christ's resurrection does not mean registering a historical fact and saying 'oh really?' without drawing any conclusions from it. It means being seized by the life-giving Spirit of the resurrection and rising up ourselves.[9]

There is no Pentecost without Easter, that is obvious. But there is no Easter without Pentecost either: that is something that still has to be understood. Easter theology and Pentecost theology are two sides of the same thing:

- life in the presence of the living Christ,
- coming alive in the powers of the new world to come,
- whole life, full life,
- shared life in community,
- life with all the living on earth,
- indestructible, eternal love:
- Where the risen Christ is, there we find this loved and lived life.

We may close this analysis of the Easter accounts with two pointers to their historicity:

1. The very individuality and variety of the accounts is an indication that the event was a real one. There was evidently no agreed-upon unification in early Christianity.

2. The tomb was empty. The disciples, the women and the Jews were all convinced of that. The only question was: Who emptied it? After the Easter appearances the disciples returned from Galilee to Jerusalem, although the city was a place of extreme danger for followers of the crucified Jesus. And they could not have held their ground with the Easter message on the streets of Jerusalem for a single hour if people had been able to point to the dead body of Jesus in the tomb. It is not the empty tomb that is evidence for the resurrection. It is the message of the resurrection that is evidence for the empty tomb. The fact that the huge church of the Holy Sepulchre should have been built over an empty tomb is a particularly unusual detail in the history of Christian piety.

The New Being of the Risen Christ

People also talk about Jesus Christ's 'new reality'. I have preferred Paul Tillich's term 'new being', so as to talk about a being which is beyond being and nonbeing.

The resurrection message is not talking about a revived corpse, nor about a life after death. As a confronting eschatological event, the resurrection from the dead takes in not only the dead Jesus but also, diachronically, Jesus' whole life history, from the manger to the cross. In the risen Christ the whole Christ is present: the child in the manger, the proclaimer of God's kingdom, the preacher on the mount, the healer of the sick and the driver out of demons, the sufferer, and the man crucified. The resurrection lends his whole life divine significance and represents what he was during the whole history of his life.[10] The person who tries to find the historical Jesus is looking for the dead Jesus, for death is the power of transience in history. It is only through the power of recollection that what is past is represented or, literally, re-membered.

In the light of the surmounting of death through resurrection, there is also a remembering representation, but it is not the remembrance of the history of someone dead; it is the recollection of the history of someone alive. The Gospels relate the life lived and the death suffered of the risen Son of God who now lives in God. In Rom. 1.4 Paul says that Jesus is declared Son of God through his raising from the dead. The Gospels relate the story of his life and death as 'the gospel of Jesus Christ, the Son of God' (Mark 1.1). They make present the life history of the risen Christ. In the Gospels, the historical way of dealing with history in the light of its transience gives way to treatment of the history of Jesus in the light of his future resurrection. What is simultaneously present in the risen Christ they again interpret in the sequence of the times. That is the answer to the riddle of why the early Christians remembered, told, and wrote down the stories about Jesus in the Gospels even though they were already experiencing and living eternal life in the presence of the risen Christ.[11]

The Inclusive Resurrection of Christ

In the modern world we have become accustomed to understanding people as individuals. But in the Gospels the history of Jesus

Christ is not told as his individual biography. It is presented in the context of the great remembrances of his people of Israel. The traditions about the salvation history of his people put their stamp on the Gospels which relate his history. For his resurrection from the dead was never understood as an exceptional fate which affected only Jesus himself; it was always grasped in collective relationships. Jesus was raised from the dead as Israel's Messiah—as the head of his church—as the leader of the new humanity—as the first born of all creation. Consequently his resurrection has a meaning for the future—for Israel, for the nations, for humanity, for the whole suffering creation. The Easter icon of the Orthodox Church shows that pictorially: Christ's resurrection begins in the world of the dead. He draws up Adam with his right hand and Eve with his left, and with them pulls humanity and the whole sighing creation out of the realm of the dead into the new transfigured world of the eternal life of the new creation. So we may say that Jesus' death on the cross was solitary, and exclusively his death, but his raising from the dead is inclusive, open to the world, and embraces the universe, an event not merely human and historical but cosmic too: the beginning of the new creation of all things.[12]

The Overcoming of Sin, Death and Hell

With the overcoming of the disciples' crucified hope for the future and the shaken confidence in death of the women at the tomb, the early Christian belief in the resurrection acted in the ancient world like an explosion of hearts and senses. It attacked with elemental force 'the powers of this world': the power of sin, the inescapability of death, and the hopelessness of hell. The risen Christ became the power of protest against these godless and inhumane forces. We already sense this certainty of victory in Paul's chapter about the resurrection, 1 Corinthians 15.

With the raising of the crucified Jesus from death, the one condemned according to Jewish and Roman law and crucified with Roman violence has been justified by God, and with that the powers that have executed him have been proved wrong: 'And he will destroy every rule and every power' (1 Cor. 15.24). The raising does not justify the crucifixion; it justifies the crucified victim of Roman power politics. That is why in the end the murderers will not triumph over their victims. If the crucified Jesus is God's just and righteous One, then there is divine justice for all the people who suffer violence here. The one who guarantees it is the crucified and now risen Christ.

'The last enemy to be destroyed is death', proclaims Paul (1 Cor. 15.26). 'Death is swallowed up in victory', says the Easter hymn of the earliest Christians which Paul quotes in 1 Cor. 15.55. The shaken confidence in death is transformed into jubilation over the eternal life in which death is swallowed up. What emerges from this is the vista of the new creation in which death will be no more (Rev. 21.4). As the later Christian martyrs proved, the Easter faith also overcomes the fear of death which violent rulers use to coerce powerless people, and the demonic fear which they disseminate. If God has raised the one executed by the power of the Roman state, and if he has given him all power in heaven and on earth, then for believers the emperor cult comes to an end, and what follows is a humanization of political power. In the long run, the intense political significance of the cross led to the elimination of political idolatry, and to the public duty for rulers to render a public account for their use of political power.

Not least, belief in the resurrection perceives that Christ has destroyed hell: 'Hell, where is thy victory?' (1 Cor. 15.55). On the one hand, 'hell' means experiences of being forsaken by God, lack of perspective, and destructive torment; but on the other hand it also means the place of punishment for the wicked and godless in the world of death. The raising of Christ has overcome not only eternal death but these hells too. The death of God and the dark night of the soul have been surmounted. Christian Easter hymns sing about the destruction of hell.[13] Since Christ's 'descent into hell', there has been hope where every prospect has disappeared:

Tu es factus spes desperatis—you have become the hope of the despairing.[14] No one is 'damned to all eternity' any more.

To sum up what has happened through the living God in the raising of Jesus from the dead, and to express it philosophically:

Nonbeing has been annihilated, death has been abolished, sin—the separation from God—has been overcome, and hell destroyed. These negations of the negative are the presupposition for a positive position which is indestructible. Out of the surmounting of nonbeing by being, new being emerges.

6

The Resurrection of the Body

Many people think that, somehow or other, life will go on after death, but they find it difficult to believe in a resurrection of their bodies, fragile, weak, sick and mortal as they are. The media confront us daily with pictures of the victims of accidents, with murdered, sick and dying bodies, in war with body counting and body bags. Can we set a hope for a resurrection of the body against these experiences?[1] Modern medicine transplants bodily organs, treating the human body like a machine which can be set going again with the help of spare parts, and which also functions— although we have all in fact learnt to look on human beings as a totality of body and soul, and to respect them as such. How can anyone believe in the resurrection of the body, and what consequences could this belief have for our dealings with the body?

The patristic church inserted the phrase about the 'resurrection of the body' into the Apostles' Creed although even then this idea ran counter to the general spiritualizing trend of Hellenistic and Roman culture. In our Western civilization, where everything is objectified, it appears even more incomprehensible and offensive. Why did 'the resurrection of the body' make its way into the context of the Christian hope and find a place in the creed?

An initial reason, I believe, lies in the general thrust of all biblical statements about God's purpose: 'All the works of God end in bodiliness', declared Friedrich Ötinger, and I would add: on this earth. God created human beings out of earth, we are earthly beings, God's Word became 'flesh'. Christ lived bodily among us, God's Spirit is poured out 'on all flesh'. How should God's history with those he has created not end in a resurrection of the body and an eternal bodily life?

Resurrectio carnis?

Many people have wracked their brains over the question of how to translate *resurrectio carnis*. The translation 'flesh' seemed embarrassing to many people, because it sounded like 'flesh and blood'. So they translated it into English by 'body' because that sounds more personal. Finally the Catholic and Protestant churches in Germany agreed on the translation 'the resurrection of the dead' because that sounds as personal as 'the living and the dead' in the second article of the Apostles' Creed. So this is what we now have in the creed. But does it mean the same thing? If we go back to the Hebrew root of 'all flesh', we find that the phrase *kol' basar* means all the living, as in Noah's covenant, which was made 'with you and your descendants after you, and with every living creature' (Gen. 9.9–10). According to Isa. 40.5, at the end 'the glory of the Lord shall be revealed, and all flesh shall see it together'. These universal dimensions of life get lost if we only have human beings in view. In a 'resurrection of the flesh' human beings will be redeemed together with the whole interwoven fabric of all the living, and the living space of the earth. Paul was still aware of this when he heard 'the sighing of creation' which, together with us, yearns for the redemption of the body (Rom. 8.19–22).

I would suggest talking about *the resurrection of life*, instead of a resurrection of the dead, the body or the flesh. By the living, lived body we do not mean the desouled body as an object, as a set of scientifically objectified organs and the medical treatment of them; we mean the experienced and lived body with which I am subjectively identical: I am body—this body is I myself, this is my bodily gestalt or configuration, and my life history. Life in this sense means the life that is lived, not unlived, the life that is affirmed, not denied, the life that is loved and accepted. Real life is the bodiliness which I *am*: unlived life is alienated bodiliness which I *have*. How would it be if in the creed we were to talk about the resurrection of the lived life? We should then accept dying too as a part of life, and believe in the victory of life over death. We can then affirm that eternal life will be lived in the transfigured body. 'The body will rise, everything belonging to the body, the identical body, the whole body' wrote Tertullian emphatically in his famous treatise *De Resurrectione Carnis* (after 212 c.e.): '*Resurget igitur caro, et quidem omnis, et quidem ipsa, et quidem integra*'; and he declared that the flesh was the key to salvation: '*Caro cardo salutis.*' For God has 'appeared in the flesh' and in the lived life we encounter God.

But in saying this we come up against a difference in gender.[2] How do men experience their body, and how do women? According to ancient notions, the woman's body, with its capacity for giving birth and its rhythms, was accused of being sometimes unclean and of being in general a source of temptation, weaker than the male body, and unreliable. Throughout the Middle Ages runs the idea that the human being as the image of God only begins beyond the body, at the topmost peak of the soul, *ubi sexus nullus ist* —where there is no gender. But according to the story of creation we have to accept that men and women in their full bodiliness are made in the image of God, and have to rejoice in the living God body and soul (Ps. 84.2).

Ideas about a resurrection from the dead presuppose death, and what is being thought of is quite clearly a bodily resurrection. Instead of 'raising' Paul can also say *zoopoiesis*, meaning the giving life to mortal bodies through the spirit of life which 'dwells' in them (Rom. 8.11). Paul also shows awareness of the special nature of the woman's body, with its ability to give birth, when he writes: 'The whole creation has been groaning in travail till now' (Rom. 8.22). In 1 Cor. 15 he calls the same process 'changing', transformation, and in Phil.

3.21 he looks to the 'glorious (transfigured) body of Christ'. If we take the word *zoopoiesis,* we mean the lived life; transformation presupposes life as 'minted form which takes shape as it lives', as Goethe wrote. Transfiguration, finally, anticipates the transmutation into the beauty of the divine life. According to all these ideas, what comes into being after death in the place of mortal life is not a different life. It is this mortal, this lived, and this loved life which will be raised, healed, reconciled, completed, and thus find its divine destiny; for 'God created man for eternal life' (Wis. 2.23).

The Eschatological Moment

When is this supposed to happen? The 'raising of the dead' is a universal eschatological symbol. All the dead are meant. The 'annihilation of death' is the cosmic equivalent of this anthropological idea. For Christian faith, the process of the raising of the dead and the annihilation of death has already begun with the raising of Christ from the dead. The process is continued through the Spirit, the giver of life, until it is completed in that eschatological moment when the dead are raised (1 Cor. 15.52). At that moment eternity breaks into time, and what comes into being is the eternal present.[3] At that moment all the times become simultaneous. 'Before the face of God time is not counted ... Hence the first man Adam is as close to Him as will be the last to be born before the Final Day. For God seeth time not according to its length but athwart it, transversely', explained Martin Luther.[4] That is to say, the eschatological moment takes place *diachronically,* throughout and across the times. What follows, conversely, is that all the deadly sins of men and women reach as far as the eschatological moment. The raising takes place immediately after the death of every individual person. 'The individual resurrection of the dead takes place in and with death', says the *Ökumenische Glaubensbuch* of 1973. From the hour of death until the resurrection to eternal life is only a moment.

It is not easy to formulate well-founded ideas about eternal life which are relevant for life here. When we search for a temporal concept of eternity, we come up against the question: Plato or Boethius?

If we follow Plato, we experience time as a moved sequence of fleeting and irrecoverable moments in life. That is life as *chronos*. According to Greek understanding, *chronos* is a brother of death, *thanatos*. Transitory time is the time of death. If time is what is transitory, then, as Augustine concluded, eternity, as its opposite, is what abides—what does not pass away.[5] Paul intensifies the distinction between time and eternity by talking realistically about the perishable and the imperishable (1 Cor. 15.53). If we apply this antithesis between time and eternity to eternal life, then we can certainly think the negation of time, but we cannot conceive a timeless life, for the life of the living is life in time. Consequently eternal life is often described as eternal rest. If that is applied to God, the concept of a timeless eternity makes God an unliving God without relationship. But the God of the biblical traditions is a living God, who has relationships in time to his temporal creations. His eternal life is the source of all the living. For that reason theologians from Aquinas to Karl Barth have given preference to the concept of eternity which Boethius put forward, rather than to the Platonic concept, and for Boethius *Aeternitas est interminabilis vitae tota simul et perfecta possessio*:[6] eternity is the unlimited, whole, simultaneous and perfect possession (or enjoyment) of life.

Here eternity is measured against the concept of life, not life against the concept of eternity. Applied to God, God's eternity then means God's unrestricted and perfect livingness and his inexhaustibly creative fullness of life. Applied to human beings, eternal life means unrestricted livingness, perfect fullness of life in unrestricted participation in the life of God. 'Through nature, human beings remain wholly human in soul and body; through grace they become wholly divine in soul and body', said Maximus Confessor.

If we apply this concept of eternity as fullness of life to the experience of time, the perspective changes. We do not look back sadly to lost time, to the past which cannot be brought back, and to the eternal death which swallows up everything that passes away with time. We look forward to the time that is coming to meet us, a beginning time in which the fulfilled time of eternal life is heralded. Our gaze changes from the deadliness of life to what Hannah Arendt called its 'natality', its 'birthliness'.[7] To put it in pictorial terms: time as it is experienced in the evening and in parting gives way to time experienced in the morning and in greeting. That is the experience of time in creation: 'And the evening and the morning were the first day' (Gen. 1.5). *Chronos* disappears and is replaced by *kairos*. For *kairos* is a brother of life, *zoe*. Empty time becomes full-filled time, and the fulfilled life here becomes the foretaste of the eternal and perfect enjoyment of life.

Lastly, we come to the relevance of the resurrection hope for bodily life here. The person who loves life in the light of the resurrection hope becomes capable of happiness. All the senses come awake, the understanding and the heart become open for the beauty of this life. But with this love for life we also become capable of suffering, and feel the pains, the disappointments and the trouble of this mortal life. Ultimately speaking, the life of people who love comes alive from within, and is vulnerable to what meets them from outside. We experience what life and death really are when we love, for in love we go out of ourselves, become capable of happiness and at the same time can be hurt. We can easily make the countercheck: the person who ceases to love life becomes apathetic and indifferent. For him nothing matters. He does not rejoice over anything, and he sheds no tears. He lets the world go by as if it were not there. Earlier, people called this the death of the soul. Today we might talk about zombies, walking corpses, people who are spiritually petrified.

Rejected, unlived, denied life is life that has been missed, and life that is dead. What we then experience is death before we have lived. The biblical image about the grain of corn brings this out particularly well. If the grain of corn is not sown and planted in the earth 'it remains alone' (John 12.24). It shrivels up and loses its capacity to live. That is death before life. That is denied, unlived and unfruitful life, a hopeless death.

A New Spirituality of the Senses

Today we are learning a new spirituality of the body and the senses. The mysticism of the soul is now being followed by a mysticism of the body. The mystical renunciation of the sensory world is being followed today by a new awakening of the senses and of the attentive life. The Spirit, the Jesus, who makes us live does not merely free the soul from sadness. It also liberates the body from tensions. It heals not only traumatic memories but psychosomatic illnesses as well. In a great sadness after the loss of someone we have greatly loved, we feel that all our senses have been quenched. We no longer see colours; the world round us looks grey. We no longer hear any melodies; everything is monotonous. We no longer taste anything; everything is insipid. It is as if our feelings have died. A distance grows up between us and the surrounding world like a glass wall. We become indifferent and turned to stone while we are still alive. That is what the Spanish mystics called 'the dark night of the soul'. If then, in the divine Spirit, through other people, or through a blossoming tree—I am talking about an experience of my own in a prisoner of war camp in 1945—we once more experience the unconditional love for life, then joy in living awakens in us. We perceive the beauties of the brightly coloured world again, we hear the melodies of life once more, we recover our sense of taste, and feelings draw us out into the world. We leave behind us the shell into which our soul had withdrawn. Our senses wake up, and we live life. That is the new sensoriness which belongs to the new spirituality of the body. In both we become aware of the coming springtime of creation. And in this way the 'resurrection of the body' acts upon our physical and sensory life here and now.

7

The Resurrection of Nature: The New Creation of All Things

The Catholic liturgy for Easter Eve enjoins the reading of the first creation narrative, Genesis 1. That is a wonderful sign: the world begins with a 'resurrection'. It is called out of the darkness of chaos into the light of the living cosmos. 'Thus on the very first day of creation—in the midst of the old creation—the work of the new creation flashes up. In this way creation acquires an eschatological character from the beginning, for in this way it can be seen as a great "promise" on God's part.'[1] With this, its future in the kingdom of God is created. All created things are true promises of their completion. Creation out of chaos is like a resurrection, and the resurrection from the power of death is like a new creation. The God who makes the dead live is the same God who calls into existence the things that do not exist (Rom. 4.17). The God who has raised Jesus from the dead is the creator of the new being of everything created. Resurrection and creation belong together, for the raising of the dead and the annihilation of death are viewed— and rightly so—not only as surmounting the consequences of the Fall, but also as the consummation of creation-in-the-beginning. In both resurrection and creation the negative is negated and the positive perfected. The light of Christ's Easter appearances was already viewed from early on as the daybreak colours of the first day of the new creation. Later, people called Sunday—the festival of Christ's resurrection—the 'eighth day', following the Sabbath, and the 'first day' of the Christian week. In this creation radiance the risen Christ appears as the first born of creation (Col. 1.15), who reconciles everything in heaven and on earth. That is the beginning of cosmic Christology, in which we understand the raising of Christ not only as God's eschatological act *in history* but also as the first act of the *new creation* of this transitory world into its true and abiding form. Resurrection is not only the meaning of history. It is the meaning of nature too.

Resurrection—The Meaning of Nature

By 'nature' we mean the present disrupted condition of creation, which is full of beauties and full of catastrophes. But we understand this nature as God's creation, because we trust in the faithfulness of its creator and perceive its capacity for transformation in the direction of its goal. What has Christ got to do with nature? Paul already talks about Christ as the mediator in creation: 'For us there is one God, the Father, from whom are all things and for whom we exist, and one Lord, Jesus Christ, through whom are all things and through whom we exist' (1 Cor. 8.6). If all things exist 'through Christ', then he manifests not only the Messiah of history but also the Wisdom of the whole creation as it creatively was at the beginning. It follows that the forces of nature are no more to be worshipped as gods than are the idols of the human world, such as emperors or capital (1 Cor 8.1–13). Sun, moon and stars are God's goodly creations but they are not gods. In the sovereignty of the risen Christ, people are freed from the deification of natural forces, and from the fear of them. Christ brings human beings into harmony with God's good creation. Orientation toward the forces of nature, which are themselves in need of redemption, does not help.

In practice, what followed from this cosmic Christology was that the Christian congregations in the multifaith cities of the ancient world did not come forward as one of the numerous religious groups of an until-then unknown deity. Instead they acted as a peace-conferring and uniting community of the creator and redeemer of all things. What they wanted was not a new religion but a new world. What they brought was not a new cult but new life. Their missionary task was not a competitive religious struggle but the peace of the cosmos and the reconciliation of humanity. The Christ proclaimed was expected not just as the Lord of believers but as the redeemer of nature too. The church was to understand itself as the beginning of the reconciled cosmos, and as an anticipation of the new creation of all things. In this respect it is a microcosm for the macrocosm which is destined to be the place of God's indwelling. This does not mean the churchification of the world; what is in view are Christ's cosmic dimensions. As the body of Christ the church has always been the representative of the whole creation. 'The Most High does not dwell in houses made with hands; as the prophet says, "Heaven is my throne and earth my footstool. What house will you build for me, says the Lord, or what is the place of my rest? Did not my hand make all these things?"' (Acts 7.49–50, following Isa. 66.1–2). God is worshipped in the temple of his whole creation. It is towards this that every Christian church and cathedral is aligned. It is only as the house of the whole creation that the Christian community is more than one religious society among others. If Christ is not perceived in all the things of nature as the Wisdom of creation, then he is not rightly perceived in the church either. Christianity is designed to be the healing beginning of the healed creation in the midst of a disrupted and sick world.

Matter with Future

In the eighteenth century, the first Enlightenment taught a simple materialism, conceived of in mechanical terms. Like Descartes, it viewed the objective world merely geometrically, as *res extensa*, and like Lamettrie saw the human being as a machine. But in the nineteenth century a new dialectical materialism came into being which tried to mediate the human subject and the object nature to each other, in order to understand the human being as nature, and nature in human terms. The young Karl Marx wrote: 'Among the characteristics innate to matter, movement is the first and most important, not merely mechanical and mathematical movement, but even more movement as drive, as the vital spark, as tension, as the torment—to use Jakob Böhme's expression—of matter.'[2] Here the borrowings from Paul's image in Romans 8 about the sighs and groans of creation are unmistakable. Twentieth-century philosophers such as Ernst Bloch developed this romantic concept of matter further, in the light of the theory of open systems and process philosophy.[3] Matter is minted form which develops. Matter is not just existing reality; it is always at the same time the potentiality of its own self. Its forms are not fixed, permitting the facts about them to be determined, but can be found in the movements of communicative and anticipatory processes with other material forms. Every determination of a material state is a human intervention into an open process. Matter is involved in processes of continual alteration, with a certain past and a still uncertain future. So with Whitehead and Bloch we can talk about a *Prozessmaterie*, or matter in process. All formed matter—and that is the only kind we know—is matter with future. But what future?

The modern sciences read nature in the light of anthropocentric concerns: nature is supposed to become the home of humanity. Nature is to find its future in human civilization, by which it will be dominated, utilized and preserved. The true symbols of nature, which were earlier called *signatura rerum*, are today viewed and processed as information, and are interpreted anthropocentrically. But can the alienation between human beings and nature be overcome if present-day human beings are alienated from themselves, and if their own essential nature is still hidden from them? Alienated human beings will find no harmony with nature.

Natural theology always read 'the book of nature' theocentrically and interpreted it eschatologically. All created things point to their creator: 'The heavens proclaim the glory of God'. At the same time they point beyond themselves, in the future of their redemption, to their true and abiding form in the kingdom of God. Human beings are created beings too, and in their development are aligned towards the future of God's kingdom. 'It does not yet appear what we shall be, but we know that when it does appear we shall be like him (God), for we shall see him as he is' (1 John 3.2). What emerges from this is not a historically attainable home of identity for human beings and nature, but a shared historical path pointing towards a common future. Human beings who long for 'deliverance from the body' will find fellowship with the creation which sighs under transience and yearns for the glory of God. The *signatura rerum* will be read theologically in cosmology, and anthropology will be read with eschatological hermeneutics. That is a way of reading nature in the light of its eschatological resurrection.

The 'Resurrection of Nature'

The young Karl Marx had this vision about the meaning and goal of the world's history: 'Hence *society* is the perfected unity of the essence of human beings with nature, the true resurrection of nature, the realized naturalism of the human being and the realized humanism of nature.'[4] He could conceive of a deliverance of nature from its alienation only as its resurrection into the world of human beings. But for him that did not mean the extension of human domination over nature, and nature's subjugation to human will, but also a reciprocal interpenetration of human beings and nature: without the naturalism of the human being, no humanism in nature, and conversely: without the humanism of nature no naturalization of the human being. But this essential unity between human beings and nature is supposed to take place in the perfect, classless society, free of domination. True communism is supposed to overcome not only the contradictions in human society, but also the contradictions between human beings and nature, and even the contradictions in nature itself. Otherwise the expression 'resurrection of nature' would be meaningless. Like Ludwig Feuerbach, the young Marx idealistically misjudged evil and failed to recognize death. But when he used the word 'resurrection' he could have known that this presupposes the death which has to be overcome. A 'humanism of nature' is not a 'resurrection of nature'; it is merely the appropriation of nature by human beings. This does not lead to nature's resurrection but often to its death. The catastrophe of Chernobyl and the progressive climate catastrophe are the signs of our time.

But if a resurrection of nature is inconceivable in a society of mortal human beings, what can such a resurrection of the natural world lead to? Traditionally, we think of a world beyond this one in a heaven of the blest or an Elysium of pure spirits. But that is closer to Plato than it is to Jesus and the New Testament. The resurrection of the dead takes place on this earth, and leads those who have been made alive to 'a new earth according to his promise in which righteousness dwells' (2 Peter 3.13). The kingdom of God is not just a kingdom in heaven; it comes 'on earth as it is in heaven'. Resurrection and eternal life are God's promises for the human beings of this earth. That is why a resurrection of nature too will not lead to the next world, but into the this-worldliness of the new creation of all things. God does not save his creation for heaven; he renews the earth. 'God's kingdom is the kingdom of the resurrection on earth.'[5] That puts all those who hope for a resurrection under an obligation to remain true to the earth, to respect it, and to love it as they love themselves. The earth is the stage of God's coming kingdom, and so resurrection into God's kingdom is the hope of this earth.

Are there any pointers in the created world to this future of resurrection? I believe that all created beings are created in the direction of this future, for the consummation of creation 'in the beginning' is the feast of creation in God's creation Sabbath. The seventh day of creation has no evening. God blesses everything he has created through his resting presence. On the Sabbath he is present to all. It is the Sabbath which distinguishes the concept of creation from the concept of nature. A Sabbath doctrine of creation is aligned towards the consummation of the created world in God's eternal presence. The resurrection of the dead, the annihilation of death and the resurrection of nature are the preconditions for the eternal creation which shares in the indwelling of the eternally living God. Creation 'in the beginning' is aligned towards this earth. Afterwards 'the whole creation groans in travail together with us' (Rom. 8.22–23), and that is the true resurrection of nature.

8

Life against Death

Death is not only the natural end of a mortal life. The destructive powers of death reach deep into personal, social and natural life. Lived life is every day a struggle against death and death's beginning in the petrification of the soul which leads to death. Every morning life must be affirmed and loved anew, since it can also be denied, refused and rejected. The will to live can switch over into psychosomatic programmes of self-destruction.[1]

The powers of death make themselves felt in *social life* through rejection, isolation and growing loneliness. If the social resonance is withdrawn from us, if we are not only mentally hurt and injured in our sense of self-worth, then bodily disturbances are the result as well. Psychogenic death is not infrequently followed by suicide, into which people are driven through isolation. Social life too is a struggle against death, a fight for recognition against possible and feared rejections, a waiting for respect instead of defeat because of social coldness.

Through exploitation, oppression and alienation, the powers of death reach deep into *political life*. Major decisions have incalculable consequences for the little lives of millions, even if this does not appear. They make life difficult and often impossible. The weak, the poor and the sick struggle literally for survival every day. Before our very eyes the failure to render help on the political level contributes to mass deaths in Cambodia, Rwanda, Darfur, and other places where death is rife.

Finally, all peace treaties, disarmament agreements and conventions about the use of nuclear weapons have as their tacit presupposition the fact that each partner wants to live. Mutual deterrence only works if all those concerned want to survive. What happens when one of the partners has no wish to survive, but wants to die in order to destroy this world? The suicide terrorists belonging to the Islamic world are as yet no more than organized individuals in the struggle against the West. But what happens if whole nations become suicide assassins?

What happens if the present global economic system should prove to be humanity's ultimate suicide programme, which is what the threatening climate catastrophe could suggest? The individual social and political will to live can turn into death drives. Then everything one does no longer ministers to life but to self-destruction. The very question as to whether humanity should survive or should rather disappear from this earth as a failed evolutionary development is a sign that among human beings the will to live is not a matter of course, and that the survival of humanity is not even rationally convincing. It can be affirmed only as a prerational premise.[2]

Life and death cannot be affirmed simultaneously but at most successively, when the time for the one or the other has come. But life and death can be rejected simultaneously, if both the one and the other have become a matter of indifference and one has become resigned, or dreams about another world of the soul, over against life and death. If we want to love life without reserve we must fight against death and the powers of death in the midst of life, and must not surrender to them.[3] In order to fight against death and not to give up, we need faith that death can be overcome. The resurrection hope gives us courage for a life in unreserved love here, and this love reflects the hope for the future of eternal life there. The resurrection hope justifies life against the claims of death. It manifests humanity's destiny to survive. It gives the prospect of victory in the daily struggle of life against death. Christ's resurrection comprehends God's 'yes' to life and God's 'no' to death, and awakens our vital energies. 'Jesus is the defiance against poverty, against sin and misery', wrote Christoph Blumhardt.[4] And for that reason Christians are 'protest people against death'.

The origin of the Christian faith is once and for all the victory of the divine life over death: the resurrection of Christ. 'Death is swallowed up in victory': that is the heart of the Christian gospel. It is the gospel of life. Where Christ is present there is life and there is hope in the struggle of life against the powers of death. In creative love for the life we share we do not just experience life's natural energies; we also already experience 'the powers of the age to come' (Heb. 6.5). 'In him was life, and the life was the light of men' (John 1.4). The Gospel of John is stamped by this theology of life. 'The life was made manifest, and we saw it, and testify to it, and proclaim to you the eternal life which was with the Father' (1 John 1.2). That, I believe, must be the heart of the Christian message in the twenty-first century. Jesus didn't found a new religion; he brings new life into the world, the modern world too. So we do not so much need interfaith dialogues, interesting though they are. What we need is a common struggle for life, for loved and loving life, for life that communicates itself and is shared, life that is human and natural—in short, life that is worth living in the fruitful living space of this earth.

9

God's Kingdom Is the Kingdom of the Resurrection on Earth

The extent to which Dietrich Bonhoeffer was influenced by Christoph Blumhardt (1842–1919) and his kingdom of God theology is not much known, and yet the parallels between Blumhardt and Bonhoeffer cannot be overlooked. Both understood the kingdom of God as being 'the kingdom of the resurrection on earth'.[1]

The Kingdom of God on Earth

Blumhardt writes: 'The goal was initially an earthly one, not as we Christians think a heavenly one but a heavenly one on earth … so that God's name may be hallowed on earth, so that there may be God's kingdom on earth, and so that his will may be done on earth. The earth is to proclaim eternal life … God on earth. I have no God in heaven: that is the God whom the angels have. I want to pray here below. I must have God there. The earth is the stage of God's kingdom … For the kingdom of God stands in direct relationship to the earth; it lives now, with the earth … The Saviour in this world. God's goal is this world. Jesus is the defiance against poverty, sin and all misery.'[2] 'Nature is the womb of God. It is from the earth that God will come to meet us.'[3]

And then Bonhoeffer. In 1932 the young Dietrich Bonhoeffer gave a splendid lecture on the petition 'Thy kingdom come.

The prayer of the Christian community for God's kingdom on earth.' 'Only the person who loves the earth and God in one can believe in the kingdom of God.' We are no 'backworldsmen'. Christianity is not a 'religion of backworldliness'.⁴ 'Christ … does not lead people to a religious flight from the world into worlds behind the world; he gives the earth back to them as their faithful sons.' 'The person who loves God loves him as the Lord of the earth just as it is: the person who loves the earth loves it as God's earth … The person who loves God's kingdom loves it as God's kingdom on earth.' 'The hour in which the church prays today for the kingdom pledges it to faithfulness to the earth, to misery, to hunger, to dying.'⁵

The theological faithfulness to the earth of Blumhardt and Bonhoeffer is a reply to Nietzsche's accusation in his *Zarathustra*, and is at the same time a criticism of the Christian religion of redemption, the reduction of salvation to the salvation of the individual soul, and the nineteenth-century piety which was concentrated on that. Against the slogan 'only those will be saved', Blumhardt put Jesus' saying: 'Seek first the kingdom of God'—and the kingdom of God includes social salvation and the salvation of the earth.⁶

'What does it mean to "interpret in a religious sense"?', asked Bonhoeffer, and answered: 'I think it means to speak on the one hand metaphysically, and on the other hand individualistically … Does the question about saving one's soul appear in the Old Testament at all? Aren't righteousness and the Kingdom of God on earth the focus of everything?'⁷ We find word for word parallels with Blumhardt: 'The other world is closed to us: God has given us no insight into it. Why not? Apparently because we are supposed to keep our eyes turned to this world, so that we can bring truth and justice here on earth, to God's glory.'⁸

Bonhoeffer writes: 'It is not with the beyond that we are concerned but with this world as created and preserved, subjected to laws, reconciled, and restored. What is above this world is, in the gospel, intended to exist *for* this world.'⁹

Resurrection against Death

At the centre of Blumhardt's hope for the kingdom of God on earth is not the Kantian idealism of nineteenth-century liberal German Protestantism, but the overcoming of death in the resurrection of Christ from the dead. This is the challenge to the destiny of death: 'We are protest people against death' for 'death shall be no more' (Rev. 21.4). The living God and death are irreconcilable antitheses. The hope of resurrection is part of the seeking for the kingdom of God, since the abolition of death is an irrelinquishable component of that kingdom. It is the fault of the religion of redemption to come to terms with death, and to expect eternal life only on the other side of death in a heaven of the saved. With Christ's resurrection the purification of the earth from 'sin and death' already begins now. God's new world is already beginning in the midst of the old one. 'Death as the idol of Christianity. Our beloved Christianity rushes to meet death as its real redeemer, its idol, to which it offers its hymns and prayers … Against this of course all the words of Scripture are helpless: "I will swallow up death for ever…" Death, where is thy victory? Hell, where is thy sting?' That is Blumhardt's ironic lament.

According to Bonhoeffer, Christians are faithful to the earth because they 'fix their gaze on the strange place in the world at which they perceive, astonished, the breaking of the curse, God's most profound Yes to the world … the resurrection of Christ. Here the wonder of wonders has taken place. Here the law of death has been broken, here the kingdom of God itself comes to us on earth.' And then follows the statement which for Bonhoeffer remained fundamental until his death: 'God's kingdom is the kingdom of resurrection on earth.'[10] In his letters from prison he comes back to this: 'The decisive factor is said to be that in Christianity the hope of resurrection is proclaimed, and that that means the emergence of a genuine religion of redemption, the main emphasis now being on the far side of the boundary drawn by death. But it seems to me that this is just where the mistake and the danger lie… The difference between the Christian hope of resurrection and the mythological hope is that the former sends a man back to his life on earth in a wholly new way which is even more sharply defined than it is in the Old Testament.'[11] After their engagement, Bonhoeffer wrote to his fiancée, Maria von Wedemeyer: 'May God give us [this faith] daily; And I do not mean the faith which flees the world but the one that endures in the world and which loves and remains true to the world in spite of all the suffering which it contains for us. Our marriage should be a yes to God's earth, it should strengthen our courage to accomplish something on the earth.'[12] He reinforced this unconditional 'yes' to God's earth in the prison cell from which he was to go to his death. His 'yes' to the earth is founded on his hope of resurrection and his preparedness to participate in 'the suffering of God in the life of this world'.

PART THREE

GOD IS RIGHTEOUSNESS AND JUSTICE

10

No Monotheism Is like Another: The Dissolution of an Inappropriate Term

The term *monotheism* sounds clear enough, but in fact it is open to many interpretations. The religious phenomena which it describes as a unison are no less polyphonic than the ones called polytheism. Anyone who talks about monotheism is like someone who sees only a wood everywhere without being able to distinguish between the different trees. He has failed to approach the phenomena closely at all, and knows nothing. If we want to employ the term usefully, it has to be explained. But if a term needs more explanation than it itself is capable of explaining, it is not very serviceable. We shall try to make this need for explanation clear, so that we can dispense with the term.

Who invented the term, and what was it used for? Can we transfer one religious phenomenon to others without blurring the differences? Monotheism is translated as 'belief in one God'. But this does not tell us anything about the nature of this divine unity. Nor—whatever the nature of this divine unity may be—does the term say anything about its religious, cultural or political consequences. What is the theistic *monas* and what is its effect? What point can it have to sum up the religions of Judaism, Christianity and Islam as 'monotheistic religions'? What intention lies behind the attempt to bring together all the 'world religions' into as abstract as possible a transcendent point of unity in infinity?

If we look more closely from the angle of the history of religion, we shall discover that each so-called monotheism is different. No 'monotheism' is like any other. So what is the point of this overriding term, detached from the actual differences?

Seen logically and rhetorically, 'monotheism' is merely a term of relation, intended to exclude its opposite, 'polytheism'. 'Theism'— a term without content—is analogous. It only has a meaning inasmuch as it excludes its opposite, 'atheism'. But what deity is meant with the term 'theism' is left open: it can be mono-, heno-, poly-, pan-, or panentheism, or whatever theism happens to be in question. As these portmanteau terms show, what we are dealing with here are the logical problems of 'the one and the many' and 'the one and the other'; but nothing more than that. And what has that to do with the many-faceted and complex religious phenomena? On what do these terms shed light, and what do they obscure?

A Primal or Ur-Monotheism?

The term 'monotheism' dates from the period of the Enlightenment, and was probably coined by David Hume, as a way of characterizing the Persian religion of rule.[1] He was not thinking of Judaism, Christianity, and Islam. On the steles set up by Xerxes at the frontiers of his empire stood:

'I am Xerxes, the great king,
King of Kings,
king of the lands
in which all manner of men dwell,
the king of this earth far and wide'

To what extent is that meant in a monotheistic sense? Rule over the world belongs to the one God in heaven; lordship over the different peoples and countries belongs to his image on earth: one God—one king—one universal empire. That is the religious idealization of power: the more power the more divinity. And so the earthly ruler is declared to be God. As the Son of Heaven, the Son of God, and the God Emperor he stands over against his subjects, and demands religious worship and absolute obedience.

The notion that the one God in heaven has to have the one ruler on earth as his correspondence, and that the divine universal sovereignty has to be matched by political rule over the earth, is age-old political theology. We find it in the Chinese ideology of the emperor as the Son of Heaven, in Japanese state Shintoism, and in Persian, Babylonian and Egyptian myths of rule. Echnaton's state, with its sun worship, is a good example of this political mono-theism. Yet it was never more than a utopia, because there was never a worldwide empire that went undisputed. An encounter—ironical in the context of world politics—took place in 1245 at the court of the Mongolian ruler Genghis Khan in Karakorum. Two Franciscans from Rome came before the Khan hoping to convert him. He responded:

> Dei fortitudo, omnium hominum imperator. Praeceptum aeterni Dei: In coelo non est nisi unus Deus aeternus, super terram non sit nisi unus Dominus Chingis Chan, filius Dei. Hoc est verbum quod vobis dictum est.[2] [The might of God, the ruler of all men. The precept of the eternal God: In heaven there is none but the one eternal God, upon earth there shall be none except the one Lord Chingis Chan, the Son of God. This is the word I say to you.]

The Franciscans took this answer of the Mongolian emperor back to 'God's representative on earth' in Rome, who legitimated his religious power in a very similar way.

In the Western world, Aristotle reduced the correspondence between metaphysical and political monotheism to a definition.[3] In Book 12 of his *Metaphysics* he puts forward the view that the deity—the *theion*—is one, indivisible, immovable, impassible, immortal and perfect. The universe has a monarchical structure. It resembles a pyramid, with a solitary apex. Aristotle closes his metaphysical exposition with a quotation from the *Iliad*: 'Being resists wrong rule: The rule of the many is not good. Let one be Lord.' In Homer the last sentence is the political call with which Agamemnon unites the Greek city states to do battle against Troy. Whether in his *Metaphysics* Aristotle was thinking of his pupil Alexander the Great we do not know. But ever since then, the political monarchy of the ruler has been supposed to correspond to the cosmic monarchy of God. The worldwide empire can only be one. Once the monotheistic reason for political power is advanced, imperialism is the inescapable claim. Like the deity, who determines everything while being himself determined by no one, the *imperator* rules all human beings and is ruled by no one. His sovereignty is absolute. But it is not arbitrary, for it has to conform to the will and laws of the deity. Consequently the obedience of his subjects is unconditional but not blind, since they have to observe the divine will and the divine laws. Political monotheism arrived at its final form in the absolute states of the Enlightenment period, the states in which there was religious and confessional unity: according to Louis XIV's tenet, '*un roi—une foi—un loi*'—one king, one faith, one law. In the Hitler dictatorship it sounded more secular but was no less religious: 'one people—one Reich—one Führer'.

Another form of primal monotheism or ur-monotheism is the *religion of patriarchy*. By cultural patriarchy we mean the male ordering of authority, property and inheritance which has been the general rule among human beings almost everywhere since the beginning of historical times.[4] Here there is no need for us to trace this back through cultural history. We shall only look at Roman-Christian patriarchy, because this still often prevails today. The Roman *pater familias*, the father of his family, occupied the position of a monarchical ruler in his family and household, and possessed unlimited, lifelong power over everyone who belonged legally to the family unit: women, children and slaves. Where these people were concerned he occasionally even had power over life and death, the *potestas vitae necisque*. The Roman father of a family corresponded to the Roman father gods and to the later father of the gods, Jupiter, acting as the household priest. The Caesar was seen as the *pater patriae*, the father of his country, and ruled as priestly king or priestly father, the *pontifex maximus*. On the one hand these titles reflect the people's expectation of protection by the ruler, and on the other his unrestricted power: the father of his country is omnipotent—*pater omnipotens*. In Lactantius's writing about 'the Wrath of God', we can clearly see how the Roman idea of the father has been transferred to the Christian God: the one God is both Lord and Father, his power being fatherly and also supreme. 'We should love him because he is the Father, but we should also fear him because he is the Lord ... In both persons he is deserving of worship. Who would not love the Father of his soul with a proper childlike reverence? Or who without punishment could disdain the one who as the ruler of all things has the true power over all?'[5]

It is not difficult to see how this double Roman concept of God as 'God the Lord' and 'God the Father' put its stamp on the Christian picture of God in the West. The catechisms tell us that God 'is to be feared and loved' above all things; and in the history of Western culture the father's authority over the household always had these two sides as well. The man is the master of the house and the father of the family, and has the final power of decision in all the questions that arise. He is also 'the head' of the woman and her lord and master, she is his 'body' and subject to him (1 Cor. 11). Christian theologians from Augustine and Thomas Aquinas down to Karl Barth have defended patriarchal monotheism with these alleged biblical arguments. But what has this patriarchal God got to do with the Abba mystery of Jesus? What has Jupiter, in whose name Pontius Pilate had Jesus crucified as a rebel against the Roman imperium, to do with the Father of Jesus, for the sake of whose name Jesus was crucified? Nothing at all!

Was There a Covenant Monotheism in Israel?

Theologically speaking, Israel was born through the Exodus from slavery in Egypt into the promised land of liberty. As the first commandment says, God is called Israel's Lord because he liberates, not because he legitimates political or patriarchal rule. Israel's God is a subversive God, so Israel's liberator, deliverer and the giver of its living space has nothing whatever to do with political primal monotheism or ur-monotheism. On the contrary. It is true that the explanations always stress that Yahweh freed Israel from Egyptian slavery. But if we are clear about what Egypt meant religiously at that time, then what the God of Sinai, the God of Moses, freed his people from was Egyptian theocracy. Then the God of the Exodus stands counter to political ur-monotheism as it was cultivated in the kingdom of the godlike Pharaohs. Jan Assmann indeed supposes that 'Moses the Egyptian' took over his monotheism from the sun worshipper Echnaton.[6] But we have to accept that there is a very great distance between Echnaton and the God of Moses before we can use the term 'monotheism' for both. What has Echnaton's sun god to do with the God of the nomads who were Israel's patriarchs? It is a point worth noting that in Egypt the Pharaohs called themselves after the gods in whose name they ruled—Echn*aton*, for example, or Tutench*amon*—whereas Israel called God after the people to whom he had revealed himself: the God *of Abraham*, the God *of Isaac*, the God *of Jacob*. The God who 'has *seen* the affliction of his people who are in Egypt, and has *heard* their cry and has *come down* to *deliver* them and to *bring them out*' (Ex. 3.7–9) has nothing to do with Amon or Aton. According to Psalm 8 he does indeed belong to 'the assembly of the gods', but there he is the great alternative to the gods of power and sacrifice. They demand the surrender of human beings—this God surrenders himself *for* human beings. Those gods look upon the glory and splendour of rulers and priests in the palaces and temples; this God looks on the afflicted, 'sees' their suffering, and enters their prisons in order to bring them out.[7]

The experience of the liberating God is followed by the experience of the covenant between the people liberated and this God. With his *self-determination* 'I will be your God and you shall be my people', God commits himself finally to the people of Israel. Since Israel owes its existence to Yahweh's election and liberation, it is self-evident that it can worship 'no other gods' besides this God. That is not an absolute, universal monotheism. Other peoples have other gods, but Israel is not to have these 'other gods' 'besides' Yahweh. Even the famous Shema Israel (Deut. 6.4f.) says only: 'Hear, O Israel, the Lord *our God* is one Lord'. God's covenant with his people excludes other gods, but initially only for Israel.

God's self-determination to be Israel's covenant God implies his *self-limitation*. It secures Israel's freedom in the covenant with God. The commandments are commandments whose observance guarantees the freedom won through the Exodus. This too runs counter to ur-monotheism with its religious idealization of supreme power and obedience. It is true that at the time when Israel was an independent state, as it was under Solomon, there was also a theology of kingship, taken over from Egypt. But in Israel this theology was always limited by the people's covenant with God. However, for most of its history Israel was not politically independent. It lived in dependency on the great powers. Consequently the powerless little state was far removed from imperialist ur-monotheism. It is only in the eschatological hope of the great prophets that we first encounter the idea that one day the God of Israel will be the God of all the nations, and that his righteousness and justice will guarantee eternal peace on earth. But what counted for Israel in its history of suffering was the affirmation: 'O Lord our God, other lords besides thee have ruled over us, but thy name alone we acknowledge' (Isa. 26.13). So it was certainly not the case that Israel viewed its God as 'the all determining reality' and as the Lord of heaven and earth who already ruled with almighty power.

But Israel knew that God of its covenant as its companion on its way and the fellow-sufferer at its side. Part of God's covenant with the people of his choice was the promise: 'I will dwell in the midst of the Israelites.'[8] The *indwelling* God—that is the Shekinah—shares Israel's joys and sufferings, its persecutions and its hopes. If the divine indweller among the Israelites is compared with the creator of heaven and earth, one must either talk about a bipolar concept of God, as Abraham Heschel does, or with Franz Rosenzweig speak of an inner self-differentiation in God himself.[9] The one God whom Israel confesses is then an inwardly self-differentiated God. His unity is diffused in history and is united in the hope for his universal unity. Every Shema Israel prayer 'unites' God if it links the Shekinah within us with the God who is over all. It is only in the kingdom of God that there will be universally united what here has become dialectically divided in the history of Israel and can only be stated severally.

If we bear in mind the way in which Israel's belief in God is constituted—God's self-determination, his self-limitation, and his indwelling in Israel—it immediately becomes clear that the term 'monotheism' is inappropriate and explains nothing.

Trinitarian 'Monotheism' in Christianity?

Christianity arose neither out of a political religion of rule nor out of a patriarchal family religion. It certainly adopted both forms in the course of its history, but the document of its origin speaks a different language. At the centre stands the person and gospel of Christ, not a general concept of God. In the community of Christ, believers have a *trinitarian experience of God*: God is the Father of Jesus Christ. In the community of Christ believers have a *trinitarian experience of life*: the Spirit of life is the Spirit of God and Christ.[10]

In the community of Christ, Christ's God becomes the God of believers. Jesus' exclusive 'Abba' mystery opens out, becoming 'Our Father'. When Jesus discovered the Abba mystery of God, and himself in that mystery as 'the beloved Son', he left his family and began to live among the poor of the people (*ochlos*) (Mark 3.31–35). So 'the Father of Jesus Christ' has nothing to do with the father of a family, or with what in German is called 'the Fatherland'—one's own country. He is not a God of the powerful; he is a God of little unimportant people. What we experience in him is not power heightened into supreme power and almighty power, but the love which empties itself and is creative in so doing. It is not the self-giving of human beings to God which becomes the liberating experience of God; it is the self-giving of God to human beings and all he has created. This self-giving is so strong that God's very nature is seen not as power but as love: 'God is love' (1 John 4.16). The love which God himself is, is almighty because it is unconquerable. From that love 'nothing can separate us' (Rom. 8.31–39). The experience of the wide space for living which opens up in the divine love excludes every idea about a divine universal monarch. W. H. Vanstone brings this out in his poem:

> Here is God, no monarch he,
> thron'd in easy state to reign.
> Here is God, whose arms of love
> aching, spent, the world sustain.[11]

Energies for living awaken in the person who is loved. So out of God's love, people in the community of Christ receive the spirit of new life. In the Old Testament, *ruah* is the divine creative force and the creative energy for living (Ps. 104. 29, 30). According to the testimonies of the New Testament, 'the grace of Christ' and 'the love of God' and 'the fellowship of the Holy Spirit' act together in the experience of redeemed and reborn life. The persons who act together in this way are personally distinguished: Christ—God—Spirit; but they are bound together in fellowship in the unified movement for the redemption of created beings for eternal fellowship with God. In Christianity the new experience of life acts in as liberating a way as did the Exodus experience in Israel. But whereas Israel's experience was liberation from the Egyptian theocracy, here it is liberation from the godless powers of death. So Hegel was right when he called Christianity 'the religion of freedom'.

The trinitarian experience of God is defined in the Christian doctrine of the Trinity by linking the concept of God with Christology. Jesus, 'the Son of God', is one substance with the Father and the Spirit. So the unity of the one God must be further differentiated inwardly than it is in Jewish Shekinah theology. The unity cannot be monadic or numerical. God is not solitary. God is not an atom, nor is he an individual. The unity of God must itself be formulated in trinitarian terms as a 'triunity'; he is the 'threefold God'. There are three possible ways of doing this: 1. In the framework of the ancient metaphysics of substance, for a long time Tertullian's principle was accepted: *una substantia— tres personae* (one substance, three persons). 2. In the framework of the modern metaphysics of the absolute subject, Karl Barth and Karl Rahner arrived at the formula: 'one subject in three modes of being or subsistence'. 3. If we dispense with a presupposed metaphysical definition of the unity of the Godhead, either as homogeneous divine substance or as the eternal absolute subject, the unity of the three different persons can only be conceived perichoretically, as in the Gospel of John: 'I am in the Father, the Father is in me. I and the Father are one' (John 14.10; 10.30). The unity is brought about by virtue of the mutual indwelling of the divine persons. For this, the mutually indwelling persons must at the same time be understood as inviting spaces that confer dwelling. It is only this perichoretic concept of the unity of the triune God which offers a correct definition of the trinitarian experience of God. For then the unity of God is not a solitary, transcendent vanishing point; it is an inviting, accepting unity which unites with itself. God's unity is a communicating unity, not an ultimate, indivisible one. Neither circle nor triangle are its appropriate geometrical symbols, for the love which is the essence of the triune God is an overflowing, all-embracing love which unites with itself: 'He who abides in love abides *in God* and *God abides in him*' (1 John 4.16). In love God throws himself open to become the dwelling space of those he has created, and those he has created take God into themselves.

For Christianity too, the universality and totality of the God of Christ belong within *eschatology*. With his raising from the dead, God has installed Jesus as the Lord of his kingdom. Consequently in history this kingdom takes the form of a servant, and is termed the lordship of love. In history it is disputed.[12] Like death, 'angels, principalities and powers' are still really existing hostile powers. In principle, it is true, God has already put everything under his Christ's feet, but 'we do not yet see everything in subjection to him' (Heb. 2.8). The completion of that which began when Christ was sent into this world belongs to the eschatological drama which Paul outlines in 1 Corinthians 15: 'As in Adam all die, so in Christ all will be made alive, first Christ, then those who belong to Christ when he comes—then the end, when he will hand over the kingdom to the Father, and will abolish all rule and authority and power … The last enemy to be destroyed is death. Then the Son too will be subject to the One who has subjected everything to him, so that God may be all in all' (1 Cor. 15.22–28). Then the triune God will become the all-one God and his glory will interpenetrate and illumine all things. It is only then that it will be possible to call God 'the all-determining reality'. It is only then that it will be possible to talk about a divine unlimited omnipotence, omnipresence and omniscience. But in history these sovereign attributes of God are determined, restricted and formed by Christ.

Can this trinitarian-eschatological concept of God—or better: this divine history—be called 'monotheistic'? If Christianity is termed *monotheistic*, then this word explains nothing but obscures the best.

Is the Islamic Belief in God Pure Monotheism?

The most severe challenge to Christian theology was, and still is, *Arianism.* The Alexandrian theologian Arius described Christ as God's first created being, but not as the only begotten Son of God. He did so not in order to belittle Christ but in order to maintain the undivided divinity of the one God. His option in favour of pure monotheism made of Christ a moral teacher, a prophet and a model, but deprived his suffering on the cross of its redemptive efficacy as divine suffering for the reconciliation of the world. Although the patristic church decided against Arius and in favour of Athanasius, and hence for the trinitarian concept of God, Arius has always had his followers in Christian history. In the Reformation period it was the Socinians, and in modern times the Jesus humanists. For these, being a Christian and belief in God diverged, and still do. Today they prepare the way for the Islamization of the Christian concept of God. But that is to take the wrong path.

The concept of God in the Koran—the concept which Mohammed taught—is closest to the monotheism which at the beginning we called primal or ur-monotheism.[13] *'Allah akbar'*: God is one and other than him there is no God. God is the ever greater God, God is the Creator of all and the All-Merciful. To him believers owe entire, undivided devotion: Islam. The infinite, eternal, one God has no 'Son' beside him. He has his prophets in Judaism and in Christianity, Moses and Jesus; but Mohammed is 'the seal of the prophets', that is to say he is the last, the perfect, the absolute prophet. That makes Islam the final, apocalyptically absolute religion.

'God did not beget—God is not begotten' wrote Muslims to the Christian church in the countries they conquered. They accused the Christians (as they do still) of believing in three gods: tritheism. Muslims certainly respect Judaism and Christianity as 'religions of the Book',[14] but the one God they worship is superior to the God of Israel and the Father of Jesus Christ in that he is universal and total, and makes his worship—Islam—the final redeeming project for all peoples and the whole earth.

True Islam is as undivided as Allah is almighty. There is no separation between religion and politics, belief and law, religious life and family life. That is to say, on the foundation of its belief in the one God, Islam is theocratically aligned. Islamic theocracy can be either the rule of a caliph or the rule of the mullahs—to put it in terms of the Christian analogies, it can be a state church or a church state. But a separation between religion and politics, the religious society and civil society, is a new experience for Islam in modern society. The Islamic theocracy is imperialistically aligned as a matter of course, for only one single rule over the world in the one single worship of the one God can correspond to that one God. No more than Christian mission, does Islamic mission have to be spread by force, as it was in the Middle Ages; in today's world it can also work through conviction.

That brings us to the theological problems about Islamic monotheism.

1. If the one eternal God is indivisible, how can he impart himself? But he has finally imparted himself in the Koran. Is then the Koran, as God's word and communication, as eternal as God himself? In that case there would be not only the one God but as well as him what he eternally imparts in the Koran. But if God imparts himself in the Koran, then his unity is not monadic or numerical; it is a unity differentiated in itself, a unity which is in a position to impart itself. If, on the other hand, the Koran is not the eternal word of the one God, then it is the work of human beings, subject to its time, and open to, and in need of, historical-critical interpretation. Consistent monotheism would have to demythologize the Koran and transpose it from the divine sphere into the human one, from the eternal to the temporal. But would Mohammed then still be apocalyptically 'the seal of the prophets'?

2. The God of Islam is not only the one God, but also the one God of all; but Islam, seen historically, is particularist. The 'house

of Islam' embraces neither all peoples nor the whole earth. That is the reason for Islamic eschatology. Of course the God of Islam will at the end be the one God of all; but in history this is not yet the case: there are believers and there are those who are still unbelievers, so there is the one God and Satan. In Mecca this Satan can be ritually stoned, as a mythical figure representing the enemy of God, but he can also appear politically as 'the great Satan', the United States of America, and 'the little Satan', Israel. As the enemy of God, he must in any case be fought against with all possible means.[15] But in this case the alleged pure monotheism of Islam has a dualistic basis. The one does not exist without the other. Anyone who believes in the power of God and the power of Satan can surely not be viewed as a pure monotheist. Islamic monotheism is a dualistic conflict-monotheism. That becomes clear from the rigorous friend-enemy thinking of the Koran where believers and unbelievers are concerned. Radical monotheism— in Christianity and Judaism too—always leads to just such an apocalyptic conflict dualism. But if consistent monotheism ends in the apocalyptic dualism of God and Anti-God (Satan), and if there is therefore a dualistic monotheism, how unequivocal is the concept monotheism really?

Monotheism: Exclusive or Inclusive?

Generally, every monotheism is viewed as exclusive. Monotheism excludes polytheism. The one God permits no other gods besides him. For that reason religious societies which are termed *mono-theistic* are usually intolerant towards the gods of other religions. According to the stories in the Old Testament, belief in Yahweh forbids the worship of Baal and the fertility gods. For 'the Lord' 'idolatry' is an atrocity, and must be put down as the worst of sins. According to 1 Kings 18, the prophet Elijah personally slew four-hundred-and-fifty priests of Baal. During periods when it missionized by force, Christianity systematically destroyed heathen sanctuaries. Political Islam acted in the same way in India, destroying the Hindu temples with fire and the sword, so that today only ruins give us an idea of their original beauty. At the same period, on the island Elephanta off Bombay the Christian Portuguese tried to destroy the Vishnu and Shiva statues. In these religions, which rest on personal belief and not on general experience, for every individual there is only a *monogamous* relationship to God and his religious community.

We see the Hindu world of the gods depicted in every temple. Can even this polytheism be monotheistic too? That is quite possible, and is also so interpreted by religious scholars in India. There is an *inclusive monotheism* too, which becomes possible with the help of the manifestation idea. Shiva appears in ever new forms: as dancer, as warrior, as hermit, and so forth. The One, Unnameable, Unknowable—the divine—manifests itself in the different forms of the great gods Vishnu, Brahma and Shiva. What confronts us in the many figures of the gods is the One Deity. The divine manifests itself comprehensively in forms as protean as life itself, and as polyphonous as the nature that surrounds us. It never appears as itself in only one single form. For that would destroy life and annihilate nature.

It is only in the many that the one can show itself. Consequently Indian polytheism may be held to be the true inclusive form of monotheism. It demands no belief and no personal commitment; it demands only attention to the encounters with the many forms of the divine in daily life. Hindu polytheism is an experiential religion which is so bound up with the experiences of life and nature that it superelevates and intensifies them, as we can see in the many festivals. The polyphonic world of the gods makes Indian life vibrate, and gives it its kaleidoscopic festivity.

It is seldom that people in the Asiatic countries have a monogamous relationship to only one deity or only one religion. In Japan there is the 'three religions movement', which can take in popular Shintoism, Buddhism and Christianity. In Taiwan there is a 'five religions movement'. To be on good terms with all the gods through little sacrifices lends life security. The gods do not disapprove of religious polygamy.

If even polytheism can be understood as inclusive monotheism, what does the term *monotheism* then really tell us?[16]

11

Shekinah:
The Mystery of God's Presence
in Judaism and Christianity

The Question: Where Is God?

I am not a historian, and not a biblical scholar either. I am merely a Christian theologian. That is to say, I am a Christian who struggles with his experiences of God: with the experience of God-forsakenness and with the experience of having been found by God when I was lost. In thinking about my experiences, I went to school to Jewish philosophers (or theologians) and learnt from them at least as much as I did from my theological church fathers.[1]

There was first of all the philosopher Ernst Bloch, with his still amazing *Principle of Hope* (1959).[2] From him I learnt to seek the divine mystery not just up above us in heaven, and not just within us in the ground of our being, but *before us,* and ahead of us, on our way into the unknown future. That is the God whom Paul calls 'the God of hope' (Rom. 15.13).

Then afterwards came Franz Rosenzweig, whose *Star of Redemption* (1921, 1930) I came increasingly to appreciate and love.[3] What moved me most deeply was his interpretation of the Shekinah, God's indwelling among his people Israel, as their companion on the way and their fellow sufferer in the exiles of this world and in its persecutions. That is the empathy of the Eternal One who 'will dwell in the midst of the Israelites'.

I should like to talk about both these things: about the Merciful One who shares our suffering, and about the Holy One who goes ahead of us and leads us to the eternal home of identity. But the presupposition for both these experiences of God is the descent and self-lowering of the Eternal One into our earthly and transitory world—the immanence of the transcendent God. Or in the words of the prophet Isaiah (57.15): 'I dwell in the high and holy place, and also with him who is of a humble and contrite spirit.' It is not just for us that it is important to experience the nearness of God in what happens to us. It is important for God too, for he wants to live among us and on this earth for ever and ever.

In the first part of this chapter I shall talk about the history of God's indwelling in the temple on Zion, in the holy city and among his people, and not least in the midst of the redeemed creation. In the second part I shall then go on to pick up ideas about the Shekinah which we find in Gershom Scholem, Franz Rosenzweig and Hans Jonas. In the third part I shall go into the mystery of God's presence in the Christian New Testament and in present-day theology, ending with the question about the eschatological Shekinah in the new creation.

Shekinah Theology in Scripture

By Scripture I mean what in Christianity is called the Old Testament. I don't read this Scripture and the New Testament one after the other, so that the one appears as what is 'old' and the other as 'new'. I read them together and parallel to each other, as testimonies to the single eternal divine history and its promises about the future.

Ideas about the descent and indwelling of God belong to *temple theology*.[4] The temple is the place where God's presence is experienced in the cult: it is the place where heaven opens and comes down to earth. 'This is the house of God and this is the gate of heaven' (Gen. 28.17). So the temple is also the centre of the world: on Mount Zion, Israel's God takes up his dwelling as the lord of the world. From Zion, justice and righteousness will go out to the world of the nations. 'The Lord dwells *in heaven* and in *his sanctuary.*' In this temple theology we already find a twofold presence of God: the one who embraces the whole universe dwells at the same time in the Holy of Holies of the little temple in earthly Jerusalem.

The history of the people of Israel whom God brought to Jerusalem is familiar and I shall only briefly recapitulate it. From the mountain of God, Horeb, God comes down to Moses and goes ahead of his people in a pillar of cloud by day and a pillar of cloud by night, leading them into the promised land. He 'dwells' in the transportable ark of the covenant, until David brings the ark to Zion and Solomon builds the temple for it. From that time on, 'God's indwelling' is present in the centre of the temple, in the centre of the city and the country, and in the centre of the people.

But what happened to the Shekinah when the Babylonians destroyed the city and the temple in 587 B.C.E.? Did the Lord withdraw his earthly indwelling into his heaven? That would have been the end of his covenant and the end of Israel's election. Or did his Shekinah remain 'dwelling in the midst of the Israelites', going into the Babylonian exile with the imprisoned people? Then the Shekinah itself would be itself homeless, humiliated, persecuted—and in need of deliverance! The second answer, as I believe, has preserved Israel's faith in God throughout its exiles down to the present day. It is the new experience of God's nearness in the alien land and in the country of the godless. It is the experience of God as Israel's companion on its way and the sharer in its sufferings. But how is that conceivable? I believe that the *Torah* took the place of the ruined temple, and *remembrance* replaced the cult, and *obedience* sacrifice: 'Where two or three bend over the Torah, the Shekinah is in the midst of them.' That does not mean that the gaze towards Jerusalem and Zion was lost, but because of the experienced presence of the Shekinah it became—as we can read in the great exilic prophets—the gaze of hope for the *new* Exodus, the *new* Jerusalem and the *new* creation. And there is more in the new than there ever was in the old.

In the exile, the remembrance of the exodus which had once led to Jerusalem and to Zion comes alive again. It is not a 'remembrance of things past'. These are remembrances of God's promise. Like the time of the exile, the time of the exodus was a time without a temple and without a home. Consequently in the exile the indwelling of the Lord 'in the midst of the Israelites' becomes important again. It becomes part of the foundational covenant formula:

'And I will dwell among the people of Israel,
and will be their God.
And they shall know that I Yahweh am their God,
who brought them forth out of the land of Egypt
that I might dwell among them'. (Ex. 29.45–46)

'I will dwell among the children of Israel,
And will not forsake my people Israel'. (1 Kings 6.13)

In the rabbinic literature written after the second temple had been destroyed by the Romans in 70 C.E., the God who 'indwells' the persecuted and scattered people takes on more human features. God 'the Lord' is experienced as 'Israel's servant'.[5] He carries the people with its sins: 'He lifted them up and carried them all the days of old' (Isa. 63.9). The Shekinah binds himself to Israel like a twin brother; Israel's shame is the Shekinah's pain too: 'In all their afflictions he was afflicted' (Isa. 63.9). 'I will be with him in trouble', says Ps. 91.15. And when in his torment a person falls dumb, what does the Shekinah say? 'My head is heavy, my arm is heavy': so says a kabbalistic writing. Ps. 23.4 already talks about a consoling accompaniment 'in the valley of the shadow of death'.

According to Elie Wiesel, the Midrash tells this moving story: 'Lord of the world, it was you who scattered us throughout the peoples and is it now you again who brings us back? ... And the Holy One, blessed be He, said to the children of Israel: When I saw that you had left my home, I left it also, so that I might return there with you.'[6] In Israel's exile and sufferings, the Shekinah shows the participating side of God, his ability to suffer.

This theopathy is not a poetical anthropomorphism; in the *pathos of God* as Abraham Heschel has interpreted it[7] it becomes real. It is the passion of God. The Eternal One goes out of himself and comes down and dwells among the people of his choice, making their fate his own.

But at the same time God's Shekinah, which has been banished with the people, presses towards its return to the holy city from its exile. 'Thus says the Lord', says Zechariah 8.3, talking about the second temple: 'I will return to Zion, and will dwell in the midst of Jerusalem, and Jerusalem shall be called the faithful city, and the mountain of Yahweh Sabaoth the holy mountain.' From this the prophet Ezekiel develops his great vision of the future, the temple of the end time, in which the Lord 'will dwell for ever in the midst of the Israelites' (Ezek. 40–49). This final indwelling brings the full glory of God into the city and the whole creation. The world becomes the new creation, which will endure. In the *new* temple, the *new* Jerusalem and the *new* creation the logic of hope tells us that there is always 'more' than there ever was in the old. What was transient will become what abides eternally, and what was destructible will become indestructible. Consequently the expected 'return home' of the Shekinah from the foreign land is ultimately speaking not after all a return to the old, but a journeying forth into what is new.[8] What is remembered is caught up and preserved in hope, and what is past is surpassed in the future. If this were not so, the misery of an earlier time would repeat itself endlessly.

The Interpretation of the Shekinah in Contemporary Literature

This brings us to the interpretation of the Shekinah in the literature of the present day. I shall look at Gershom Scholem, Franz Rosenzweig and Hans Jonas.

1. Is the Shekinah God's first creation, like God's Wisdom (*hokmah*) according to Proverbs 8, or is it one of God's attributes? If we follow Gershom Scholem's Kabbalah interpretation, it is neither a divine creation nor a divine attribute; it is *God himself in his presence* at a particular place in the world.[9] At the same time there is a distinction between God and the Shekinah: Scholem says, quoting: 'Then the Shekinah stood up before God and said to him …'.[10] 'For the medieval philosophy of Judaism the Shekinah as a manifestation of God was certainly present, and present precisely as something distinct from God himself.'[11] Is it in the metaphysical sense a hypostasis of God? We come closer to the differentiation in the unity of God if we look at the *sephiroth* tree of the Kabbalah in the book Sohar: here the three-times-three *sephiroth* which are related to each other are followed by the tenth *sephirah*, which is related to the earthly world. It is called Shekinah.[12] Here the unity of God is differentiated in itself and structured; it is not a monadic unity, and it is a self-communicating unity, not an ultimately indivisible one. The unity of God embraces the whole divine *pleroma* or totality, 'the fullness of the Godhead'.

This brings us to Franz Rosenzweig's interpretation of the Shekinah. Is the Shekinah a self-differentiation of God's? Rosenzweig sees it as follows:

The Shekinah, God's descent to human beings and his dwelling among them, is thought of as a separation which takes place in God himself. God cuts himself off from himself, he gives himself away to his people, he suffers with their sufferings, he goes with them into the misery of the foreign land, he wanders with their wanderings ... Inherent in God's surrender of himself to Israel is a divine suffering ... God himself makes himself in need of deliverance.'[13]

How does this deliverance of God come about, and who delivers the 'exiled God'?

The Jew fulfils the endless customs and precepts (of the Torah) 'for the uniting of the Holy God and his Shekinah' ... To acknowledge God's unity (in the Sh'ma Israel)—the Jew calls it: uniting God. For this unity is, in that it becomes, it is a becoming unity. And this becoming is laid upon the soul and in the hands of human beings.[14]

God's self-differentiation and his self-surrender to Israel in the Shekinah finds its correspondence in the homecoming and deliverance of the Shekinah through Israel's obedience to the Torah and its acknowledgment of God. That is an ancient metaphysical figure or pattern: God goes out of himself—God returns to himself again. That is the way Hegel also saw the self-realization of the absolute Spirit in world history. Hegel called the history of God which takes place in world history 'God's biography'. Rosenzweig, on the other hand, talks about the Shekinah's 'odyssey', as if the indwelling God had 'gone astray' and had lost sight of the goal of his surrender to his people. In Hegel the 'self-realization of the absolute Spirit' is in the hand of the Absolute, even if its medium is the history of human beings. This was just what Ernst Bloch wrote at the same time, in 1921, in his *Spirit of Utopia*. 'Only the wicked exist through their God; but the righteous—God exists through them, and in their hands is laid the sanctification of the Name, the naming of God himself.'[15] The *kiddush hashem*—the sanctification of the Name—'delivers' God from his alienation.

I would not dispute this, but would only ask whether there is then ever an ultimate prospect of redemption, as long as human beings are at once evil and righteous? If the Eternal One has laid his earthly fate in the hands of us ambivalent, uncertain beings, does redemption, then, perhaps never come?

3. Hans Jonas, finally, has made out of Rosenzweig's 'odysseys of the Shekinah' a 'myth' of world history:

> In the beginning, out of his inscrutable choice, the divine Originator of being, decided to surrender himself to chance, risk and the endless multifariousness of becoming. And did so wholly: since the Deity entered into the adventure of space and time, he held back nothing of himself … So that the world might be, and might be for itself, God renounced his own being; he divested himself of his divinity so that he might receive it back again out of the odyssey of time, laden with the fortuitous harvest of unforeseeable temporal experience, transfigured or perhaps disfigured by that experience…' [16]

Where does this journey lead, this adventure of God's in the odyssey of time?

> With the appearance of the human being, the Transcendence awoke to itself and from that time accompanied what he did with bated breath, hoping and beseeching, with joy and with grief, with satisfaction and disappointment.[17]

> After God had given himself wholly into the developing world, he had nothing more to give; now the giving-back lies with the human being.[18] … In our hands we literally hold the future of the divine adventure on earth, and we dare not fail him.[19]

In Jonas, the end of God's journey through the world is uncertain. The journey can succeed, but it can also fail. That depends on us human beings. It is not only the fate of our world which is in our hands; it is also the fate of God, who has emptied himself into our world. Since he has laid the sanctification of his name in human hands, God is no longer almighty. But then what hope is there that we shall succeed in what God, the ground of all being, expects of us? If God has given himself into the world 'wholly' and without reserve, then there is no transcendence except that which awakens in our consciousness. For Jonas, God remains *a single,* undivided subject; he does not differentiate himself from himself. So is Jonas subjugating God to the freedom of human beings? Is he therefore making him indifferent towards the victims of evil and the perpetrators of evil? Whereas Rosenzweig holds fast to the transcendence of the holy God beyond his surrender of himself in the Shekinah, in Jonas this transcendence lies wholly in the hands of the human being. So does this mean that God is journeying into the becoming of this world without a goal?

I have the impression that Jonas has moved far away from the biblical Shekinah, and has put his modern 'myth' in its place. And yet traces of Shekinah thinking can be perceived in his theology.

Does Shekinah theology contravene the almightiness of God? Must God give himself up in order to be able to indwell his finite created being? Kierkegaard offered the best solution for this problem:

> Only Almighty power can withdraw itself by surrendering itself, and it is just this relationship which constitutes the independence of the recipient. So God's almighty power is his goodness. For goodness means giving oneself totally, but in such as way that in almighty fashion one withdraws oneself, making the one who receives independent. All finite power creates dependency. Almighty power alone is capable of creating independence, of bringing forth from nothingness what is given inner permanence in that the almighty power withdraws itself.[20]

God is almighty in that God has power over himself. Only God himself can restrict God. Only God himself can withdraw himself in order to allow something other to exist besides him and with him. God's almightiness consists of his liberty. Consequently his descent and his indwelling, his becoming human and his surrender do not mean an emptying of his almighty power; they are its most wonderful expression.

Shekinah Theology in the New Testament

The Christian experience of God springs from the perception of God's presence in the person of Jesus Christ, in the self-giving of his life and in his resurrection into our future. This perception of Christ is also the source of the experience of the divine Spirit who dwells in believers and their community. This Christian experience of God stands in the light of Israel's Shekinah experience, and was interpreted from the beginning with Shekinah ideas.

The Christ hymn in Phil. 2.5–11 sees Christ's history as God's emptying of himself in order to redeem the world from its remoteness from him:

> Have this mind among yourselves which is yours in Christ
>   Jesus,
> Who, though he was in the form of God,
> Did not count equality with God a thing to be grasped,
> but emptied himself, taking the form of a servant,
> being born in the likeness of men.
> And being found in human form
> he humbled himself and became obedient unto death,
> even death on a cross.
> Therefore God has highly exalted him
> And bestowed on him a name
> which is above every name.

This history begins with the 'divine form' of Christ in heaven and ends on earth with 'the form of a servant' on the cross on

Golgotha. The incarnation of Christ presupposes the self-emptying of God and, as the consequence, his 'humbling of himself'. The goal of the self-humiliation is the redemption of the universe and the exaltation of all created being into the glory of God, as the hymn says at the end. But there are two divine subjects here: the Son of God humbles himself, becomes human like us, lives among us, and dies a violent death—and God the Father raises him from the dead, exalts him, and receives from him the redeemed world.[21]

Everywhere in the New Testament Christians see in Jesus 'the indwelling of God'. That is why they said later that 'In him the whole fullness of deity *dwells* bodily' (Col. 2.9) and 'The Word became flesh and *dwelt* among us, and we beheld his glory, glory as of the only Son from the Father, full of grace and truth' (John 1.14). They try to describe the mystery of God's presence in this person and in his history with a whole series of titles: Son of God and Son of man, Messiah and Servant of God, Lord and Saviour. But the point is always on the one hand the perception of God's Shekinah in this person, in his presence and in the space in which he lived, and on the other the experience of deliverance from our remoteness from God. We can perceive these two movements— away from God and towards God—in the Jewish Shekinah; now, in Christian experience, they are projected into the history of Christ: his lowering of himself into our world of forsakenness and violence, and his exaltation into the divine world of righteousness and justice and eternal life. These two movements comprehend the whole history of the world and are not restricted to the individual person of Christ. On the contrary, they highlight Christ's universal significance.

If we compare Jewish and Christian ideas about the Shekinah, we discover the following:

What they have in common is:

1. God's descent into the world and his indwelling among human beings;

2. The self-differentiation of God out of which this self-
   surrender of God proceeds;

3. The participation of the Shekinah in the fate of human
   beings and its capacity for suffering in the exile of the world.

What differs is:

1. There the Shekinah is in the people of Israel—here
   in the person of Jesus Christ; there the Shekinah is linked
   with the name of Israel—here with the name of Jesus
   Christ.

2. There the Shekinah suffers out of solidarity with the
   people, and leads the people home—here the Shekinah
   dies and is raised.

3. There, by virtue of his indwelling, the Eternal One
   delivers scattered Israel—here the Incarnate One gives
   himself up to death for the redemption of the world.

If we look more closely at Shekinah thinking in the Christian
Scriptures, we always find the idea of a *mutual* indwelling:
God is in Christ—Christ is in God; Christ is for us—we are
in Christ; God's Spirit dwells in us—we live in the Holy Spirit.
Later, the church fathers described this with the Greek term
perichoresis.[22] What this means is the mutual indwelling out of
which a unity-in-the-difference and a difference-in-the-unity
proceeds. The Eternal One and his earthly Shekinah are different
and yet one, because the one indwells the other.

On the first level, perichoresis describes the unity of Jesus the
Son of God with God the Father—that is to say, the unity of the
Shekinah with the eternal God. In the words of the Gospel of
John: 'He who has seen me has seen the Father' and 'I and the
Father are one,' for 'I am in the Father and the Father is in me'
(14.10, 11; 10.30). In John 17.21, in what is known as the high
priestly prayer, Jesus prays: 'That they may all be one; even as thou,
Father, art in me and I in thee, that they also may be in us, so
that the world may believe that thou hast sent me.' Through their
reciprocal indwelling, the Father and the Son form an inwardly

differentiated unity.[23] They give one another mutually the living space for the mutual indwelling. So God's unity is not infringed. Nowhere is there any talk of three gods. But this unity of the one God also comprehends his Shekinah among human beings, and in the indwelling the unity opens itself in order to receive into itself human beings and the created world, so that they may participate in it. The inwardly differentiated unity of God is an inviting unity, like the 'broad place where there is no cramping' (Job 2.16; *cf.* also Psalm 31.8).

On the second level, perichoresis describes the unity of Godhead and humanity in the person of Jesus Christ. This is not a matter of two who are by nature similar being bound together in inward community. Here are two different natures—that is, the one and the other. In Christian terms this describes the 'descent' of God and the 'dwelling' of the Eternal One in our earthly time. That is undoubtedly God's greatest mystery: his closeness, which embraces us, his presence in our world, far from God as it is, and his accompaniment on our odysseys in this world. Emanuel, 'God with us'—with us, the godless and God-forsaken. That is the name for the wonder which Christians experience in the fellowship of Christ.[24]

On the third level, perichoresis describes the indwelling of God's life-giving Spirit in believers and in their community. 'We are the temple of the living God; as God said, "I will dwell among them, and they shall be my people".' With this quotation from Israel's covenant formula (2. Cor. 6.16), Paul picks up Israel's idea about the Shekinah and with it interprets the experience of the indwelling divine Spirit among Christians. For him this is not just a spiritual experience; it is a bodily one too: 'Do you not know that your body is a temple of the Holy Spirit within you? So glorify God in your body and in your spirit' (1 Cor. 6.19, 20). In saying this he is urging Christians to bodily, earthly, social and political obedience to God's commandments, in accord with his righteousness and justice.

Christ—Companion on the Way and Fellow Sufferer

That brings us to the interpretation of the self-surrender and suffering of Christ in present-day literature. When I try to understand the presence of Christ in the light of the Jewish Shekinah concept, I am speaking primarily for myself.

For a long time the christological titles for Christ, such as Lord or King, were so much stressed in Christianity that his lowly status on this earth could be overlooked. It is only recently that there has come to be a widespread experience of *Christ as our brother* on our path through life, and our companion in the sufferings of this present time. He does not stand above us as Lord; he is beside us, and goes ahead of us as one of ourselves.

If God goes wherever Christ goes, then Christ brings God's fellowship to people who are humiliated, persecuted, assailed and murdered just as he was himself. His cross stands between the unnumbered crosses which line the paths of the perpetrators of violence on this earth, in the Roman Empire from Spartacus to Jerusalem, from the death camps of the German Third Reich to the 'disappeared' under the military dictatorships in Latin America. What the New Testament calls 'the sufferings of Christ' are not exclusively his personal sufferings; they are inclusively the sufferings of God's people and the sufferings of this present time. His cross stands in brotherly fashion between the crosses we have named, as a sign that God participates in our suffering and takes our pain on himself. The 'suffering Christ' has so much become one of many that all the uncounted and unnamed, forsaken and tortured men and women are his brothers and sisters.[25]

The fellowship of Christ is experienced not only as the fellowship of the humiliated Christ with us, but also as our fellowship with the Christ who was raised from the dead and exalted into the future glory. The Son of Man who finds us when we are lost takes us with him on his way to God's future. We experience this other side of Christ when we feel the energies of life and are born again to a living hope. Then we sense how 'the fountain of life' opens (Ps. 36.9) and fills us with new love for life, in spite of all the negations. Our powers are re-energized, and in the midst of the world of death we enter upon 'the path of life'. Then we live in the divine Spirit's field of force, and experience his vitalizing efficacies. Then we see this deathly world in the light of Christ's resurrection, and in the vital powers of the Spirit receive 'the powers of the world to come' (Heb. 6.5). The night of God's remoteness passes away, and the dayspring colours of God's new day are already visible (Rom. 13.12). We exist in the radiance it throws ahead of itself, and act in anticipation of God's future.

Original and true Christianity is a *movement of hope* in this world, which is often so arrogant and yet so despairing. That also makes it a *movement of healing* for sick souls and bodies. And not least, it is a *movement of liberation* for life, in opposition to the violence which oppresses the people.

If God's Spirit puts people on 'the path of life', that means *the path of righteousness*. In the Christian New Testament it is also called *the path of love*, which binds together justice and mercy. This love, hard though it is in practice, is the royal path of life. In this love there comes into being the reciprocal Shekinah of God in human beings and of human beings in God. 'He who abides in love abides *in God* and *God* abides *in him*' (1 John 4.16), for 'God *is* love'.

12

Psalm 82:
Righteousness and Justice—
The Measure of the Gods

A Sermon

Psalm 82

YHWH stands in the assembly of the gods,
in the midst of the gods he pronounces judgment:
'How long will you judge unjustly
and favour the wicked?
Give justice to the weak and the orphans,
uphold the rights of the wretched and the destitute,
free the weak and the poor,
deliver them from the power of the wicked!'
They have neither understanding nor insight,
they walk about in darkness.
All the foundations of the earth are shaken.
'I say: "You are gods
and sons of the Most High, all of you!
Yet truly you shall die like human beings,
and fall like one of the princes."'
Arise, YHWH, judge the earth,
For all the peoples belong to you!

The Assembly of the Gods

Here at last we have a real 'interreligious dialogue' when something actually happens! Not a 'parliament' of the world religions, not a United Nations assembly of 'religious leaders', not an ecumenical multifaith programme. No, the old gods and the new ones, and those who think they are 'sons of the Most High' gather together— I suppose in heaven—and dispute about their lordship over the world. A fantastic idea: let the gods finally get on with it themselves, and do what we on earth are trying to achieve with so much effort, but so fruitlessly!

This assembly of the gods is not concerned about peace. The concern here is justice, because it is justice alone which is the foundation for the earth, and justice is what the poor yearn for.

Let us now imagine that we find ourselves in this assembly of the gods. Whom do we see round us, in this congregation of the immortals?

> Over there in the right-hand corner I can see Zeus, the father of the gods, who has turned up from Mount Olympus with his wonderful Greek gods. He is surrounded by countless gods and goddesses. The young Ganymede is fanning him, to give him some fresh air.
>
> Over there in the left-hand corner I see the Indian gods appearing, with Brahma, Vishnu and Siva—and of course they have their goddesses too, and a throng of enchanting temple dancers into the bargain.
>
> But over there in the corner at the back, near the organ, it is a really solemn affair: Marduk and Ishtar are just entering, coming from Babylon, of course followed by a great procession of the whole Assyrian court.
>
> And in the fourth corner, beside the organ—yes, it really is the great Egyptian gods Ammun and Ra, Isis and Osiris, with Nut and Tot, and with them the god-like beasts. What a glorious sight!

But no—I haven't forgotten them. They aren't here yet, but I can already hear the hoof-beats of their wild herd as it comes thundering up. That is Wotan, the Germanic god, one-eyed, but carrying a tremendous spear, and beside him Thor with his mighty hammer, which strikes lightning from the clouds. They have come to us directly from Valhalla.

O Yes! 'How bright those glorious spirits shine', as Hölderlin wrote.

But down here there is also a whole throng of pretty unpleasant gods too, gods who don't want to be overlooked. These gods 'walk in darkness'. There is the horrible Moloch of the Phoenicians, who devours little children with an insatiable hunger. There is Kali from Calcutta, who prefers fresh young boys, whose skulls she then wears on a chain round her neck. The other sinister figure is called Mammon. Long before Marx, Luther considered him to be the most despicable idol on earth. What is he doing over there in his dark corner? I expect he is just planning the next 'hostile takeover' of some firm or other, and is collecting floating money in order to destabilize smaller nations in Asia, so as to thrust down even more people into poverty. The last in this horrible alliance is Mars, the god of war, who had us taught in school that *dulce et decorum est pro patria mori*—that it is a sweet and proper thing to die for one's country—and who then rejoiced over the mass graves in Verdun and Stalingrad, or wherever the nations are forced to go on sacrificing the flower of their youth to him

Yes indeed! Truly an illustrious assembly of gods and demons, both fascinating and terrible; and yet they are the ones who really judge and rule our world.

But suddenly someone stands up in this exalted ecumenical assembly and brings a charge against it. No one knows him, and he has an unpronounceable name. We say YHWH, but we know that this too is not what he is really called. He comes forward in the guise of a little mountain god from Sinai. What does he look like? I imagine him looking like John the Baptist, poor and ragged, dressed only in camel hair, and with a leather girdle; for not much else is to be had on his barren mountain. But he has a flaming passion in his heart—passion for the poor and the oppressed, and for the righteousness that brings them justice. His very appearance is a provocation, and what he has to say about 'interreligious dialogue' is nothing other than a shattering call to repentance out of the depths, addressed to these illustrious gods and goddesses in their diverse Olympic paradises, palaces and temples.

YHWH Calls the Gods to Repent

'How long will you reign unjustly and favour the wicked?' that is his indictment. Is it meant morally? Is it directed against the capricious and risqué doings of some of the gods, which the sagas of the different peoples describe so amusingly? I don't think so. The gods are certainly capricious—Homer was right about that. But they are only capricious in the way that chance in history—both personal and political history—is incalculable, and as the fate we are subject to is blind. In order to ward off the evil whims of change and the blind ragings of fate, men and women offer the gods sacrifices, to keep them in a good mood, and win their favour. *Do ut des*—I am giving you something so that you may give me something in return. That was the old commercial Roman principle for sacrificial dealings with the gods. And not just in Rome.

But there is more still behind the sacrificial cults. Because the gods rule unjustly, favouring the wicked but disregarding the poor, 'all the foundations of the earth are shaken', asserts YHWH. It is not just the caprices of chance and the blindnesses of human destiny which are dependent on the will of the gods. It is the orders of the cosmos itself as well. The system of the earth itself depends on them. It is not just life *within* these orders which is contingent; the orders themselves are contingent too. They are so fragile that human beings have to implore the good will of the gods. Why do the gods of the harvest demand the first fruits of the field? Why must the first-born children be sacrificed to the peoples' gods? Why did the Aztecs offer to their gods the still quivering, bloody hearts of their slaughtered enemies and of young men who were willing to be sacrificed?

It is because of this nameless, fathomless fear that perhaps one day nothing will grow in the fields any more, that one day no more children will be born, that one morning the sun might not rise above the horizon.

The judging and ruling of the gods dominates personal life, the political history of the world, and the history of the cosmos. If the gods are as 'blind' as chance, if they have 'neither insight nor understanding', then they will bring the whole structure of the world to destruction; then nothing is certain any more; then you can no longer rely on anything. Everything threatens to sink into chaos. The gods can confer life and blessing, but equally they can bring devastation and destruction on the world. That is why the Indian gods and goddesses always have a sunny side and a shadow side. Siva creates the world through his fiery dance—and in his dancing also destroys it again. Parvati manifests herself as the mother of life—and as Kali she devours her own children, and sticks out her bloodthirsty tongue.

Is YHWH right when he asks accusingly: 'How long will you favour the wicked?' If this is so, then it is certainly a question of life and death for human beings, and a question about the being or nonbeing of the earth.

We don't know what Zeus, Marduk, Brama, Mammon or Mars answered, if they saw and heard the little mountain god from Sinai at all. But we can imagine what their reply was, for we ourselves are still always given over to the caprices of chance and to blind fate, and we sense how the foundations of the earth 'are shaken' by the ecological wickedness of unjust economic systems, crimes which are actually 'favoured' by their gods, mammon and the rest.

What does YHWH advise his fellow gods? 'Give justice to the weak, maintain the rights of the wretched and the destitute, free the poor and deliver them from the power of the wicked.' Looking at the gods, with their greed for sacrifice, he says in simple, ordinary words: 'You gods, don't ask what human beings must do for you; ask what you can do for them! Don't demand sacrifice—bring about justice! But with what justice are they to judge? And justice for whom?'

YHWH's Righteousness That Brings about Justice

According to Israel's experience of God, YHWH, unlike the other gods, is a God who 'maintains the cause of the afflicted, and executes justice for the needy' (Ps. 140.12). He 'raises the poor from the dust, and lifts the needy from the ash heap' (Ps. 113.7). He doesn't just lay down what justice and injustice are, like human judges, so as to reward and to punish; he 'creates justice for those who suffer violence' and frees the helpless from the hand of the wicked. And for that reason the book of Job calls him 'the hope of the poor' (5.16). So YHWH is not a judge who judges without respect of persons, like Justitia, with her bandaged eyes. He is quite explicitly the advocate who takes the part of people without rights and puts to rights the unjust.

Here again we come face to face with the word 'sacrifice'. But what we are looking at now is not the *paying* of the sacrifice, but *the people who are sacrificed*, the victims. The little, unimportant people, the poor and the wretched, are the victims of the wicked, who feel that they are the darlings of their gods. The victims are the losers in our success-orientated society. The winners look down on them because, as opinion goes, 'they haven't made it'. In every society, ancient, modern or postmodern, we find these victims on the underside of the history of the powerful. But we have to seek them out; for people sitting in darkness cannot be seen. They are the people crippled by debt, the impoverished, the unemployed, the homeless, the HIV infected, the profoundly depressed and the abandoned children. Today these people are not sacrificed to the gods on bloody altars, but they are 'surplus people'.

Bring about justice for the poor; liberate these wretched men, women and children, save them from the power of the wicked who have everything going for them: that is the righteous rule of the saints in Israel. The righteous God knows the rights of the unimportant, but the gods of the wicked have no insight. They demand sacrifices, but the righteous God is concerned about the victims.

YHWH is righteous because—but also only inasmuch as—he gives their rights to the people who have no rights. More than that: the godness of the gods is to be perceived from this righteousness which sees those without rights righted. Where this justice-creating righteousness doesn't exist, there are no gods, whether they let themselves be called gods or not. God or idols: it is righteousness and justice that makes the difference. God and the gods: it is the deliverance of the poor that brings them together. For this is what YHWH expects of the exalted gods of the nations: the liberation of the oppressed.

The Poor and the Earth

Why does YHWH love the little unimportant people and not the rich? Why the losers and not the achievers, the ugly and not the beautiful? If he were to take pleasure in their misery he would not be just. But the very reverse is true. The young Luther hit the nail on the head when he said that sinners aren't loved because they are lovely; they are lovely because they are loved. Being loved really does make the ugly beautiful, and in the same way the deliverance that brings about justice makes the people without rights righteous, and the nearness of God makes the poor rich.

'Poor and needy': that is what the psalmists continually call themselves when they cry to God 'out of the deep' (*de profundis*). They are then crying out to the God who had mercy on the Israelites imprisoned in Egypt, because he saw their affliction and came down to them. The poor have nothing left to which they can appeal in order to achieve justice. God is their last hope.

But for all that, they don't have to whimper for grace, and beg for mercy. No, they actually have a right to God's help, for he has promised it to them in his covenant, promised it on his honour. This legal entitlement is not based on what they have, but on what they don't have. In their poverty and despair they have a right to God's saving justice. Because of God's 'preferential option' for the oppressed, these people vouch for him in a violent world of the wicked, because they are his, whether they know it or not.

The poor and the earth: YHWH's justice-creating righteousness has a saving significance not just for the poor in the world of human beings, but for the foundations of the earth in the world of nature too. Social justice and ecological wisdom correspond, just as social injustice and crimes against nature also go hand in hand. 'Poverty is the worst environmental pollution', said Indira Gandhi rightly. So the ones who give their rights to those without rights also save the earth, which sustains the life of us all. This modern insight is as old as Israel's psalms:

> God has established the earth and it stands fast.
> He judges the peoples with equity.

The human order is destroyed by crimes committed by the wicked against the poor; the cosmic order is destroyed by the gods who favour the wicked. Consequently the one, single justice-bringing righteousness must rule in the human world, in the cosmic world, and in the world of the gods, if the foundations of the earth are not to be shaken.

The Mortality of the Gods

YHWH's judgment on the gods who favour wickedness is unequivocal: 'You are gods and sons of the Most High, all of you!

Yet truly you shall die like human beings and fall like one of the princes.' That means that they really are 'gods', and are called to their godlike responsibility. But they haven't judged justly. They have ruled capriciously, and by doing so they lose their immortality. They fall like the political powers that be, whose wickedness they have favoured. They have become 'mortal gods'. And with this we dismiss this assembly of the gods and dissolve it.

The unheard-of thing in Psalm 82 is not the absolute claim with which YHWH judges his 'fellow gods' in this remarkable divine assembly. It is the fact that in this psalm Israel identifies the idea of the righteousness which saves the poor and brings about justice for the oppressed with the divinity of the gods, and therefore judges all gods—the God of Israel too—according to the standard of justice for those who have no rights. The poor have authority over the gods. The suffering of the oppressed is made the supreme standard—and that means the standard for 'the sons of the Most High' too. That is incredible, for it makes gods mortal and human beings immortal. Which god measures up to this righteousness? Who raises up the little people, brings about justice for the wretched, saves the poor from the hand of the wicked?

The great gods of the dazzling rulers and victorious nations 'walk in darkness', we are told. So is the God of Israel the only one who stands in the light of this saving righteousness?

No, not even the God of Israel as yet, for he has first to be exhorted to 'rise up':

Arise, YHWH, judge the earth,
for all the peoples belong to thee.

Is he sleeping, as another psalm assumes? Or has he gone away? Or is he deliberately 'hiding his face'? Who knows?

I suppose that up to then he had showed himself to the shepherd Moses, and through Moses to the people of Israel, only as the little mountain god from Sinai, but that now he is to rise up in judgment from this little people and this tiny country between Egypt and Babylon—rise in judgment on all the nations and the whole earth. Then justice and righteousness will go forth from Zion and liberate all nations, say the prophets. When YHWH rises up in his whole greatness as creator of the heavens and the earth, 'he will judge the poor with righteousness and decide with equity for the wretched' (Isa. 11.4). 'Then justice will dwell in the wilderness, and righteousness abide in the fruitful field' (Isa. 32.16). Then the whims of chance will disappear, and fate will no longer be blind, for righteousness and justice will put everything to rights: gods and human beings, heaven and earth.

Because today we are hoping for this divine uprising, we too are rising up with all our powers and potentialities against the wickedness which humiliates the poor and favours the violent, and are crying to the rulers and forces in power: 'How long will you judge unjustly and favour the wicked?'

So let our contribution to dialogue be the righteousness which raises up the unimportant, and brings justice to the poor, and liberates the wretched. Let this be our contribution to the dialogue with our own religion and with the gods of other religions, and with the powers of this godless world. Arise, God, and judge the earth, arise!

13

Sun of Righteousness:
The Gospel about Judgment and the
New Creation of All Things

Justice in Mesopotamia, Egypt and Israel

The idea that the world will end with God's final judgment is not originally a Christian concept, and not even a biblical one. Israel took over Babylonian, and later Egyptian, ideas about justice in its own independent way, and reshaped them in the power of its belief in God.[1]

The Sun of Righteousness:
The Cosmological Concept of Righteousness and Justice

In Mesopotamia the king was at once the judge and, as representative of the sun god Shamash, the executor of the divine justice.[2] This righteousness is the cosmic order of the world and life, like the light of the sun. In the morning the divine righteousness rises with the sun, and leads the country and the people along right paths. The person is righteous who guides justly; what is righteous is what is healthy; the person is righteous if he lives rightly. To live rightly can be said of plants, animals and human beings in the rhythm of the sun's light. Here, *judging* has the positive meaning of raising up, of giving life, and of healing. The king and judge has to see to it that 'the strong do not hurt the weak' and that 'orphans and widows receive justice'. He does not only have to protect the weak from the strong; he also has to protect the land from exploitation by human beings. But for his own part, he is dependent on the cosmic order. If there are natural catastrophes or famines, he is held responsible, and this can cost him his head. In this cosmological context, righteousness is an activity that brings about justice and that creates justice; it is not a righteousness that merely establishes what is good and evil, and requites it accordingly.

In Israel's psalms we find a 'solarization' of Yahweh on the one hand, and a historization of the Babylonian cosmological concept of righteousness on the other.[3] When Yahweh is extolled as the 'sun of righteousness' (Mal. 3.20), and is implored 'to arise', Israel's God is then also taking over the functions of the life-giving, healing, saving, and justice-bringing righteousness of the sun god Shamash. In the New Testament God is like the sun 'which rises on the evil and on the good' (Matt. 5.45). But because of the distinction between the creator and his creation, Israel's God is free towards the cosmos, and is not himself part of the cosmic order. In this way the Babylonian concept of righteousness is 'theologized' in Israel. God's just activity is also perceived in the contingent history of the world, not just in the constant orders of nature. Finally, in Israel's prophets we find what Gerhard von Rad has called 'the eschatologizing of historical thinking'.[4] 'The Day of Yahweh' is conceived of in a future which reaches beyond Israel's history into universal history, and is moved to the end of world history and the history of nature in general. In this way uniqueness and finality enter into the idea about the divine judgment. The last judgment will take place in all the spaces of creation, and act diachronically through all the times of created being. But the eschatological 'Day of Yahweh' will not only execute judgment on the past; it will also bring to light the future of the new creation of all things (Isa. 65.17; Rev. 21.1).

The Scales of Justice:
The Anthropocentric Concept of Righteousness

The Egyptian idea about judgment is an idea about the next world; it is not related to the cosmic justice of this one.[5] The divine judgment is judgment on the dead, a transition from this world to the world beyond. The continuity between this world and the next is constituted through reward and punishment in the world beyond for deeds and misdeeds committed here. The human being is the sum of his good and evil works. At the centre of the judgment of the dead stand the scales, with the heart of the dead person in the one pan and his acts in the other. The god Anubis tests where the pointer on the scales falls, the ibis-headed god Thoth registers the misdeeds, and the dead person is led by the jackal-headed god to judgment in 'the Hall of Truth' before the divine judge, Osiris. Beneath the scales lurks the hellish animal 'the Devourer', who waits for the condemned. That is what we see depicted on a papyrus dating from the New Kingdom or Empire. Sometimes the condemned person is boiled in a cauldron before the hellish beast devours him, sometimes he is thrown into the pit of fire or beheaded by demons. In contrast, the realm of the blessed is an Elysium. Through this paradise flows a stream whose banks are clothed in luxurious vegetation. Even in paradise the blessed still work, but their harvest is always a sumptuous one.

In Egypt, Ma'at is the quintessence of justice and truth. In this world, the human being is the sum of everything he does. His deeds are requited in the next world with rewards and punishment. There is no personality apart from the individual's deeds and misdeeds. Everyone is 'on his own' in the Hall of Truth in front of Osiris and his forty-two assessors in the court. The verdict is pronounced on the basis of the weight of the heart. The weighing is undertaken by Anubis, who later mutated into the archangel Michael when in Christianity Osiris was replaced by Christ. The law according to which the deeds are weighed and judgment is passed emerges from the many assertions of innocence which the dead have to put forward to the court. They are all offences and crimes against life, against ancestors and gods, and against the person's neighbour.

At the centre of the judgment of the dead are the scales, with the heart of the dead person in the one pan and the symbol of truth in the other. Anubis tests where the pointer falls, the ibis-headed Thoth registers the offences committed by the dead person, who is led to the court by the jackal-headed god. The Devourer lurks beneath the scales, waiting for his prey—the one who is perhaps going to be damned. (Taken from a Book of the Dead *dating from the New Kingdom)*

If we compare the ideas of justice in Babylon and Egypt, we find on the one hand the concept of a justice which puts things right, which saves and heals, and on the other hand a justice which assesses and requites. In the Old Testament too there are ideas about a divine wrath which reacts to human wickedness and punishes the godless; but the prevailing ideas centre on God's creative righteousness and justice. 'Bring about justice for me!' is the appeal to the God who 'creates justice for those who suffer violence'. In Babylon the divine justice has social, earthly and cosmic dimensions, but in Egypt it is related only to human beings, and in human beings only to their deeds and misdeeds, not to their sufferings, and not to their natural, bodily existence as God's creation either. In Babylon we find a justice which holds the universe together and enlivens it. In Egypt the judgment of the dead individualizes human beings. Each person is completely on his own. In Babylon the divine justice protects the weak and the victims. In Egypt justice punishes or rewards the people concerned.

If we look for a moment at the Christian pictures of the last judgment in the medieval churches, we immediately see how much the Egyptian judgment of the dead has put its stamp on these representations of 'judgment according to works', and how little the Old Testament concepts about YHWH's creative justice have found an entry into Christian ideas about judgment. The Christian representations of judgment are indistinguishable from Islamic ideas: there too each individual must for him or herself appear before Allah and be given the book recording his or her acts. The good acts too are weighed with just scales. If a person's good deeds weigh heavily, he enters bliss. The person whose deeds are weighed in the balance and found wanting, goes into the pit of raging fire (Sura 21.47; 101.5). That brings us to the question: what is really Christian in our traditional ideas of judgment? Is it not highest time to Christianize notions about the last judgment and to evangelize their effect on present-day life, so that we can cry joyfully, 'Maranatha, come Lord Jesus, come soon' (Rev. 22.20)?

The Last Judgment according to Christian Tradition: The Final Reckoning

If we open Heinrich Schmid's handbook of Lutheran orthodoxy, *Dogmatik der evangelisch-lutherischen Kirche* (1893), on page 470 we read the following:

> De extreme judicio: The Last Judgment follows on the raising of the dead. It marks the end of the world. The dead will be raised, the living transformed. The time is hidden from us. But it is preceded by signs: the power of Satan, manifested to the greatest degree, the increased self-assurance and godlessness of human beings.
>
> The judgment will be presided over by Christ, who will appear to all visibly and in glory, to the godly as their longed-for consolation, to the godless as the supreme terror. Then everything they have done will be manifested to all, both the good and the evil, and judgment will be passed on them inasmuch as the godly will be taken up into the kingdom of glory, while the others, the ungodly, will be cast into the realm of eternal darkness.
>
> Scripture calls the place of torment hell; scripture calls the place of blessedness heaven.

For Paul Althaus in his article 'Gottes Gericht', or 'The Divine Judgment' (RGG[3] II, 1421–1423), the justice in the divine judgment is punitive, retributive justice: 'God calls them (human beings) to account, and passes judgment on them in recognition and condemnation, in reward and punishment.' At the last judgment 'the believer must flee from God's judgment to Jesus Christ, who "saves us from the wrath to come"' (Rom. 5.9).

But that then means that God's judgment at the end of the world belongs to the sphere of the law, which requires good deeds and forbids evil ones. The law is the presence of God's coming judgment. It is a judgment according to works. The transition from this world to the next proceeds by way of reward and punishment. The human being is nothing more than the subject of what he does, the good deeds are permanently rewarded, the evil ones are kept for ever in the torments of hell. Whereas Lutheran orthodoxy makes Christ the judge who rewards and punishes, Althaus distinguishes between the God the judge, and Christ, the defender of believers.

Unlike human courts, where sentences differentiate, in this idea about the divine judgment the sentences are only two: eternal life or eternal death, heaven or hell. If we then ask in surprise what happens to the goodly visible creation, the earth, and God's other earthly creatures, the answer is that everything will be burnt to ashes. The structure of this world will no longer be required when the blessed in heaven see God directly, without any mediation through other created things. That is the *annihilatio mundi,* the annihilation of the world; only heaven and hell are left.[6] That is 'the end of the world':

> *Dies ira, dies illa:*
> *Solvet saeclum in favilla.*

The Contradictions

In my view, this notion about judgment is extremely hostile to creation. Is God the judge then supposed to be in contradiction to God the creator? And if it is the same God, doesn't God the judge destroy the creator's faithfulness to those he has created? Whether this be a case of a self-contradiction in God himself, or whether it is a matter of different Gods, the biblical trust in God is destroyed. The idea about an annihilating, criminal court of justice is, as I see it, an extremely atheistic picture.

The Christ with the two-edged sword in his mouth who exercizes retributive justice towards human beings, with rewards and punishment, is unrecognizable. He has nothing to do with

Jesus of Nazareth, the preacher on the Mount, the healer of the sick, and the forgiver of sins. This retributive judge cannot be the Christ who was crucified for us and who has risen ahead of us. Faced with the universal judge whom Michelangelo painted in the Sistine Chapel as a hero belonging to the ancient world, or as an athletic Olympic winner, who would arrive at the idea that this could be the poor man from Nazareth?

The picture of the God who judges human beings in wrath has been the cause of much spiritual and psychological damage. It has poisoned the idea of God instead of leading to trust in him. Among the dying it has intensified the fear of death through fears of hell. The picture of God's punitive judgment was always a threatening message. It has plunged some into profound self-doubt and has led others to an incensed rejection of belief in God in general.

As a result, modern theological interpretations of judgment have ceased to put the God who judges in wrath at the centre. It is now the human being who takes responsibility for himself. No one will go to heaven or be sent to hell against his will. It is a person's own decision, which is followed by the one or the other consequence. So the picture of the last judgment is nothing other than the final endorsement of human free will: 'Nevertheless it is our conviction that the reality of hell (and indeed of heaven) is the ultimate affirmation of the reality of human freedom', said the Doctrine Commission of the Church of England in 1995.[7] If this is the case, then human beings are the masters of their own destiny, and God is only the executor or accomplice of the person's own decision. If he believes, God will take him to heaven; if he does not believe, God will send him to hell. So doesn't this make God superfluous? Belief in the freedom of the human will replaces belief in God.

The Sunrise of Christ's Righteousness and Justice

But there is a completely different approach to the idea about the great final judgment: injustice cries out to high heaven; the victims do not remain silent; the murderers find no rest. The hunger for justice and righteousness remains a torment in a world of unvoiced cries. The victims cannot be forgotten; in the end the murderers must not be allowed to triumph over them. The expectation of the divine judgment which will bring about justice was originally the hope of the victims of injustice and violence. The divine judgment was the counter-narrative and the counter-picture of the oppressed which was set over against the world of the triumphant perpetrators of violence. The victims, the powerless and the unfortunate hope for the judge 'who will establish justice for those who suffer wrong'. Israel's psalms of lament are an eloquent witness to the conviction that 'to judge' means to establish justice. God's supreme justice will 'create' justice for the victims of wickedness, will raise them up out of the dust, will heal their wounded lives, and put to rights the lives that have been destroyed. The victims wait for God's creative justice, which will bring them liberty, health and new life. They are waiting, not for a judgment based on works but for a *judgment based on the suffering of the sufferers.*

It was only later and under foreign influences that in the biblical writings this saving deliverer of victims came to be turned into a universal criminal judge, who judges according to good and evil, and no longer enquires about the victims. A victim-orientated expectation of saving justice was turned into a perpetrator-orientated moral judgment based on the justice whose purpose is retribution.

In order to Christianize the ambivalent ideas about judgment and to evangelize their meaning for the present day, I am assuming that the original experiences of God in Israel and in Christianity are experiences of creative, saving and healing righteousness and justice, and that ideas about the coming last judgment have to accord with these specific experiences—not with general religious notions about retributive justice, and the general human longing for vengeance. That being so, we have to ask the following questions:

Who is the judge at the last judgment? According to the Christian ideas of the New Testament, judgment day is 'the day of the Son of

Man' and Jesus, the Son of Man, has come 'to seek the lost' (Luke 19.10; 6; Matt. 8, 11). Anyone who thinks that there are people who are lost and whom he has not found, discounts Christ, and declares that he is incapable, and not very successful. The day of YHWH is 'the day of Jesus Christ' (Phil. 1.6). It is the day of days, when the crucified and risen Christ will be manifested to the world and the whole world will be manifested before him. 'We must all appear before the judgment seat of Christ' (2 Cor. 5.10). On that day both will emerge from their concealment into the light of truth—the Christ who is now hidden in God, and the human being who is unfathomably hidden from himself. The eternal light will manifest Christ and human beings to each other. What is now still hidden in nature will also become clear and lucid, for men and women are bodily and natural beings, and belong together with nature. We cannot be isolated from the nature of the earth, not in the resurrection, and not even at the last judgment.

But as whom will Christ be manifested? Surely not as the avenger or retaliator, but as the crucified and risen victor over sin, death and hell! To him have been given 'the keys of death and of hell' (Rev. 1.18). Why? Surely so that he can throw open what has been closed! He will be manifested as the living one, as the first-born from the dead, and as the leader of life. Perhaps in his picture of the last judgment in the Sistine Chapel Michelangelo did not paint a judge at all, but a transfigured Son of man in his bodiliness, the first in the resurrection of humanity and nature.

What is the righteousness by which Christ will judge when he is manifested as the risen victor over sin, death and hell? Surely it cannot be any righteousness different from the one which he himself proclaimed in his gospel and practised through his fellowship with sinners and tax collectors. Otherwise no one would be able to recognize him. The coming judge is the one who was judged and put to death on the cross.[8] The one who will come as judge of the world is the one 'who bears the sins of the world' and who has himself suffered the sufferings of the victims of injustice and violence. About him we can say with Paul: 'Death is swallowed up in victory (the victory of life); Death where is thy sting? Hell where is thy victory?' (1 Cor. 15.55.). The divine justice which Christ will bring about for all human beings and for all things will not be the justice that establishes what is good and what is evil; nor will it be the retributive justice which rewards the good and punishes the wicked. It will be God's creative justice, which brings justice for the victims and puts the perpetrators right. The victims do not have to remain victims to all eternity, and the perpetrators do not have to remain perpetrators forever. The victims of sin and violence will receive justice. They will be raised up, put right, healed and brought into life. The perpetrators of sin and violence will receive a justice which transforms and rectifies. They will be already transformed inasmuch as they will be redeemed only together with their victims. They will be saved by the crucified Christ, who will encounter them together with their victims. They will 'die' to their misdeeds in order to be 'born again' together with their victims to a new, common life. Paul expresses this transforming grace with the image of fire: 'If any man's work is burned up, he will suffer loss, though he himself will be saved, but only as through fire' (1 Cor. 3.15). The image of the end-time 'fire' has nothing to do with the stake or with the apocalyptic destruction of the world through fire. It is an image for God's love, which burns away everything which is contrary to God, so that the person whom God has created will be saved.

As the coming judge of the victims and perpetrators of sin, the risen Christ will bear the suffering of the one and the burden of the other, so as to bring both out of the rule of darkness into the light of God's kingdom.

What is the purpose of Christ's judgment? When the victims are raised up and the perpetrators are put right, the purpose is not the great reckoning, with reward and punishment; the intention is to bring about the victory of the creative divine righteousness and justice over everything godless in heaven, on earth, and beneath the earth. This victory of the divine righteousness does not lead to the separation of human beings into the saved and the damned, or to the end of the world; its purpose is to lead to God's great day of reconciliation on this earth. On judgment day 'every tear will be wiped from their eyes', the tears of suffering as well as the tears of remorse, for 'there will be no more mourning, nor crying, nor pain any more' (Rev. 21.4). 'Earth will be purified from the being of sin and death'.[9] The shadows of sin disappear with the power of death. The powers of annihilation will be annihilated. So the last judgment is not the end of God's works, nor is it the last thing of all; it is not last but penultimate. It is only a first step in a transition from transience to nontransience. What is final is only the new, eternal creation, which will be brought into being on the foundation of righteousness. Because the judgment serves this new creation of all things, its righteousness is not a righteousness related to the past, which merely establishes what is done and requites it. It is a creative righteousness related to this future, a righteousness which creates justice, heals and rectifies. The judgment is not at the service of sin and death, as if it were the great settling of an account. It serves the new creation. The end of the old world-time in the judgment is nothing other than the beginning of the new world-time in 'the life of the world to come'. It was the fault of Christian tradition, in picture and concept, in piety and doctrine, to look only at the judgment on the past of this world, and not to perceive, through and beyond that judgment, God's new world, and in consequence of this omission it failed to believe in the new beginning in the end.

Perpetrators and Victims? Of course the evil committed and suffered is not always distributed between completely different people and groups of people. Victims can become perpetrators too, and in many people the perpetrator side and the victim side are inextricably intertwined. It is all the more important to perceive that the coming judge judges us as perpetrators, and raises us up as victims—rejects the Pharisee in us and accepts the sinner in us, and in this way reconciles us with ourselves.

Dimensions of Judgment. The judging of victims and perpetrators is always a *social judgment.*[10] We do not stand before the judge just on our own and dependent on ourselves, as we do here in criminal courts, or in nighttime torments of conscience. In that other judgment the perpetrators stand together with their victims, Cain with Abel, Babylon with Israel, the violent with the helpless, the murderers with the murdered, the persecutors with the martyrs. For the history of human suffering is indissolubly bound up with the history of guilt. The conflicts which make the one a victim and the other a perpetrator are always social and political conflicts which are unsolved or insoluble. As we saw in the Auschwitz trials and in the South African truth commissions, the victims have long memories because they are tormenting memories; but the perpetrators have only short memories, if they remember at all. Terrorists can become ex-terrorists, we say, but the victims always remain victims. So in order to arrive at the truth the perpetrators are dependent on the memories of their victims. They must listen to their accounts and learn to see themselves with the eyes of their victims, even if this is terrible and destructive. To raise up the oppressed is one side of the truth; to make the blind see is the other side.

In Israel's stories about God, the higher justice is often invoked with the words: 'May the Lord judge between you and me!' (Gen. 16.5; 31.53; 1 Sam. 24.13). God is invoked as a 'justice of the peace' in human conflicts. That is the way he is supposed to judge between the poor and the rich, the high and the low: 'Behold, I judge between sheep and sheep' (Ezek. 34.17), so that the herd can live in peace again. The petitioners in the psalms are also calling to God for judgment in social life when they ask the tormenting question why everything works out well for the godless while the people who remain faithful to God are persecuted. God is supposed to judge between believers and the ungodly. A judgment about social life is supposed to put right the disrupted relationships between people and nations; its intention is not to reward or punish individuals: 'God will judge', as the saying goes.

This means that we ought to imagine the last judgment as a peaceful arbitration whose purpose is the furtherance of life, not as a criminal court which decides over life and death. If the purpose of the last judgment is to put right the disrupted social conditions in the community of creation, then we can put our hope in the coming divine 'justice of the peace'. When ideas about punishment are used in the New Testament, we can interpret them in the light of the new creation of all things which the judgment is designed to serve.

> The Day of Jesus Christ will be the Last Judgment which clears away the rubble. The salvation of human beings, even though they have sinned, is the Last Judgment and at the same time the mercy which brings life, resurrection and rebirth.[11]

> One thing must be said in response to the notion customary in pious circles: Judgment has not just a negative meaning but above all a positive one. That is to say, it will not merely destroy but will above all save. It is the annihilating No to all the powers that are contrary to God, and the dissolution of the world of evil, but it is the saving and fulfilling Yes of creation: 'Behold, I make all things new'.[12]

So wrote Christoph Blumhardt, and called it his 'confession of hope':

> That God might give up anything or anyone in the whole world—about that there can be no question, neither today nor in all eternity … The end has to be: Behold, everything is God's! Jesus comes as the one who has borne the sins of the world. Jesus can judge but not condemn. My desire is to have preached this to the lowest circles of hell, and I will never let myself be confounded.[13]

If judging in the final judgment is a social judging, then it is a *cosmic judging* too—not just ultimately speaking but indeed in the first instance; for the coming Christ is also the cosmic Christ (Col. 1.15–17). The Psalms already call upon YHWH: 'Arise, O God, judge the earth' (Ps. 82.8; 96.13). All the disrupted conditions in creation must be put right so that the new creation can stand on the firm ground of righteousness and justice, and can endure to eternity. That means the relationships between human beings as well as the relations between human beings and the world of the living in the earthly community of creation. Not least, it means the disruptions which make all created being, even apart from human beings, sigh and long for redemption. Since all created beings have been given a specific free sphere for their own activity, as Genesis 1 describes, disruption and chaos is a possibility among them all.

In the vista of the new creation of all things, God's judgment is concerned not only with poor human beings and their little sins, but with a cosmic transformation of all things into their enduring form. The first creation (Rev. 21.1) is a creation everywhere threatened by chaos. According to the picture language of the Bible, chaos thrusts into the creation of light and the earth in the form of 'night' and 'the sea'. In John's picture language in the book of Revelation, in the new creation of all things there will no longer be any 'night' or 'sea' because the radiant glory of God will illumine everything, and its light is Jesus Christ 'the Lamb' (Rev. 21.23). Then everything created will share in the eternal being and in God's eternal livingness. According to 1 Corinthians 15 and Revelation 21 this is a truly fundamental change in the constitution of the cosmos and of life. God will dwell in everything and be 'present in all'.[14] Paul's concern in 1 Corinthians 15 and Philippians 2 is *the universal glorification of God*. This embraces the *universal reconciliation* of human beings and the *bringing again of all things* into the new eternal creation. Otherwise God would not be God.

Nothingness will be annihilated, death will be slain, the power of evil will be dissolved. What will be dispelled from all created beings is sin, the misery of separation from the living God; hell will be destroyed. It is only the negation of the negative which provides the foundation for the indestructible position of the positive. And this is the beginning of the kingdom of glory.

Because the resurrection of Christ opens up the vista of a world without death and without hell, the problem whether all will be redeemed, or only a few, solves itself of its own accord. The Christian idea of universal salvation is based on cosmic Christology, according to which 'death will be destroyed' (1 Cor. 15.26) and hell annihilated.[15]

Ps. 96. 10–13 gives a wonderful description of the 'last judgment' as an image of hope:

> Say among the nations, The Lord reigns!
> Yea, the world is established, it shall never be moved;
> he will judge the peoples with equity.
> Let the heavens be glad, and let the earth rejoice,
> let the sea roar, and all that fills it;
> let the field exult, and everything in it!
> Then shall all the trees of the wood sing for joy
> before the Lord, for he comes,
> for he comes to judge the earth.
> He will judge the world with righteousness,
> and the peoples with his truth.[16]

Dialectical Universalism

Finally, let us look at the present-day practice which is the consequence of this future expectation. How do we make present to ourselves the coming righteousness of Christ?

Armageddon

An American friend asked his pious grandmother about the end of the world, and she answered with the mysterious and terrible name 'Armageddon'. According to Rev. 16.16 this means God's final struggle with the devil, which is generalized today into the struggle between good and evil, and which ends with the victory of the good. Out of the Manichean idea about the end, American fundamentalists have developed a modern, fantastic scenario about the final struggle. Examples are Hal Lindsay (*The Late Great Planet Earth*, 1970, more than 30 million copies sold) and Tim La Haye and J. B. Jenkins (in the Left Behind series, more than a million copies sold from 1995 onwards). What were still, at the time when these people wrote, the Red armies of the Soviet Union and China will march on Jerusalem, but will be destroyed beforehand in the valley of Armageddon by U.S. atomic bombs and, if the armies are too numerous, by hydrogen bombs. Then Christ will come from the clouds and will appear on the pinnacles of the third temple, and will establish his Thousand Years' Empire. Those who belong to him will be 'snatched away' from the misery of the end time, so that they may return with him to build the new world.[17]

What does that mean for the present? It establishes and justifies friend-enemy thinking as an existential political category, which was just what the Nazi constitutional lawyer Carl Schmitt demanded in the political theology with which he wanted to combat Bakunin's anarchism. Whereas Bakunin maintained that there was 'neither God nor state', Carl Schmitt countered that only 'God and state' can save us in the final struggle.[18] This was also the view of President Ronald Reagan, who believed in 'an Armageddon in our generation'—a nuclear one. For him, the Soviet Union was 'the evil Empire'. For this purpose George W. Bush invented the 'axis of evil' which was supposed to extend from Iraq to North Korea. 'America is at war', he proclaimed after September 11 and 'he who is not for us is against us'. But it was not any country that had attacked the United States; it was the criminal Islamist band Al Qaeda. So America will remain 'at war'. What war? What is meant is the apocalyptic war: Armageddon has already begun![19]

Friend-Enemy Thinking

The customary expectation of judgment in Christianity and Islam has a very similar effect on the present. If the end of the world is God's judgment on believers and unbelievers, with a double outcome, believers going to heaven and unbelievers to hell, then the present is inescapably dominated by religious friend-enemy thinking. Since for unbelievers there is no hope, they can already be punished with contempt or terror here and now. Unbelievers are the enemies of believers because unbelievers are the enemies of God. To kill and be killed for God is the greatest thing in the life of militant believers, who want to become blessed martyrs. But is their God a God of life or is death their God? 'You love life, we love death', said the Taliban mullah Omar, and the same could also be read in the writings claiming responsibility for the mass murder in Madrid.

The Separation of Believers from Unbelievers

To anticipate the last judgment by dividing people into believers and unbelievers (with the possible persecution of the unbelievers as God's enemies) is wrong, because it is godless. God is not the enemy of unbelievers, nor is he the executioner of the godless. 'God has consigned *all* men to disobedience, that he may have mercy upon *all*' (Rom. 11.32). So we must view and respect all human beings, whatever they believe or don't believe, as those on whom God has had mercy. Whoever they are, God loves them, Christ has died for them as well, and God's Spirit works in their lives too. So we cannot be against them. To quote Christoph Blumhardt once more: 'My father once wrote to me that I should make it a rule wherever I go and am, to look on everyone as a believer, never to doubt, never to talk to him in any other way. To this my soul assented. If a Mameluke comes, I call him a believer, I never see him as an unbeliever. The objective belief that God believes in me, and that if God believes in me, I can believe in him—for me that is faith.'[20]

In his doctrine of reconciliation (CD [IV/2]) Karl Barth followed Blumhardt.[21] The all-embracing hope for God's future is based on the boundlessness of love. Why should we take the different belief, disbelief or superstition of other people more seriously than God's mercy on them? That was a theme for Christianity in the atheistic East German state, the GDR. Our dealings with people of other religions cannot be any different. The differences between believers, people of other beliefs and unbelievers exist, but they are caught up and absorbed in the frame of reference which is God's mercy on all.

Can this universalism be realized through a global ethic resting on the golden rule, 'Do as you would be done by'? After all, this rule can be found in both Confucius and the Bible. But it only works between equals and people who are equally strong. In a violent world of victors and defeated, the strong and the weak, winners and losers, it will have no force, for what have the victors to fear from the defeated, the strong from the weak, and the winners from the losers? In this violent world the golden rule is a utopia, even though it is undoubtedly a fine one.

Partisanship for the Victims of Injustice and Violence

Christian universalism is no hindrance to partisanship for the victims of injustice and violence, but promotes it. In a divided and hostile world the universalism of God's mercy with all can only be vouched for by way of the familiar preferential option for the poor. God himself acts in history with a bias in favour of the victims, so that through them he can save the perpetrators too. This is borne out by Mary and Jesus and Paul.

In the Magnificat, Mary sings: 'He puts down the mighty from their thrones and exalts those of low degree; he has filled the hungry with good things, and the rich he sends empty away' (Luke 1.52–53).

Jesus calls the weary and heavy-laden to himself, accepts sinners and lets the Pharisees 'go empty away'.

For Paul, the community of Christians is itself a witness to this one-sided activity of God on behalf of all human beings: 'For consider your call; not many of you were wise according to worldly standards, not many were powerful, not many were of noble birth; but God chose what is foolish in the world to shame the wise, God chose what is weak in the world to shame the strong, God chose what is low and despised in the world, even things that are not, to bring to nothing things that are, so that no human being might boast in the presence of God' (1 Cor. 1.26–29).

And that is why we sing:

'Sun of righteousness arise, triumph o'er the shades of night.'

A Coda

In the ancient patriarchy of Aquileia in Italy, universal redemption was taught by way of special rituals and a special theology of Easter Eve (Easter Saturday), when Christ 'descended into hell' in order to break down its doors and to deliver the despairing. The fourth-century *Credo Aquileiensis* runs:

> *Cum rex gloriae Christus infernum debellaturus intraret*
> *et chorus angelicus ante faciem eius portas principium tolli*
> *praeciperet,*
> *sanctorum populus qui tenebatur in morte captivus*
> *voce lachrimabili clamaverat:*
> *Advenisti desiderabilis*
> *quem expectabamus in tenebris*
> *ut educeres hac nocte vinculatos de claustris.*
> *Te nostra vocabant suspiria*
> *te larga requirebant lamenta*
> *tu factus es spes desperatis*
> *magna consolatio in tormentis.*
> *Alleluia.*

[When Christ, the king of glory, entered the underworld to destroy it, and the angelic choir called upon the princes to lift up their gates before his face, the people of the saints, held captive by death, cried out with tears: Thou hast come, O desired One, for whom we have waited in darkness so that this night thou might lead us captives out of the dungeon. To thee our sighs have risen, thee we sought with abundant lamentations. Thou hast been the hope of the despairing, the mighty consolation in our torments. Alleluia.]

The port of Aquileia had close connections with Alexandria. Origen's ideas about universal redemption arrived in Aquileia by way of Rufinus. The symbol for this was 'the arc of Marc'. The Gnostic writing, the Shepherd of Hermas, described Christ's descent into hell. On Easter Eve the so-called 'knocking rite' took place in the basilica in Aquileia. The priest went from door to door in order to symbolize Christ's breaking down of the gates of hell. The wonderful mosaics on the floor of the basilica depict the story of Jonah, as a metaphor for the redemption of the universe. The mosaics also show Jewish-Christian influences from Alexandria, and Gnostic ideas taken from the Pistis Sophia in Nag Hammadi are also evident. In the early centuries people in the patriarchy of Aquileia were very well aware of the differences from Rome shown in these fragments.[22]

In Poland, the Lublin Catholic theologian Waclaw Hryniewicz pleaded for research into the history of Christian teaching of universal salvation and its acceptance in a book entitled "The Hope of Salvation for All: From an Eschatology of Fear to an Eschatology of Hope."[23] He shows that in the ancient Syrian and Persian churches the hope for universal reconciliation was taught, and was very much alive.

Postscript about the Universal Theology of Grace and the Particularist Theology of Faith and the Universal Glorification of God

Every theology of grace tends towards universalism because it issues for God's sake in the triumph of grace. Every theology of faith tends towards particularism because it starts from the decision of the believer, and hence issues in the separation of believers from the unbelieving. The theology of grace makes us humble and unites us with all human beings, for 'God has consigned all men to disobedience, that he may have mercy upon all' (Rom. 11.32). The theology of faith, in contrast, is in danger of self-righteousness on the part of believers towards nonbelievers, because the difference between them depends on the human beings themselves. These traditional differences can be surmounted if the salvation of the world is seen in *the universal glorification of God*, and if it is theocentrically orientated, not anthropocentrically.

In this outline of a new version of the expectation of the last judgment, I have only entered into the biblical tradition of Paul and the deutero-Pauline epistles Ephesians and Colossians. I recognize that Matthew, the Synoptic Little Apocalypse [Matt 24-25; MK 13], and the book of Revelation talk about an anthropocentric dualism rather than about a theocentric universalism. For me, the casting vote was given by the Old Testament concept of divine justice for victims and the all-rectifying judgment of God. The different biblical traditions about judgment cannot be harmonized. A decision has to be made on the foundation of theological arguments.

14

The Triune God

The New Trinitarian Thinking

Ever since Augustine and Thomas Aquinas, trinitarian thinking in the Latin church of the West has proceeded from the self-consciousness of the one God.[1] By way of Hegel, this approach proved very convincing for modern theology: in his self-consciousness God makes himself his own object, and identifies himself with himself. His unity is a unity dialectically differentiated in itself. So the revelation of God can be understood as 'God's self-revelation', which was the way the young Karl Barth presented it: God reveals God through God.[2] In his 'self-communication' God remains the subject of himself; that was how Karl Rahner conceived it.[3] This development of the trinitarian concept from the concept of the self-consciousness of the absolute subject can be undertaken without reference to the divine history to which the Bible witnesses,[4] and can only with difficulty be used to interpret the biblical history of God. Is, then, Jesus 'the Son of God' the Father's self? Is God's life-giving Spirit the identity of the Father with himself?

The new trinitarian thinking, in contrast, starts from the interpersonal and communicative event of the acting persons about whom the biblical history of God tells.[5] It has to do with Jesus the Son, and with God whom he exclusively calls 'Abba, my dear Father', and with the Holy Spirit who in fellowship with him is the giver of life. The differentiation between Father, Son and Spirit describes the rich relations of the divine reality of the biblical history of God: the Father reveals the Son, the Son reveals the Father, and sends the Spirit of life from the Father. The Father communicates the Son, and the Son reveals the Father, and the Spirit of the Father radiates from the Son into the world. We could go on, so as to tell the history of the divine plenitude in the richness of its relationships as the New Testament depicts them. The new trinitarian thinking has no desire to conceptualize this history in order to replace history by concept, but wants to define the trinitarian concept of God in such a way that it interprets this divine history, leads into it and deepens it.

For this we have tirelessly to work on the concept of God.

The One Name of God

Even when we hear the name of 'the Father and the Son and the Holy Spirit', as the Christian baptismal formula runs, we sense that there must be a wonderful community in the reality of God. The Father, the Son and the Holy Spirit are so different that they are named one after the other and are then joined together through the narrating 'and'. But these are not three names. It is the one name of God, into which believers are baptized and in which people are received into the trinitarian history of God.[6] Consequently it is three persons that are named, not three gods. The one name of God joins the divine persons and makes the community between them nameable. In the sanctification of the one name of God, Christian faith is one with the faith of Israel, as the first petition of the Lord's Prayer shows. It seems to me worth thinking about that the unity of the triune God is described through the name, not through an ontological term.[7] This leap into a different category is important for every biblically based doctrine of the Trinity. It prevents our concepts of God from turning into idols which take the place of God's presence, which is unfathomable because it is so near. God can be invoked but not defined.

The Triune God

That brings us to a brief, critical survey of the terms used in theology for the trinitarian mystery of God.

We call the divine mystery a 'triunity' (*Dreieinigkeit*) when we start from the three persons and want to stress their unity. We speak of 'the threefold God' (*Dreifaltigkeit*) when we start from God's unity and wish to look at the three persons in which this unity 'unfolds' itself, since it is a unity differentiated in itself. In Germany, Protestant Christians give preference to the word *Dreieinigkeit*, 'triunity', whereas Catholics more often use the word *Dreifaltigkeit*, 'threefoldness'. To speak of the threefold God sounds modalistic, while on the other hand triunity has a tritheistic flavour. To describe God as the 'three-in-one'[8] is not very helpful, because it puts the unity numerically on the same level as the threeness of the persons. I would also suggest avoiding the designation the 'thrice-personal God'[9] because that relates the three to the one personal God and makes one think of the figure of a body with three heads. But whatever concept of Trinity we use, we are expressing with it that God is not a solitary lord of heaven who subjects everything to himself, as earthly despots have always done in his name. Nor is God a cold, dumb force of destiny, who determines everything and is touched by nothing. The triune God is a God in sociality, rich in inner and outward relationships. It is only of the living God that it is possible to say that 'God is love', for love is not solitary, but presupposes those who are different, joins those who are different, and differentiates between those who are joined. If 'the Father, the Son and the Holy Spirit' are bound together through eternal love, then their unity consists in their oneness with each other. They form their unique divine community through their self-giving to each other. By virtue of their overflowing love they go beyond themselves and open themselves in creation, reconciliation and redemption for the other, different nature of finite, contradictory and mortal created beings, in order to concede them space in their eternal life and to let them participate in their own joy. So how ought we to think of the trinitarian unity?

Perichoresis

Shekinah: The Biblical Approach

We have the concept of the Shekinah from Israel's exilic and post-exilic theology. It means God's 'indwelling'. It belongs from the beginning to God's covenant with Israel: the one who promises 'I will be your God' also promises 'I will dwell in the midst of the Israelites'.[10] God's Shekinah itself becomes homeless together with the people and wanders with it through the exile of this world until one day, united with the Eternal One, it comes to rest and fills the whole world. According to Franz Rosenzweig's interpretation, the idea of the Shekinah involves the concept of a self-differentiation in God: 'God separates himself from himself, he gives himself away to his people, he suffers with their sufferings, he goes with them into the misery of the alien land, he wanders with their wanderings.'[11]

This Shekinah theology deeply marks the background of New Testament Christology as it developed. 'The Word became flesh and dwelt among us' (John 1.1); in Christ 'dwells the fullness of God bodily' (Col. 2.9); the Holy Spirit 'dwells' in our bodies and in the community of Christ as if in a temple (1 Cor. 6.19). These indwellings of God in Christ and in the Christian communities point beyond themselves to the cosmic Shekinah, when God will be 'all in all' (1 Cor. 15.28). According to Christian theology, incarnation and inhabitation have their foundation in God's kenosis. Through his 'lowering of himself' the infinite God is able to dwell in the finite being of creation.

Perichoresis: The Patristic Approach

The idea about perichoresis, the reciprocal indwelling, derives from the theology of the Greek fathers. With this, it becomes possible to conceive of a community without uniformity and a personhood without individualism. The semantic history of the term has been well researched.[12] The substantive means 'whirl' or 'rotation'; the verb means a movement from one to another, passing round and going round, surrounding, embracing, enclosing. In the New Testament it occurs only twice (Matt. 3.5; 14.35), and in both places it means only 'the surrounding world'. The first to use the word theologically was probably Gregory of Nazianzus, John of Damascus made it the key concept for his Christology, and then for the doctrine of the Trinity too. In Christology, perichoresis describes the mutual interpenetration of two different natures, the divine and the human, in the God-human being Christ. The examples offered are red-hot iron, in which fire and iron interpenetrate, or Moses's burning bush, which 'was not consumed'. In the doctrine of the Trinity, perichoresis describes the reciprocal indwelling of the like-natured divine persons Father, Son and Spirit. John of Damascus wanted to conceptualize the Johannine unity of the Son with the Father—'I am in the Father, the Father is in me' (14.11), 'he who sees me sees the Father' (14.9). Jesus the Son and God the Father are not one and the same, but are one in their reciprocal indwelling. The perichoresis of the divine persons describes their unity in a trinitarian way, not with the metaphysical concepts of divine substance or the one absolute subject. Its application both to the two natures in Christology and to the three persons in the doctrine of the Trinity shows the fruitfulness of the concept. It makes it possible to link not only 'the others' of the same species but also 'the other' in a single species without admixture. Whereas the three divine persons form their perichoresis through homologous love, it is by virtue of heterologous love that divinity and humanity are joined in the God-human being.

The Latin translation of the Greek word *perichoresis* was first of all *circumincessio*, and later also *circuminsessio*.[13] The first translation indicates a dynamic interpenetration (*incedere*), the second an enduring, resting indwelling (*insedere*). The Council of Florence (1438–1454) finally formulated a dogmatic definition which was supposed to serve the ecumenical unity of the Western and the Eastern churches:

> *Propter hanc unitatem Pater est totus in Filio, totus in Spiritu*
> *Sancto;*
> *Filius totus est in Patri, totus in Spiritu Sancto;*
> *Spiritus Sanctus totus est in Patre, totus in Filio.*
> *Nullus alium aut precedet aeternitate,*
> *aut excedit magnitudine, aut superat potestate.*[14]
> [On account of this unity the Father is wholly in the Son,
> wholly in the Holy Spirit; the Son is wholly in the
> Father, wholly in the Holy Spirit; the Holy Spirit is
> wholly in the Father, wholly in the Son. No one pre-
> cedes the other in eternity or exceeds the other in
> magnitude or is above the others in power.]

On the perichoretic level, therefore, in the Trinity no one person takes precedence over the others, not the Father either. Here the Trinity is a nonhierarchical community. We can speak of the Father's 'monarchy', if at all, only on the level of the Trinity's constitution, but not in its perichoretic life. In the Trinity it is not the monarchy of the Father but the perichoresis which is 'the seal of its unity'.[15] Nor is it the Holy Spirit, which in the unity of the Father and the Son constitutes 'the bond of unity' (Augustine) for the Trinity. This view would reduce the Trinity to a binity or dual-ity, and would rob the Holy Spirit of its own personhood. It is not any single subject in the Trinity which represents the unity; it is the triadic intersubjectivity which we call *perichoresis*.

The Latin words *circumincessio* and *circuminsessio* express a double sense of the trinitarian unity: movement and rest. We arrive at the same result if we use the Greek verbs *perichoreo* and *peri-choreuo*. Then the words describe the mutual resting in each other, and a round-dance with one another.[16] Grammatically, however, *perichoresis* derives from *perichoreo*, not from *perichoreuo*. But as an apt description of the shifting round dance of three persons it can quite well be used. What is meant at all events is that in the Trinity there is simultaneously complete rest and complete turbulence, a little like what we find in the eye of a hurricane or in a circle.[17] On the level of the trinitarian perichoresis there is complete equality between the divine persons. No one of them precedes the others in eternity. It is not even possible to number them, and to call the Holy Spirit 'the third person' in the Trinity.

Each person 'moves' in the two others. That is the meaning of their *circumincessio*. So the trinitarian persons offer one another reciprocally the inviting space for movement in which they can develop their eternal livingness. For living beings there is no personal freedom without social free spaces. In the transferred sense that is also true of the divine persons in their perichoresis. They move with one another, and round one another, and in one another, and change 'from glory to glory' without leaving what is transient behind. We can compare this with circular movements or with kaleidoscopic plays of colour. In their eternal mobility the trinitarian persons merge with the free scopes they give one another, without being absorbed into one another. In their *circumincessio* they are at once persons and the spaces for movement. In the human sector we call these spaces social spaces, in which others can move. In transferring this to the divine level we have to proceed from a unity of physical and moral spaces, for the perichoresis is as primal as the life of the trinitarian persons.[18]

Each person exists outside itself in the two others. It is the power of perfect love which allows each person to go out of itself to such an extent that it is wholly present in the others. This means conversely that each trinitarian person is not only person but also represents the space for living for the two others. In the perichoresis each person makes itself 'dwellable' for the two others, and prepares the wide space and the dwelling for the two others. That is the meaning of their *circuminsessio*. So we should talk not only about the three trinitarian persons but at the same time about the three trinitarian spaces in which they mutually exist. Each person actively indwells the two others and passively gives space to the two others—that is to say at once gives and receives the others. Divine being is personal *Da-sein*—existence or 'being there', social 'being-with', and—in the perichoretic sense—'being-in'.

The perception of their perichoretic unity leads not least to a new version of the trinitarian concept of person. Boethius's definition was: *persona est individua substantia naturae rationalis* ('person is the individual substance of a rational nature'). This has traditionally been employed, but it is useless, because in the perichoresis the trinitarian persons cannot be individual substances or individuals resting in themselves and existing from themselves. They are rather to be understood as ex-static hypostases. We need a perichoretic concept of *person*.[19] This goes even beyond the communitarian concept of person—*persona in communione*—because it takes its stamp from the reciprocal indwelling. By virtue of their selfless love, the trinitarian persons come to themselves in one another. In the Son and in the Spirit the Father comes to himself and becomes conscious of himself; in the Father and in the Spirit the Son comes to himself and becomes conscious of himself as Son; in the Father and in the Son the Holy Spirit comes to himself and becomes conscious of himself.

If we see the trinitarian unity perichoretically, then it is not an exclusive unity, closed within itself. It is an open, inviting and integrating unity, as we see from the way Jesus prays for the disciples to the Father: 'that they may also be in us' (John 17.21). This indwelling of human beings in the triune God corresponds entirely to the reverse indwelling of the triune God in human beings: 'If a man loves me, he will keep my word, and my Father will love him, and we will come to him and make our home with him' (John 14.23). As has been said, perichoresis binds together not merely others who are the same in kind but also others who are different in kind. According to Johannine theology, God and human beings indwell each other mutually in love: 'He who abides in love abides in God, and God abides in him' (1 John 4.16). Paul formulates the ultimate eschatological vista as God's cosmic Shekinah, when God will be 'all in all' (1 Cor. 15.28). Then all created beings will be 'deified' in the eternal presence of the triune God, as Orthodox theology says, following Athanasius—that is to say, all created beings will find their 'broad place where there is no more cramping' (Job 36.16) in the opened eternal life of God, while the triune God will come in the transfigured new creation to his eternal dwelling and rest, and to his bliss.

I have called the inviting, integrating and uniting community of the triune God 'the open Trinity',[20] and have dissociated it from the images of the closed Trinity represented by the circle or triangle. The Trinity is 'open', not out of deficiency and incompleteness, but in the overflow of love, which gives created beings the living space for their livingness and scope for their development. C. G. Jung rightly discovered in many pictures of the Trinity a 'fourth person' in the Virgin Mary, but wrongly turned this into the archetype of a 'quaternity'.[21] In fact Mary is really a symbol for saved humanity and the new creation of all things. It is for that reason that she finds her living space in the divine Triunity. That means that the open Trinity is the inviting environment for the whole redeemed and renewed creation, which for its own part then becomes the environment for the divine indwelling.

The Trinitarian Experience of God

A few years ago I discovered in Granada in Spain an old Catholic order I had never previously heard anything about. They call themselves Trinitarians, were founded in the eleventh century, and ever since then have devoted themselves to 'the liberation of captives'. Originally that meant buying the freedom of enslaved Christians from Moorish prisons, but not these only. The arms on the church of the Trinitarians in Rome, Saint Thomas in Formis, show Christ sitting on the throne of glory; at his right hand and his left are

prisoners with broken chains, on the one side a Christian prisoner holding a cross, on the other a black prisoner without a cross.
Christ frees them both and takes them into fellowship with himself
and one another. 'Trinity' was the name for this original liberation
theology, more than eight hundred years ago.

But what has the doctrine of the Trinity—which many people
think sounds so 'abstract' and 'speculative'—to do with the praxis
of political and social liberation theology? How can the adoration
of the Holy Triunity become a leavening force for the liberation
of persecuted, imprisoned and forsaken men and women? If we
ask about the inner theological connection between 'Trinity' and
'liberation', we shall first have to identify the Christian experience
of God as a trinitarian experience of God, and shall then have to
come to the trinitarian structure of the fellowship of Christ, and of
life in the Holy Spirit.

It is easy to see that the Christian experience of God has a
trinitarian structure if we look at the early Christian benediction
formula which Paul cites in 2 Cor. 13.13:

The grace of our Lord Jesus Christ
and the love of God
and the fellowship of the Holy Spirit
be with us all.

1. The trinitarian experience of God begins with the experience of undeserved and unexpected grace in the encounter
with Christ and fellowship with him. In Christ, 'one of the
Trinity becomes human and suffers in the flesh'; and for that
reason Christ is for human beings the gateway to the experience
of God. Through faith in Christ their life in the Trinity begins.
Faith is trust in God's promise. This conveys the experience of
grace which liberates the victims of sin, and the perpetrators
of sin, from the destructive power of evil, and draws them into
the community of God. This happens through Christ, the brother

in humiliation and the redeemer from guilt. In the community of Christ, the new, freed life begins, with the great 'yes' of God's love for those he has created.

2. In fellowship with Christ, the Father of Jesus Christ becomes our Father too, and we begin to believe in God for Christ's sake. Jesus called God exclusively 'Abba', my dear Father, and in fellowship with him believers become God's children, who—driven by the Spirit—address God with the same intimate word 'Abba'. When Jesus discovered this intimate mystery of the present God—probably at his baptism—he left his family, and found his 'family' in the poor, forsaken people (*ochlos*) in Galilee. Those who follow him and call God 'Abba', dear Father, do nothing other. But that means that 'the Father of Jesus Christ' has quite different functions in the life of Christ and those who are his from the father in the family religions of the ancient world, with their patriarchal structure. Christ's 'Abba' has nothing to do with the Greek father of all, Zeus, and even less with the Roman father of the gods, Jupiter, or the authoritative 'father of the family'.[22] Even if in the Roman Empire the Father of Jesus Christ and Jupiter later came to be fused in the concept of God, the irreconcilable difference between them still remains; for between the God of Jesus and the Roman lord god Jupiter stands the cross on Golgotha, on which in the name of Jupiter Jesus was executed under Pontius Pilate by the Roman occupying power, even though Pilate certainly 'knew not what he did'. Even though, ever since Lactantius, in Roman Christianity 'Father and Lord' became one and the same in the concept of God, so that God had to be 'both loved and feared', Paul always differentiated in trinitarian terms between 'God the Father of Jesus Christ' and 'Christ our Lord' (1 Cor. 1.3 and frequently). God is the Father of Jesus Christ; Christ is our Lord and liberator; and through Christ, in our relationship to God, we come to him as God's children come to their Father in heaven. Catholic devotion has always distinguished between 'God the Father' and 'the Lord God'.

3. The 'fellowship' of the Holy Spirit is certainly in the first instance the Spirit's fellowship with believers.[23] But apparently there is ascribed to the Holy Spirit in a special way the conferring of community between different people through his creative powers; for his eternal presence gives the fellowship of the Father with Christ, and on the other hand the walls of separation and the enmity between people are broken down, so that we can term the Spirit 'the go-between God' and 'the fellowship God'. The experience of the Spirit joins Jews and Gentiles, Greeks and barbarians, men and women, the old and children in a new community of equal and free people. And beyond that, the experience of the Spirit extends 'to all flesh' that is to say to all living things, and lets nature burgeon and bloom in the dawn of the spring of the new creation of all things.[24] Consequently it links human revival too with the expectations of sighing nature. 'Fellowship' or community seems to be the particular nature of the Holy Spirit and its creative energies, just as 'grace' determines the special nature and specific action of the Son, and 'love' the nature and the efficacy of the Father.

The interaction of divine grace, love and fellowship brings into being the trinitarian experience of God. Christ accepts us in unconditional grace, God the Father loves us with unconditioned love, the Spirit brings us into the community of all the living. The three persons operate in a differentiated way, but act together in a unified movement, creating new life which in its newness is eternal.

The Trinitarian Experience of Community

The other side of the trinitarian experience of God is the trinitarian experience of the fellowship of the church. Here the classic text is Jesus' high priestly prayer in John 17.21:

That they may all be one
Even as thou, Father, art in me, and I in thee,

That they may also may be in us,
So that the world may believe that thou hast sent me.

The disciples' fellowship with each other for which Jesus prays is to correspond to the mutual indwelling of the Father and the Son in the Spirit—or so it will be permissible to add. Here the trinitarian fellowship of God is the primal image, the church its reflection.[25] That is the first dimension in Jesus' prayer. 'That they may all be one' is the motto of the ecumenical movement towards the visible unity of the church; for we assume that this prayer of Jesus' has been heard, and that in this prayer all the divided churches and Christians are already 'one'. It is important to stress that the unity of the church 'corresponds' to the perichoretic unity of the three divine persons, and therefore not to any one person of the Trinity. The church is supposed to correspond neither to the Father, nor to the Son nor to the Spirit, each for itself, but to the eternal perichoresis. That is what Cyprian meant with his much-quoted saying: the church is 'a people brought into unity from the unity of the Father, the Son and the Holy Spirit.'[26] The community of the church derives from the coefficacy of the Father, the Son and the Spirit. Paul surely already had this trinitarian cooperation in mind when in 1 Corinthians 12 he traced the fullness, energies and ministries of the congregation back to a threefold foundation:

There are varieties of gifts, but the same Spirit;
and there are varieties of service, but the same Lord;
and there are varieties of working, but it is the same God
   who inspires them all in every one. (12.4–6)

It is only if we see the unity of the Trinity in the perichoretic interplay of the three divine persons that we can understand the second dimension in Jesus' prayer: 'that they also may be in us.' That is the mystical dimension of the church's fellowship. It does not just 'correspond' to the trinitarian unity of God; but it also 'exists' in the triunity of God which is open to the world; for through the efficacy of the Father, the Son and the Spirit it is taken into the inner mystery of God. The open space of the perichoretic sociality of the triune God is the church's divine living space. In fellowship with Christ, and in the energies of the life-giving Spirit, we experience God as the wide space which surrounds us from every side and leads us to the free unfolding of the new life. In life-affirming love, we exist in God and God in us. The church is not the space for the indwelling of the Holy Spirit alone; it is the space for the whole Trinity. The whole Trinity is the church's living space, not just the Holy Spirit.

What does the community that corresponds to the triune God and lives in him look like? We find the classic text for this in Acts 4.32–37:

> The company of those who believed were of one heart and soul, and no one said that any of the things which he possessed was his own, but they had everything in common … There was not a needy person among them.

This so-called early Christian communism was not a social programme; it was the expression of the new trinitarian experience of sociality.[27] These Christians put their community above the individual and above their individual private possessions. They no longer needed these possessions in order to make their lives secure. In the spirit of the resurrection their fear of death disappeared, and with it the greed for life. And so they had enough, more than enough. This community ends the competitive struggle which turns people into lonely individuals, and the social frigidity of a heartless world disappears.[28] What comes to an end with this community is also 'the strong hand' of the state, which forcibly keeps people from becoming a 'wolf' for someone else. This community can settle its affairs by itself. It is true that historically speaking 'early Christian communism' did not last long, but it has by no means disappeared completely. In the Christian monastic communities and in the radical Protestant communities of the Hutterites and 'the brethren', and among the Mennonites and the Moravians, communities of this kind can be found down to the present day. In Latin America, in the new base communities, people are experiencing the trinitarian fellowship with God. That is why at their meeting in July 1986 in Trinidade, Brazil, as Leonardo Boff reports, they put on their placard the slogan: 'The Trinity is the best community'.[29]

'The Trinity is our social programme.' This thesis goes back to Nicholas Federov, a friend of Dostoevsky. I assume that he was seeking a third way between the autocracy of the Russian tsar and the anarchism of Kropotkin.[30] For him, the holy Trinity in God and its resonance in the *sobornost,* or spiritual community, of the Russian church were models for a truly humane society in liberty and equality. The problem of how to link personal liberty and social justice has dominated European societies ever since the French Revolution, and has not been solved down to the present day. Federov argued that the unity of the triune God shows just such a unity of person and community in which the persons have everything in common apart from their personal characteristics and differences. So a human community that corresponds to the triune God, and lives in it, must consequently be one without privileges, and one where liberties are not infringed. The persons can be persons only in community; the community can be free only in its personal members. It ought to be possible to harmonize personal liberty and just community if we look at the triune God and his resonance in the church, provided that the church, ecumenically united, can come to understand and present itself as the avant-garde of the redeemed humanity which has been liberated from its divisions and enmities.

Federov never succeeded in realizing his ideas in the Russia of his time, but what he had in mind can point the way forward today. For the last 200 years Western industrial society (and now modern industrial society in general) has seen one thrust after another towards individualization. The last of them is called 'postmodern'. But an 'individual' is not a person; according to the Latin word, the individual is something 'finally indivisible', the equivalent of the Greek word 'atom'.[31] As the end product of divisions, an individual has no relationships, no characteristics, no memories and no name. It cannot be articulated. A person, in contrast to an individual, is a human existence in the field of resonance of his or her social relationships and history. The person has a name, with which he or she can be identified. A person is a being in community. The modern thrust towards individualization in society gives rise to the suspicion that a modern individual is the product of the old Roman precept for domination, *divide et impera*—divide and rule. Individualized people are easily open to domination by political and economic forces. Resistance, with the aim of protecting personal human dignity, is only possible if people join together in communities and socially speaking determine their lives for themselves. These few indications may be enough to show the public relevance of the trinitarian concept of God for the liberation of individualized men and women, and the relevance of the trinitarian experience of community for the development of a new sociality.

Trinitarian Experiences of Space

Does the concept about the trinitarian indwelling mean the end of the eschatological exodus? Does the theological path lead from hope to homecoming, and from the setting forth to resting permanence? Have we not arrived at the goal once we have found ourselves in God and God in us? No, that cannot be the case. On the contrary, the concept of the trinitarian indwelling deepens the eschatological hope and strengthens the historical exodus. Good symbols for the mobilizing presence of God in history are the 'cloud and fire in the Exodus'.

And the Lord went before them
by day in a pillar of cloud
to lead them along the way,
and by night in a pillar of fire
to give them light,
that they might travel by day and by night. (Ex. 13.21)

God's presence among the people does not lead them to a rest in the wilderness, but puts them on the road to the promised land. His presence throws this history open; it does not end it. God 'dwells in the midst of the Israelites' as their companion on the way and their leader, for he sees the goal ahead. God's presence in Israel is his Exodus-Shekinah, and later his Exile-Shekinah.

In this presence of God in history we find a *perichoresis* of the times: his future in his present, and his present in his future.

In the New Testament too the presence of the risen Christ is understood as the presence of the coming one.[32] His present and his future are interlaced. It was not a good idea when Rudolf Bultmann set presentative and futurist eschatology over against each other, and decided for the presentative one.[33] Even the theologians who wanted to harmonize the two by calling the one 'now already' and the other 'not yet', did not make things any better, because they described present and future in concepts of time seen as *chronos*. And chronologically, every 'now already' and every 'not yet' ends in the 'no longer'. But *chronos* is interrupted by the *kairos*, and finally surmounted in the eschatological moment when the dead are raised. It was Bultmann's error to follow Kierkegaard and to see the kairos in time (2 Cor. 6.2) as 'the eschatological moment', whereas Paul first uses the designation eschatological 'moment' for the moment of the resurrection of the dead (1 Cor. 15.52): 'in a moment, in the twinkling of an eye'. The person who considers that the kairos in history is the 'end of history' lets world history come to a close in meaningless nothingness, and has given up every hope for the world.

In closing, let us turn to some fundamental ideas in a trinitarian eschatology.

We in Christ—Christ in Us

If we understand Christ perichoretically as person and as space, we can discover in this formula both the fellowship of Christ and the living space of Christ. If 'we are in Christ', then Christ is the living space of believers, and their space in the new creation. 'With Christ' means the divine space in which believers are, heart and soul. They no longer live egocentrically in themselves, but excentrically in Christ. Christ is the new centre of their lives and their divine space for living.

'It is no longer I who live, but Christ who lives in me', says Paul in Gal. 2.20. This acknowledgement already brings us to the formula's other side: 'Christ in us.' Here Christ is the person and we are his living space. That can apply to the individual person as a believer or to the community of believers, as the parable about the vine in John 15 says: 'I am the vine, you are the branches. He who abides in me and I in him, he it is that bears much fruit' (John 15.5). But the indwelling of Christ goes beyond human life and purposes to make the whole creation his living space.

If Christ is the divine living space in which we exist, then we have to imagine this space as a moved and moving space. In the vista of the coming kingdom of God (1 Cor. 15.28) the space of Christ is open like an anteroom. 'Your life is hid with Christ in God. When Christ who is our life appears, then you also will appear with him in glory' (Col. 3.3–4). The risen Christ takes us with him on his way to his future. So whoever is 'in him' is in the space in which he moves.

'*Christ in us*' makes 'us' the anticipation of redeemed humanity, and the overture to the new creation of all things.

'*We in Christ*' brings us into the space of movement of God's coming kingdom.

We in the Spirit—The Spirit in Us

We experience the presence of the Holy Spirit together with the community of Christ, and the structure is similar. Even in what we have said about 'place', God's Spirit is both person and space. What comes into being is our perichoresis with the divine Spirit.

If we find ourselves 'in the Holy Spirit', we sense God's Spirit as the vitalizing field of force which wakes to life our powers for living. We see the divine Spirit as the light which illuminates everything, as the heartwarming stream of love in us, and as the gale of wind which seizes hold of us. The Pentecostal Spirit is the same Spirit as Yahweh's *ruah*, which awakens life in the created world. According to Heb. 6.5, in the energies of the Holy Spirit we experience 'the powers of the world to come'. The living space of the Holy Spirit is the anteroom to the new world ahead, and the true symbol of God's coming beauty which will redeem the world.

If we look at the other side, we discover the divine Spirit 'in us'. Here the Spirit is person, and we become his living space in the world—the temple and body of the living Spirit. 'You are the temple of the living God; as God said, "I will live in them and move among them … and they shall be my people"' (2 Cor. 6.16, following Lev. 26.12). Here the Shekinah promise to Israel is related to the indwelling of the divine Spirit in the community of Christ. But the Spirit wants to go further. Its aim is to make eternally living not just human beings but 'all flesh'—that is to say, everything that lives. The whole creation is to become the temple of the indwelling energies of the Spirit, and is to find bliss in charismatic fullness of life.

'*We in the Spirit*': here we are persons, and the Spirit is our living space.

'*The Spirit in us*': there the Spirit is person, and we are its living space and its dwelling.

All in God—God in All Things

The nearness of God the Father—Abba—is to be found everywhere where human beings experience the Spirit's powers of life in the fellowship of Christ; for in the fellowship of Christ they find the Father and experience the Spirit, just as in the Spirit they find Christ and the Father. That is the reason why ultimately the living spaces of Christ and the Spirit lead to the perfected space of the new creation, in which God will be 'all in all'(1 Cor. 15.28).

But what is the nature of this perfecting? In the end will God become the eternal living space of those he has created, or will the new creation become God's final living space 'on earth as it is in heaven'?

'We do not know whether God is the space of his world or whether his world is his space. But from the verse "Behold, there is a place by me" (Ex. 33.21) it follows that the Lord is the space of his world but that his world is not his space': so says the old Midrash Rabbah.[34] This answer seems to me one-sided, because it passes over the experience of God's Shekinah among his people. If God the Father is also simultaneously person and space, it is easier to understand his eternal kingdom in perichoretic terms rather than monarchical ones.

'*All things in God*': here God is the living space of his world, the space which receives everything and takes up everything. Then all created beings find in God their 'broad place where there is no more cramping'. As Psalm 139 says, God encompasses those he has created from every side. Here the predicate for God is MAKOM.

'*God in all things*': there God finds his space for living and dwelling in his new creation: 'and God will dwell with them', and all created beings will participate in the indwelling living-ness of God. In the indwelling presence of God the new creation will become the eternal creation. Here the predicate for God is SHEKINAH.

I should therefore like to answer the old rabbinic question in the following way. The redeemed creation finds in God its eternal living space, and God finds in redeemed creation his eternal dwelling place. The world will dwell in God in a worldly way and God will indwell the world in a divine way. God and world will interpenetrate each other mutually, without destroying themselves or being absorbed into each other. That is the eschatological perichoresis of God and world, heaven and earth, eternity and time. God's eternal joy over his redeemed creation and the eternal song of praise of everything created is the end of every eschatology.

In closing I should like to draw attention to an image of the perichoretic doctrine of the Trinity. It is Andrei Rublev's wonderful icon painted in the fifteenth century in Orthodox Moscow. The three divine persons are sitting at table. Through the tender inclination of their heads and the symbolic gestures of their hands they show the profound unity in which they are one. The chalice on the table points to the self-giving of the Son on Golgotha for the redemption of the world. The situation is the moment before the incarnation of the Son for the redemption of the world. The image goes back to the story (Genesis 18) in which Abraham and Sarah receive 'three men', entertain them lavishly, and receive from them the confirmation of the divine promise of a son, a promise over which Sarah admittedly laughs, because of her advanced age. They had 'entertained angels unaware', explains the later interpretation. They have encountered the triune God, declared later Christian theology. Rublev leaves out Abraham and Sarah, and paints the 'three angels' in such a way that we cannot discern which of them represents the Father, which the Son and which the Spirit. In this way there came into being this wonderful social image of the unportrayable triune God.[35]

15

Face to Face:
A Meditation on the Seeing of God

Eye hath not seen ... the things which God hath prepared for
them that love him.
— (1 Cor. 2.9)

The man that looks on glass
on it may stay his eye,
or if he pleaseth through it pass
and then the heaven espy.
— George Herbert[1]

We shall begin by looking at the sensitivity of the human senses,
then turn to physiognomy in order to come to arrive at the field
of vision, and shall only then advance to the seeing of God 'face
to face', the eternal bliss of all believers and for the mystics among
them the ultimate goal of supreme rapture.

The Human Senses

Seeing—recognizing—wondering—contemplating and, along
these stages, perception: that means entering into the light of truth:
'In thy light we see light' (Ps. 36.9). The sense to which these verbs
refer is human perception from afar, through the eyes, the medium

being light. The more immediate sense is hearing, and its medium is sound. That brings us to the closer senses in general. We notice what smells good or bad in our proximity, but our sense of smell is weak; every dog smells more. We taste what is on the table or in the wine glass, at best with the tip of the tongue, and develop our taste. Every child wants to taste things first of all, because it has not long been weaned from its mother's breast. And, not least, we feel the world outside us with the skin of our whole body, and make it out with the tips of our fingers. In feeling, we develop our feelings. Through touching and feeling we come 'into contact' with other people. The mediaeval doctrine of the senses therefore declared that the skin's tactile sense is of all the senses the original and fundamental one for the human being. For further 'contacts' with the outside world the human skin has developed the taste cells, the organ of smell, hearing, and finally the eyes. But the most intimate encounter is the erotic ecstasy in which we love and are loved, and then with all our senses.

What is experienced here is a unity in difference and a difference in unity. It is a reciprocal interpenetration, and a mutual indwelling, for which the concept of perichoresis is one of the most appropriate descriptions. When Adam sleeps with Eve, the Hebrew word says that he 'knew' her. This 'knowing' evidently links the remote sense of seeing with the most intimate, closer sense of loving, and joins the ecstatic astonishment of union with perception of the other for his or her own sake. The ecstatic form of subjectivity becomes the highest form of perceived objectivity. The 'knowing' through looking and loving embraces the whole wealth of human life in its sensoriness, if we take both meanings of the word 'know'.

Knowing and Loving

That brings us to the necessary differentiations in the processes of knowing. *Knowing* is guided by preconceived concerns. Modern reason, which after its emancipation from wisdom, *phronesis*, was developed into instrumental reason, wants to know in order to 'grasp', to dominate. Consequently, according to Kant, reason 'has insight only into that which it produces according to its own concepts'. To perceive in this sense then means to know, and know leads to can—to 'know how'. We know something with our hands: we want to know something in order to 'lay hold of it'. If we have found a concept for something, we have 'seized' its meaning, we 'have it', we possess it and control it. We have at all times what we have perceived 'in our grasp', it is saved in data banks and the internet.

The ancient reason of the philosophers and church fathers perceived things with their eyes, and when they understood them, they presented them in the disinterested notion of pure theory. We acquire enduring knowledge by contemplating. We look at a flower so long until we see *the* flower. We watch a sunset until we perceive *the* sunset per se. Through this tarrying contemplation, the perceiving person participates in the object perceived, enters into it and corresponds to it. Pure perception transforms the perceiving person into what is perceived—not, conversely, the thing perceived into the perceiving person, as in the modern concept of reason. The concern that prompts and guides the perception is not the desire to rule and possess, but the community with what is perceived in a shared world. We perceive in order to participate. Consequently we perceive only insofar as we are prepared to let the object be as it is, and are ready to respect our human counterpart simply for himself. *Tantum cognoscitur quantum diligitur,* said Augustine rightly: 'We only know in so far as we love.' The person who cannot love understands nothing.

In love we forget ourselves and put ourselves in the other person's place by perceiving and respecting his or her difference. Anyone who in other people loves only himself and what resembles himself does not see the others. Like is not at all known by like, for what is no different is a matter of indifference. Only what is different awakens, when we encounter it, the stimulus of 'coming to know'. So the person who knows objects and human counter-parts only on the pattern of his own preconceived concepts sees, hears and feels solely himself wherever he is. He remains impris-oned in his egosolitariness, and is completely obscure to himself. It is only by virtue of love that we perceive something different and become curious. And if we become curious, we also become prepared for change. Unless we open ourselves in this way, cogni-tion deteriorates into a pure recognition of what we already knew in any case. This certainly endorses us, but it is boring too.

Wondering and Seeing

Anyone who wants to discern something must learn to see. Anyone who wants to see must be alert and attentive, must 'take it in', look closely, look at it and pause while he looks. He must not look away or lose himself in something distant. Both eyes concentrate on the object, focus on it, or look the other person in the eye. Concentrated looking is intensified in astonishment and fear. If we suddenly meet something unexpected we are plunged into a state of wonder or fear. If we are frightened we draw back in order to protect ourselves; in wonder our senses open themselves for the spontaneous impression. If we are 'impressed' then we are at first bewildered, and still cannot grasp what we see because we must first develop new viewpoints in order to process the new impres-sions. What is truly astonishing is always 'groundless', and takes place 'in the moment'. The perception which arises from wonder is therefore called *intuitive perception*.

In astonishment we perceive things, happenings and other peo-ple for the first time. There is no way of first perceiving something except through astonishment. That is why grown-ups attribute wonder to the wide-open eyes with which children perceive the world for the first time. Adult people who no longer feel astonished at anything no longer understand anything either. Because even in the everyday world of experience, which is so much a matter of course, nothing repeats itself exactly, everything we encounter also has a unique character. The readiness to marvel at the fact opens our senses, so that we can observe the unrepeatable in the recurring, the unlike in the like, and the dissimilar in the similar. It is true that out of habit we judge 'everything that is' according to precedents and general laws, but at the same time we know that every case is different. Events remain contingent. Consequently the origin of all knowing is to be sought not in recognition but in astonishment.

In contemplation, loving perception and boundless astonishment are perfected. In contemplation we are wholly absorbed into what we are looking at. We are fascinated and as if spellbound. We forget time and space, and cannot get our fill of seeing. We want to tarry in contemplation. We are wholly concentrated and wholly present. Remembrances disappear—hopes vanish: in the moment of contemplation we are completely and wholly 'there'.

In astonishment we awake to the immediate present, in contemplation we remain there. As we look, we keep in view what we see and do not let it go. In contemplation what comes into being is not only an inward community between the thing seen and the seer, but also a fluent unity of the one in the other. The thing seen pierces deeply into the one who sees, and the seer is completely transported into the thing seen. Not least, the contemplation constantly assures itself of the untouched and untouchable independence of the thing contemplated. It is not for nothing that the mystics have talked about an *amour desinteresse*, a disinterested love. The tarrying, enduring, and therein wholly present contemplation transports the beholder into an ecstatic state of wakefulness that is more than waking. He perceives something as true, and as he does so becomes true himself, for it is one and the same light which shines in the object of contemplation and enlightens the seeing eyes.

Can one see 'the truth' itself? According to Friedrich Schiller's ballad (1795), a youth comes to Sais, seeking to see the whole truth for the sake of truth itself. Behind a huge veiled picture 'the truth' is concealed, and the oracle runs: 'Whoever with unconsecrated, guilty hand lifts the veil, he will see the truth.' 'I wish to see it, see it', cries the youth. Next day he is discovered senseless and ashen-faced. 'Woe to the one who comes to truth through guilt. The truth will never more delight him': these were his final words. Our talk about 'the naked truth' is reminiscent of this poem. The truth itself is endurable if it is veiled, but it slays the one who wrongly lays hands on it. What that 'picture of truth' was, has puzzled many people. We might think of a great mirror which revealed the unabashed youth to himself, and therefore filled him with desolation.

Face to Face

All five senses are concentrated at the front of the head, the part we call the face. The German word *Gesicht* derives from the word for seeing, and originally meant what was seen, as the old expression about the 'faces' one has indicates. The word means both 'face' and 'vision'. The field of vision is the horizon of what we see, the point of vision is the perspective from which we see it. Physiognomically, through the German word *Gesicht* the organ of sight is transferred to all the senses and their arrangement at the front of the head. The English word 'face' is Latin in origin, and simply meant visage or appearance.

The expression on someone's face is the concentration of his whole person, as the Greek word *prosopon* suggests. Whether we can really derive the ancient concept of person from the language of the theatre, as meaning mask, character or role, is uncertain, but this was already maintained in ancient Rome by Cicero. Another root may be found in legal language, in which the 'person' means the nontransferrable, responsible subject. So this cannot have anything to do with the interchangeable mask worn by the actor. Christian tradition has applied the concept of person to the indestructible and unrelinquishable nature of the human being as the image of God, meaning the personality which is addressed with his name.

A human being as a living person is first recognized when he relates to other people, and this is perceived first of all through his open eyes and his attentive face. Changes of mood are reflected in the face, and the facial expression goes together with seeing, hearing, smelling and tasting, just as do the gestures of the hands and the attitude of the body. All living speech is visibly located in the physiognomy. Consequently it is good to talk 'face to face', and not just to exchange words on the telephone or by e-mail, or to send SMSs via mobile or cell phones.

Our facial expression can reveal what we are thinking and feeling, but through our expression we can hide these things too. Every person is not just what he actually is, but is also the actor playing himself. We can be more than we seem—*esse quam videri*—but we can also seem to be more than we are. Then we present ourselves as we should like to be but aren't, or put on an act in order to appear differently from the way other people think of us, and adopt a poker face. And if we ourselves don't know who we really are, and have either lost our real selves, or have even never found them, then we seem to ourselves like actors in a play which we don't know, and in a role which we first have to invent. 'Every profound mind needs a mask', asserted Friedrich Nietzsche, undoubtedly meaning himself. To say that 'all the world's a stage' sounds convincing but the image is untenable, for if there is no other reality, a theatre is no longer a theatre. But where, then, is this other reality to be found, the reality which puts an end to the play? Is there a completely different reality in the face of which we lay aside our masks because we have been seen through, and so try to know ourselves as we are known? Or do we in principle remain so hidden to ourselves that we never arrive at an endpoint when we can put aside our masks, not even when we die, because we ourselves can never get through to the foundation?

A particularly disturbing phenomenon is the picture of ourselves we see in a mirror. There we certainly see ourselves 'face to face'. We see ourselves but we do not see through ourselves; we merely see our double and remain alone, with our own selves. Yet in myths and folk tales the human being's mirror image always has something uncanny about it, and can be deadly in its effect. In Chinese myth, in addition to the 'I' that can be seen, every person also has a hidden 'I', which is always behind him as the following phantom spirit or *doppelgänger*. The moment the person looks behind himself to what he really is, he must die. Oscar Wilde's *Picture of Dorian Gray* is a poignant witness to a deadly self-encounter of this kind. In a transferred sense, egomaniacs move everywhere only in the hall of mirrors where their images of themselves are reflected. They talk only about themselves, they only quote themselves, in other people they seek only the endorsement of their own picture of themselves. Today we call that cultivating one's image. It makes people unapproachable, and bores everyone else because they feel ignored. To exist only 'face to face' in these reflections of one's own self means deadly self-isolation.

But lovers and friends know *each other* 'face to face'. They look one another in the eye. Trustfully, they expose themselves in their weaknesses and vulnerabilities, and find mutual protection in each other. Each gives the other the human space for living which they need to develop themselves. In this way they do not just live side by side and together, but in each other too, and in mutual affection and reciprocal respect they keep their future open for themselves. Love does not invent an image of the other person and does not tie the other down to the preconceived judgments which always go together with the pictures we make of someone else. When lovers see each other 'face to face' they need no pictures; pictures would be detrimental. For pictures are representations of people who are absent. If they are present, we don't put up pictures of them. In mutual recognition we accompany the transformations of the other in the ongoing process of a shared life.

'The Lord Spoke to Moses Face to Face as a Man Speaks to His Friend'

In Moses's encounter with the God of Israel as Exodus 33 relates it, there seems to be a contradiction. The Lord speaks to Moses in the tent of meeting 'face to face', but a little later we read: 'You cannot see my face; for man shall not see me and live' (33.2). There are evidently different traditions in the Old Testament. According to the one the glory of God is so overwhelming that the person who 'looks on' God must die; according to others—and these we find especially in the Psalms—'to look upon God' brings human life to its fullness and to the most intensive form of its livingness. According to the one view, God must either veil his face, so that human beings can survive the sight of it, or human beings like Moses or Elijah veil their own faces, out of fear of 'seeing' God. According to the other view, the supreme happiness is to look upon God: 'I had heard of thee by the hearing of the ear, but now my eye sees thee', says Job in his remorse (Job 42.5), and when Moses and Aaron with the seventy elders climbed Sinai 'they saw the God of Israel … like the very heaven for clearness'. And having looked upon God, 'they ate and drank' (Ex. 24.11). What else should they do? Apparently for Israel, God has these two sides; on the one hand he is like the clearness of heaven, and on the other like a devouring fire (Ex. 24.17). But these pointers taken from tradition history do not explain why in one and the same chapter (Exodus 33) the face of God at one time brings friendship, and at another death.

It is worth trying to find a solution by way of systematic theology. For this we can pick up later concepts in rabbinic Shekinah theology, and distinguish between God as he descends to us, and God in his glory. According to Ex. 33.9, the 'pillar of cloud' in which God went ahead of his people on the way to freedom 'would descend and stand at the door of the tent, and the Lord would speak to Moses'. In this way 'The Lord used to speak to Moses face to face, as a man speaks to his friend' (v. 11). The pillar of cloud and the pillar of fire are the visible forms of God's presence at the people's exodus (Ex. 13.21–22). Just as after the temple and the city of Jerusalem were destroyed, the 'indwelling' of Israel's God went with the people into exile, in the same way it went ahead of the people at the exodus. This Exodus-Shekinah is a present form—a 'making present'—of 'the face of God'. 'My presence [Luther translates: 'my face'] will go ahead of you and with it I will guide you' (Ex. 33.14). This is not the face of God as he is exalted but the face of God in his descent, his Shekinah. If we think of it in concrete terms, then the Exodus-Shekinah has a sensory face, with which God talks to Moses. It is a divine face on the same level—eye to eye—as the human face of Moses, so it is like a talk between equals—'as if with a friend', not vertically from above to below, like a divine command to a servant.

Just because Moses sees the face of the exodus God in the guiding 'pillar of cloud', when he hears God's voice like the voice of a friend, he is seized by the longing to see the glory of the God of Israel too (33.18). But what is going to 'pass before him' is not God's glory but 'God's goodness' (v. 19). It is because of this goodness that Moses is permitted to stand in a cleft of the rock so that he may see the glory of God when it passes by, though 'from the back' (v. 23). This goodness gives Moses 'a space' beside God in which he can live, although he cannot see the face of God in his glory.

Evidently in this story about God's encounter with Moses we have to do with the face of God in two forms—with the kindly face of his Shekinah, and with the unapproachable face of his glory. But whoever has perceived—heard and seen—God in his kindly Shekinah longs for his eternal glory, for this Shekinah is the heard promise and the already-seen radiance of that glory whose light, now cast ahead of itself, is the fullness of life descried with all the senses; and it brings happiness to the whole creation. Those who 'have seen' God are called God's 'friends', like Abraham, Jacob, Moses, Job and others. Friendship with God springs from the seeing 'face to face', like to like, whether it be by virtue of God's descent into the world of our senses, or whether it be through our transfiguration into the world of his glory. So the seeing of God is already in Old Testament traditions the consummating goal. As Isaiah sees in his call vision, it comes about when 'the whole earth is full of his glory' (Isa. 6.3), and it is universal and earthly. It is not meant individualistically, and as something belonging to the world beyond, as in the gnosis of the ancient world and in the Gnostic Christianity of our own time.

'Now We See in a Glass Dimly, but Then Face to Face. Now I Know in Part but Then I Shall Know Even as I Am Known'

These brief sentences of Paul's in 1 Cor. 13.12 have become the foundational text for theological knowing in Christian faith, the *theologia viatorum*, the theology for us wayfarers. Elsewhere Paul stresses that 'we walk by faith, not by sight' (2 Cor. 5.7), and that faith comes from listening to the word of God (Rom. 10.17), but here everything is directed towards knowing through seeing. In the history of this world-time 'we see in a glass', or mirror. This is meant in the good Platonic sense: a mirror receives impressions and gives back visible images (*Timaios* 71 B). Here the knowledge of God is an indirect knowing, reflected in something else, and hence a cloudy, puzzling knowing. Because Luther was thinking of the word of the gospel which awakens faith, he translated the passage freely: 'We see in a dark (or enigmatic) word'. That leads to the difficult idea that here Paul is seeing in a 'dark word' and that the word only conveys the knowledge of God indirectly, as a mirror does. But then our proclamation of the gospel and our faith would be at best 'partial', and like everything partial fraught with uncertainties. But to understand this passage it is best to look at it in the reverse direction, so as to perceive from the goal Paul is seeking the way he takes.

'When the perfect comes, the imperfect will pass away' (13.10). How are the fragmentary and the perfect related? Their relationship is not teleological, as if the perfect were the sum of all its different parts, so that the whole would be built up piece by piece. What is perfect is not 'in its becoming', but in its coming. Its future is to be found not in the progression but in the advent. What Paul calls *teleion* here is the kingdom of God's glory, in which the whole creation will become new (Rev. 21.5). It is the 'eschatological moment' (1 Cor. 15.52) when the dead will be raised, in which *chronos*, transient time, will be transformed into simultaneous eternity. In that moment what is 'in part', the anticipatory but transitory knowledge of God in history, will end: *incipit vita nova*—a new life begins! When the eternal God appears in his unveiled glory, the indirect knowledge of God in the mirror of his words and acts in history will cease, and will be replaced by the direct seeing 'face to face'.

Because Paul makes everything point forward to the contemplation of God which is to come, he already calls what is provisional a seeing and a knowing. Indirect knowledge of God here—direct knowledge of God there; fragmentary knowledge here—perfect knowledge there. There is a continuity from here to there because in both it is a matter of seeing and knowing: initial seeing here—perfect seeing there. But there is discontinuity too, because the complete seeing of God face to face will put an end to all fragmentary and puzzling perception here, just as once we are grown up we put away childish things and forget them. The *visio beatifica*, the beatific vision, is at once an end and a consummation.

But there is another continuity as well. This does not run from here to there, but from there to here; 'Then I shall know even as I am known' (1 Cor. 13.12). God already sees us, knows us and 'sees through us' here and now, and we shall then, for our part, know God in a corresponding way.

To see and know God face to face is not simultaneous now, but it will be a simultaneous seeing and knowing then. Now it is just that God knows us from his side; then it will be a mutual knowing. It is not enough to recognize that the 'light of God's countenance' rests on us in blessing. That light is also meant to reflect the glory of God which will shine on our 'unveiled faces' (2 Cor. 3.18). In whatever ways we may otherwise think of the relation between God and human beings, here Paul is evidently insisting on complete reciprocity, as the phrase 'face to face' suggests. Why? Because it is one and the same light in which God sees human beings and human beings see God. Because it is one and the same Spirit which moves human beings into the orbit of the shining face of God, and also lets human beings, for their part, 'explore the depths of the Godhead'. Human beings who contemplate the fullness of the deity do not disappear like finite drops in the ocean of infinity, as some of the mystics have thought, and who therefore closed their eyes. On the contrary, they will with their own faces be respected and known by God, and are to meet God with open eyes, as they meet a friend.

Is this conceivable? It is possible if people become 'like God' and are deified. Then they will be able for God: 'We know that when he appears we shall be like him, for we shall see him as he is' (1 John 3.2).

The Contemplation of God and God's Presence in All Things

Since human beings are not gods but are God's creations, and will remain so, they will find the complete fullness of life not in themselves but only in God, from whose creative energy they have proceeded. It is only in God that they will find the beauty which promises not just happiness but eternal bliss. It is only in God that there is at once inexhaustible fullness and reposing perfection. Consequently Christian tradition has seen in God himself the supreme good which at the beginning awakens the desire of humanity and finally fulfils it. That finds expression in the idea about the beatific vision, and in the expectation that when the final goal has been reached, God, who created everything, will so dwell in his creation that he will be 'all in all' (1 Cor. 15.28). The two ideas about the consummation belong together.

The vision of God is not won when human beings try to rise from created to uncreated light, in order to find God in his eternity. And if they could so rise, what would they see? Luther rightly answers: a child in the manger and a man on the cross! But the vision of God becomes possible if God in his glory appears on earth and if, in his appearing, creation becomes new and the dead rise.

This coming glory of God casts its light ahead of itself in 'the dayspring from on high'. Above all other signs, this is the light of the glory of God in the face of Jesus Christ (2 Cor. 4.6). The people who believe in Christ recognize him because of that too, and when they 'see' Christ before them, they also already see the Father (John 14.9). They are enlightened—lit up—by the light of the divine Spirit, and with unveiled faces reflect the full clarity of God (2 Cor. 3.18). They no longer exist in the night when God is far off. They live in the daybreak colours of God's coming day (Rom. 13.12). In this respect, to believe means trusting in God's promise, seeing the world in the advance radiance of God's future, and living life here as a foretaste of God's fullness.

But what happens in the vision of God, and what happens to the human being in his seeing? In the contemplation we forget ourselves and are absorbed wonderingly into what is seen. We do not take possession of our opposite but surrender ourselves to him, and are so transformed that we correspond to the one seen, become like him, and participate in him. The vision of God confers eternal community with God and likeness to God. The seeing of the divine plenitude is the highest form of the love of God, the love of God for God's sake. This loving vision of God lets those who see it forget themselves, but it does not make them selfless. They do not lose themselves, and are not submerged in the ocean of the deity. They remain themselves; otherwise the seeing of God would lose its subject. The love unites those who are different and distinguishes those who are joined. Consequently the mystical picture of the marriage of the soul with the deity is a good metaphor for the intimate union, for a vision of God with all the senses, and for a 'knowing' of God in the double sense of the word; but the wedding is not the end. On earth, after the wedding the marriage begins, and in the case of God it is eternal life, face to face, and the transfiguration from glory into glory.

The vision of God confers a relative eternity on human beings through their then unhindered participation in God's eternity. It is a *participatory* eternity, in which earthly life is taken up into the divine life, and yet, though in God, still remains over against God.

The sight of God leads to *fruitio Dei*, the full enjoyment of God. It is not only the eyes which are blessed with the perception of what was hidden; it is all the senses, with which the presence of God is tasted, felt, smelled, heard and seen, so that God will be 'all in all'. In this way an eternal blessedness comes into being in the eternal life. The eternal blessedness comes about when the whole *pleroma* or fullness of the deity opens itself. That transcends earthly happiness through continually new delight and through never-ending jubilation.

This enjoyment of God too should be thought of as a *reciprocal* enjoyment. Human beings thrill to their joy in God, and God rejoices over his people as the Father rejoiced over the prodigal son. Created beings enjoy their fellowship with the creator, and the creator enjoys his fellowship with the creations who wholly correspond to him. Consequently the enjoyment of God is not reserved for the solitary soul. Those who rejoice in God will also rejoice together. They perceive each other in God and recognize each other as members of the all-embracing divine community of all things. In the great sympathy that binds all things together, people too are bound to one another in sympathy.

With 'the world in God' Hans Urs von Balthasar completed his eschatology, which he called a theodrama, and the end of it

The Last Act (1983; ET 1998). That seems to me one-sided. The full picture of the consummation only emerges when 'the world in God' is simultaneously 'God in the world', and when the indwelling of the redeemed 'in God' corresponds to the indwelling of God in the new creation. Then the perfect perichoresis of God and world comes into being as the environment in which God and human beings look upon each other face to face.

PART FOUR

GOD IN NATURE

16

Natural Science and the Hermeneutics of Nature

Do We Understand What We Know?

Jakob von Uexküll was one of the first biologists to investigate the habitats of living things. He followed up his *Streifzügen durch die Umwelten von Tieren und Menschen* ('Forays into the Environments of Animals and Human Beings') with a *Theory of Meaning*.[1] He didn't just want to observe what *is*; he also wanted to understand what it means. In a dispute with a famous contemporary chemist, he gave the following example: Let us assume that a chemist stands in front of Raphael's Sistine Madonna in Dresden and analyses it with a chemist's eye. What does he perceive? He perceives the colours but he doesn't see the picture. He is 'blind to its meaning'. And this is the way he confronts 'the face of nature' too. He sees a great deal, but understands very little. Yet—so von Uexküll concludes—life can only be understood if we understand its meaning. All the acts of living things are determined by 'feeling and reacting'. They are 'determined by their significance, not mechanically'.[2]

Today, if we are to believe the journalist prophets in the German news magazine *Der Spiegel*, we are at a turning point 'from the society of knowing to the society of understanding' (30, 2007, 125–126). True, today our scientific knowledge doubles every five years; but do we understand what we know? Excellent

189

research certainly provides data, numbers and diagrams, but it does not provide meanings. A computer can store all the data, but it doesn't understand them, because it is unable to interpret them. Mere collections of data are not yet knowledge. At bottom, a person only knows what he or she has appropriated and understood. It is only when I have understood the significance of something that I know it. Consequently we can venture to say that sciences only emerge from a hermeneutics of nature. The concern of the sciences is therefore to perceive the meaning of natural phenomena for each other, in their interrelations, and not least for human culture. Every perception presses toward understanding and it is only what we have understood that we can say we know.

Primal scientific curiosity desires to know nature for its own sake. We want to know more than we need to know in order to survive. Primal perception is based on *wonder*, as Plato stressed so unforgettably. In *wonder* we perceive natural phenomena for their own sake, and forget ourselves. Pragmatic concerns follow later. In view of today's economization of the sciences, a hermeneutics of nature which wants to do justice to nature will have to restore to their origin the interests of the modern sciences which are dominated by the need to know. There is a modern anthropocentric and utilitarian hermeneutics of nature. But we call the original hermeneutics of nature, in contrast, *the natural hermeneutics of nature*. Whereas in the one case the aim is *to know so as to dominate nature*, in the natural hermeneutics of nature the aim is *to know so as to understand*.[3]

The modern method for dominating nature has often been compared with the Roman recipe for government: *divide et impera*—divide and rule. This method led to the splitting of the atom and to the search for the ultimate, indivisible components of matter, the 'elementary particles'. Scientific reductionism is then inescapable. Yet every attempt to understand natural processes leads in the opposite direction. We then understand something when we perceive its function for its relative whole, and see its relative whole in its environment, and thus see the living thing in its habitat, the space in which it lives, and the spaces in which the living things live in their interactions with our human spaces for living. In this way we pass from the nucleus to the atom, from the atom to the molecule, from the molecule to the cell, and so forth, until we arrive at the whole organism of the earth, and to the horizons of value and belief which encircle human culture.

Do the natural sciences do violence to nature? Where it is a matter of the nature over which human beings can acquire power, violence has not merely been employed; it has also been justified. For Francis Bacon, the sciences bring Mother Nature and her children to the human being (that is to say the man) as his slave. The image is drawn from the colonialism and slave trade of Bacon's time. According to Immanuel Kant, nature is passive material, where 'reason has insight only into that which it produces according to its own concepts, … constraining nature to answer reason's own questions.' This constraining of nature was also compared with the torture through which secrets are extorted. These images of the imposition of force on nature are in line with the technology with which nature is exploited. If, on the other hand, we assume that nature has in its own way its own subjectivity, the consequence is a dialogue and exchange between human beings and nature, and a technology allied with natural forces such as Ernst Bloch envisaged.

If we want to understand, our aim should not be to dominate and exploit nature but to arrive at community with it. We investigate complex interactions, and see ourselves as part of nature. The object of our understanding is *complexity*. We do not set ourselves up as absolutes over against the nature we can perceive, as Descartes recommended; we understand our perception as a participatory link. *We want to know in order to participate.* We understand the knowability of nature as an act of its participation in us or, as people used to say, as 'the language of nature' addressed to human beings. We do not understand nature's knowability to mean its subjugation to human power.

The hermeneutics of the relationship between nature and human beings corresponds to the relationship in the human being between body and soul.[4] In the early modern world we find that a parallel is made between the subjugation of the body and the subjugation of nature, as well as between the body as a machine and the cosmos as a clockwork mechanism. But now we are becoming aware of the psychosomatic totality of the human gestalt (or total configuration) and the inner orientation of the body; for that gives us a better understanding of natural environments and habitats. 'Every environment is filled only with symbols of meaning … Every symbol of meaning in a determining subject is also a symbol of meaning for the bodily gestalt of that subject.'[5]

What can theology contribute to the present-day development of a scientifically acceptable and fruitful hermeneutics of nature?

It can first of all link up with the language in which the results of the modern natural sciences, especially genetics, are expressed. When scientists want to understand and put forward what they have discovered they often use the old metaphors of natural theology.[6] It is only when something is understood that it can be explained.

Dis-covery: Someone who discovers something hitherto unknown makes a dis-covery, as we say. It often comes to be associated with his name. He dis-closes what has been concealed, and brings to light what has been hidden. The words *dis-covery* and *dis-closure* make this clear. A discovery is not an invention, because its premise is the previous existence of the object; it doesn't produce the object now discovered. This metaphor describes the same fact as the one captured in the theological concept of revelation or apocalypse. It is only the author, the determining subject, that changes. In the one case the revealer is God; in the other, the discoverer is a human being. Natural theology is not a revealed theology. The traces and signs of the divine wisdom are hidden in nature; the human being must seek them and find them in order to take them into account. Natural theology is an indirect knowledge of God which can be discerned by human beings with their natural senses and their natural reason. It is a dis-covery of the hidden revealedness or manifestation of God in nature.[7]

The 'Book of Life' and the legibility of the world: In modern genetic research 'the book of life' is a favourite metaphor.[8] The Book of Life is an ancient Christian image for the names of the blessed who have entered into eternal life (Phil. 4.3). But the 'book of life' in the modern sense comprises the genetic sequences, as the language of all the living. When President Bill Clinton saw the sequences of the deciphered human genome, he called them the 'language in which God created life'. Even without the reference to God, the book metaphor offers a rich imagery: in the gene sequences we learn 'the spelling of life', the human genome is 'a dictionary of the human being', it is like a 'library', the 'books' are the chromosomes, the base pairs are the 'letters', the genes are the 'words'. For all that, this 'book of life' remains hard to read if only the 'syntax of life' is known, but not its semantics. Nevertheless, the book metaphor makes nature fundamentally speaking 'legible'.[9] Does it also make it correctable? Can the text of life be newly edited by human beings?

The genetic code: If we use the metaphor of the code, we are thinking of a message addressed to us in cryptic form, a secret writing which has to be deciphered.[10] The code contains the transformation rules for translating the secret text into familiar terms. The book metaphor puts the individual text in the framework of its whole, and interprets the whole in its relationship to the reader, and in a similar way the code metaphor also relates nature to human beings, and interprets signs in nature as signals to them. Nature contains a hidden message addressed to human beings. If the subject is the human genome, that is self-evident. Just as the book metaphor presupposes an author, the code metaphor presupposes a sender of the coded message, though without designating this sender more precisely. There is still a blank space in the background.

The metaphors we have described about the discovery of the book and the code turn nature into a cosmos of significant signs.[11] These must be appropriately interpreted if they are to be understood. In modern science, the human being is the perceiving and interpreting subject, and nature is the object which can be read like a book. The reference to God is therefore left open. But in thinking about the human being and nature we can also pick up the old thesis which says that in the human perception of nature, nature arrives at awareness of itself.[12] This does not limit the modern relationship between the human being and nature, but puts it in the wider cohesion of nature and the human being. Human perception and human interpretation of nature is also a natural proceeding, which has to be shaped in such a way that it is tolerable for both nature and human beings. It is only then that the blank space left open for nature's 'author' or for the 'sender' of its message is wide enough to embrace human beings and their culture too. It is only this that provides the connecting point for a theological hermeneutics of nature. And it is to this that we shall now turn.

The Idea of the Two Books: Holy Scripture and 'the Book of Nature'

The idea of 'the two books' derives from Christian tradition, and was widespread in the era before the scientific revolution. Does it offer us an acceptable point of departure for a theological hermeneutics of nature?

Generally speaking, it points to a comparison between the Jewish-Christian revelatory Scriptures and the scientific knowledge of nature, and allows us to see as God's creation the nature which the scientists investigate. More precisely, this metaphor lets us understand nature as a 'book' whose characters we can learn to read. Nature is just as intelligible as the human mind is rational. The metaphor assumes that nature has a language, and it calls the signatures of nature a 'script' which human beings can read. The interactions in nature are viewed on the analogy of linguistic information. Kepler and Galileo, however, thought that 'the book of nature' was written in numbers, not letters: the language of the great book which we always have before our eyes is mathematics. John Polkinghorne was thinking the same when he called mathematics 'the language' in which the cosmos speaks to human intelligence. But is mathematics really a science? Does it not rather belong to the humanities or to art?

Nature speaks to human beings through a language of signs which can be deciphered in the way that a language unknown to us can be deciphered. To put it theologically: all created things are creations of the divine Word: 'God said: Let there be light! And there was light.' What we get to see in nature are therefore creations of God's Word. In the beginning was the Word 'and all things were made by him that were made' (John 1.1, 3). Their perceptible reality is an expression of the eternal Logos, in which the human mind and spirit also shares. Consequently Nicholas of Cusa declared that sensory perception was an appropriate way of understanding the language of God in nature. '*Things* are the books of the *senses*. In them, the will of the divine reason is inscribed in *images* accessible to the senses.'

The Syrian Church Fathers and the Cappodocians used the idea of the two books. A certain third-century abbot Antonius said: 'My book is the created nature, one always at my disposal whenever I want to read God's words.' Basil the Great believed that our reason was so perfectly created by God that 'through the beauties of created things we can read God's wisdom and providence as if these beauties were letters and words'. For Augustine, although only the person who has learnt to read can read Holy Scripture, even the illiterate can understand the book of the universe. For Maximus the Confessor, nature and Scripture are the two robes of Christ which shone bright at his transfiguration, his humanity and his divinity: in Christ the 'two books' have the same content.

The Celtic theologian Scotus Eriugina thought that the two books were the two theophanies, the one through the medium of letters (*apices*), the other through forms (*species*). This tradition talks about the book of nature, or the book of the world or the universe, less often about a book of creation. So ever since Raimundus Sebundus the reading of the book of nature has been called *theologia naturalis* (natural theology), and this has remained general usage. The idea of the two books and their inner harmony was also supposed to express the harmony between faith and reason, and was directed against the separation of the two made by the Islamic philosopher Averroes.

Theologically, the book of nature was always read in the light of Holy Scripture. Through revelation, the wisdom hidden in nature becomes legible as the wisdom of God—which means, conversely, that only what corresponds to God's revelation according to Holy Scripture can be read and understood as divine wisdom in nature. The distinction and the correspondence are important: through the natural knowledge of God we become wise, but unfortunately not saved; through the knowledge of revelation we will be saved but unfortunately do not yet become wise. All knowledge confers community, but the direct knowledge communicated through revelation confers a fellowship with God different from the indirect knowledge of God given through nature.

We must of course be able to reverse this order of things too, and must be able to read the Bible in the light of the book of nature. Many ideas about nature found in the Bible then prove to belong to the superseded world pictures of the past eras in which the biblical writings originated. Only that which is compatible with scientific reason or which opens up for science new horizons of interpretation can count as divine revelation.

I should like to draw attention to another point of comparison between the 'two books': *memory*. The Jewish-Christian writings are undoubtedly an essential component in our common religious and cultural memory. We remember and make present to ourselves the divine revelations given to our forefathers; we remember their faith, the perils and the liberations they experienced, and the successful and unsuccessful forms of life which they created. In order to awaken faith and so as to experience life for ourselves, we interpret these things for the present and the future. Without cultural memory, peoples and nations fall sick. To destroy their memory is to rob them of their identity. The art of interpreting religious and cultural memory in the light of its importance for the present and the future is what we call *hermeneutics*. Every culture is a universe of signs, and is therefore dependent on hermeneutics for its survival.

The sciences are concerned in a comparable way with 'the memory of nature'.[13] When we gaze into the universe at night, we are looking into its past. Stars whose light arrives with us now can already have been extinguished light years earlier. Out of the background radiation, the time shortly after the big bang comes to meet us. We perceive subsequently, not simultaneously, because the speed of light is finite. What we perceive is not the universe that *is*, but the universe that was. What we see is 'the presence of the past'. In the buildup of matter and living things, nature has acquired a memory which must be called wise, because it has expelled conjunctions hostile to life and has promoted others which are compatible with it. In the cosmos since the big bang, and in life on earth since the beginning of evolution, nature has been involved in an irreversible 'history of nature'.[14]

Cultural and natural memory are not as far apart as are science and the humanities in our universities today. They have always influenced each other mutually, for ultimately speaking the cultural code of human beings is also part of the natural code, if human beings and their brains are part of nature. But because of the subjugation and domination of nature by the scientific and technological culture of human beings, the consonance between the cultural and the natural memory is not sufficiently regarded. Yet ultimately modern science belongs to the culture of humanity.

It is to a high degree conditioned by culture, and is to an enduring degree even conditioned by the Jewish-Christian religion, as we can easily see if we compare it with Indian and Chinese sciences and the attitude to nature that underlies them.

The General Doctrine of Signs: *Signatura rerum* or the Signature of All Things

The 'book of nature' can only be read if we regard nature not as a world of facts but as a world of meanings.[15] It is only when everything is full of signs that everything is also full of significance. Consequently the hermeneutics of nature is the art of interpreting the natural world of signs. In Germany this doctrine of signs in nature goes back to Paracelsus, and especially to Jakob Böhme's book, published in 1622, *De signatura rerum oder von der Geburt und Bezeichnung aller Wesen* (*On the* signatura rerum *or The Birth and Description of All Things*):

> And there is nothing in nature created or born which does not reveal its inner form (Gestalt) externally as well, for the innermost part always thrusts towards its manifestation ... Hence there is in the signature the greatest reason (*Verstand*), in which a man may not only know himself but may also learn to know the nature of all things ... Everything has its lips open for revelation; that is the language of nature.[16]

What are signs or signatures?

a)   In the doctrine of signatures or signs, nature is understood as *expression*. According to ancient Platonic teaching, every individual thing is an expression of its innermost essence. According to Christian understanding, everything is an expression of its divine Word. That is the inward dimension of things as a sign of something inherent in them or above them. Consequently natural configurations are read in a physiognomic sense: just as a face expresses the particular character of the soul, so general physiognomy is the art of interpreting configurations in the face of nature.

b) It is the character of every natural sign to be a *pointer* showing the links between things and their relationships. These also point to the relative whole, of which the things are only parts. The cross-references in the network of interrelationships, and the 'bottom-up' or 'top-down' pointers in the relative wholes, are interlaced.

c) Not least, nature's world of signs is related to the human beings who observe and who act. The signs then become *signals,* saying what the natural environment means for the human being, and what the human being means for the natural environment. In its signs nature is, as it were, a transmitter of its own signals, and not merely a receiver of the signals of human beings. That presupposes recognition of a graduated subjectivity in nature, in its living things and its various habitats.

d) Because 'the great whole' of a rounded-off and completed cosmos is not yet existent, all individual signs must also be interpreted as *prefigurations* of a future that is possible but not yet present, a future towards which everything that already exists points, and on which it is dependent. All the totalities we know are fragments of what is to come, and are therefore *anticipations* open to the future. Paul knew this: 'For we know in part and we prophesy in part. But when that which is perfect is come, then that which is in part shall be done away' (1 Cor. 13. 9–10). It is worth noting that the part-perfect relationship corresponds subjectively to the knowledge-prophecy relationship. We know what exists, and we prophesy what will come. It is also important that the perfect does not *develop* out of what is in part, but comes to meet it.

If we set aside the magic and arts of divination, as well as the astrology, which were bound up with the ancient doctrine of signatures or signs, what remains for our modern understanding is the fact that nature is a *world of forms*, and that the connections in nature consist not only of the exchange of energy but also of the exchange of *information*. The ancient doctrine of signs can easily be translated into the modern informatics of nature. The art of receiving information, interpreting it and assimilating it is hermeneutics. The primal matter of the universe is information, which is simply to say that information and reality are the same.[17]

Taking up this approach, we might say that at the beginning of nature stands the form, and form both as *forma informata* and as *forma informans*: the form is both shaped and shaping. We live in a world of reciprocal informational effects and participations. We also discover a world of *performative anticipations*: reality is formed from potentialities. That is the creative part of reality as efficacy. As Goethe wrote, life is 'shaped form which develops as it lives'.

We can grasp the sign language of the forms of life and their meaning if we consider our own bodies. We perceive internal illnesses from their outward *symptoms*. A *symptom* is the sign and expression of an illness. But these signs must not only be noted; they must also be interpreted. The interpretation takes place when the symptoms are *diagnosed*. They must not only be precisely observed; they must also be correctly interpreted, and the illness which they signify and express must be identified. Once we have understood the symptoms correctly, the *therapy* can begin. This closes the hermeneutical circle of perceiving and acting. I believe that this diagnostic-therapeutic circle can also be applied to the sciences and the hermeneutics of nature.

The Theological Doctrine of Signs

With the beginning of the modern world, the theological doctrine of signs was transferred from the cosmos to history, for in Europe, after the French Revolution, 'history' came to be the concept for reality as a whole. But if the stars no longer provide any orientation, what should we hold on to in history? We must interpret 'the signs of the times' in order to know what hour has struck.[18] The 'signature of history' is interpreted in the light of 'the signs of the time'. According to the Second Vatican Council in *Gaudium et Spes*, 'the Church carries the responsibility of reading the signs of the time and of interpreting them in the light of the Gospel'. Whereas earlier, grace presupposed nature, now it has to presuppose history. So the historical interpretation of the signs of the times takes over the function of the old *theologia naturalis*. But what Kant called the 'historical signs' which have to be interpreted are extremely ambivalent. On the one hand there are *signs of hope*, like the 'signs and wonders' in the Old Testament—in modern terms, signs of 'human nature's capacity for betterment' (which was the way Kant interpreted the French Revolution); that is to say, historical signs can be seen as *signs of progress*. On the other hand, there is the apocalyptic orientation towards *signs of the end*: 'When will this be, and what will be the sign when these things are all to be accomplished?' is the question in the Little Synoptic Apocalypse (Mark 13.4). And this is the way in which today too earthquakes, tsunamis, wars, the climate catastrophe and homosexuality are interpreted in apocalyptic communities; they are read as advance signs of the imminent end of the world.

For Christian theology *the coming of Christ* and his gospel is the one true sign of the times: 'But what are the signs of the time?' asked Rudolf Bultmann, and replied in his *Theology of the New Testament*: 'He himself! His appearance and ministry, his proclamation.'[19]

For Christian theology, the centre of its doctrine of signs is the *realized presence* of Christ in the Eucharist. According to Thomas Aquinas and the general Christian view, the Eucharist or Lord's Supper is: 1. a *signum rememorativum* of the passion of Christ, 2. a *signum demonstrativum* of present grace, and 3. a *signum prognosticon* of coming glory (Aquinas, S.Th. III q 60 a 3)—that is to say it is a commemorative sign, a demonstrative sign, and a forward-looking sign. In the unison of remembrance and hope,

Christ becomes present. The presence of the Christ who has come is at the same time the presence of the coming Christ.[20]

The Christian doctrine of the signs in history and nature will always take its bearings from this unique sacrament of Christ. Then nature appears in the light of a sacramental interpretation. By virtue of the presence of the creative, life-giving Spirit, the presence of God will be perceived in all things, just as the body and blood of Christ is present in bread and wine, and the whole Christ is present in the whole celebration of the Supper. These are the traces of God, *vestigia Dei*, in the history of nature and civilization. These are the correspondences between created beings and their creator, and the anticipations of their future true form or gestalt.

The World as Nature and as Creation: Theological Interpretative Patterns

Does it make any difference whether we see the world as nature or as creation?

Let us look briefly at what changes in the concept of *nature*. In Latin philosophy, *natura* means the essential nature of something. Today when we talk about 'the nature' of something, we mean its essential character, not its appearance. But the concept of nature in the modern sciences is different: it is aligned exclusively to the side of the thing which can be apprehended by the senses. The empirical concept of nature has no longer anything to do with the metaphysical concept of being or essence. In order to understand something, one must observe it exactly, weigh it, measure it, and so forth, but one does not think about its essential being. How did this radical transformation in the concept of nature come about? It is a historically established fact that the change arose under the influence of the theological concept of creation.

    a)   The ancient Greek concept of *physis* does not make any distinction between what is divine and what is worldly. *Physis* is the power of producing, of generation, and it is hence divine.

Understood as *physis*, the cosmos is of divine perfection. The world is a 'sphere', a self-contained system. Its time is circular, for the circle is the image of eternity. The Yin/Yang dynamic in Asia is also visually represented by the closed circle.

b) If the world is understood as creation, it cannot be divine like its creator, but has to be understood in a worldly sense. Consequently it cannot possess any divine attributes. Creation does not have the form of a sphere; its time is not circular; it is not a self-contained system. It is finite, temporal and contingent. Its foundation is not in itself but in another. As the creation of a transcendent God, it issues from God's free will and is not a necessary expression of his being, although it corresponds to that being. So it is contingent (*contingentia mundi*). It can be known only through observation and investigation, not deduced from a being or an idea. That was the theological reason for the transformation of the metaphysical concept of *natura* into the modern empirical concept of nature. This by no means contradicts the theological concept of creation, as the creationists assume; it corresponds to the theological concept and results from it.

c) According to the first creation account (Genesis 1), the whole creation is aligned towards a goal and is in no way a primal condition complete in itself. In the beginning *of what* did God create heaven and earth? Every beginning raises the question about its goal, every *bereshith* (in the beginning) has its corresponding *acharith* (in the end). Even the Sabbath of creation, with which the Genesis account closes, points beyond itself, for it has no evening.

'Thou hast made us for thyself, and our hearts are restless until they find rest in thee', declared Augustine, thus basing the restlessness of the human heart not on the Fall but on creation. This proposition became the principle of Western anthropology right down to the present day, and not only that: it is also a principle of the Western worldview. To the restless, self-transcending human mind there corresponds in a graduated way a restless, self-transcending world of nature (*mundus inquietus*). A self-transcending nature, open to the future, is the correspondence to the human soul's openness to the world. Self-transcendence is, in its own, always specific way, characteristic of all created things, because it was already given to them 'in the beginning'. All those God has created are *beginners* of their own future in God.

If, as Augustine maintained, time was created together with creation, and not just after the Fall and the banishment from an unchanging and quiescent paradise, then creation is from the beginning a changeable world (*mundus mutabilis*), a world in movement, in which every living being can distinguish between past and future, reality and potentiality. If the world were suddenly to stand still, we should no longer be able to perceive time.

d) If we call the present state of the world 'God's creation', then theologically we have to be precise: the present state of the world no longer corresponds to conditions as they were 'in the beginning', nor is the world as yet the kingdom of God, as it will be at the end. Whatever is between the beginning and the end is on the way and caught up in the transition.

If, then, we talk theologically about the present state of the world as 'nature', we mean a creation spoiled and disrupted by chaos (Rom. 8.19). It is full of beauties and full of catastrophes. And yet we believe that this world of earthquakes and tsunamis, of AIDS and other plagues, and of death, is nevertheless God's good creation, because we trust in the faithfulness of its creator, and know that he will bring it to its appointed goal.

Why is this creation of God's threatened by chaos and why has it fallen victim to annihilation? Because the creator is by no means 'the all-determining reality' of what he has created—in that case creation would be itself divine—but because he has conferred on creation its own scope for freedom and generation.[21] According to tradition, these are the so-called secondary causes (*causae secundae*) of creation: Gen. 1.11: 'Let the earth bring forth vegetation, plants yielding seed, and fruit trees'; Gen. 1.24: 'Let the earth bring forth living creatures'; Gen. 1.26: 'Let us make man .... And let them have dominion over the fish of the sea, and over the birds of the air, and over the cattle, and over all the earth ....' It is a whole warp and weft, an interwoven fabric of relatively independent creative activity on the part of the earth and human beings. But in these free spaces, the earth and human beings are creations that stand on the edge of chaos and are threatened by the forces of annihilation (Genesis 6). So in the completed and perfected creation there will be, symbolically speaking, no 'sea' and no 'night'—or, to put it realistically, no more death and no more sin.

In view of the present state of the world, which lies between order and chaos, between being and nonbeing, creation is theologically ascribed to continuous creation (*creatio continua*). In continuous creation God preserves those he has created, in spite of everything that threatens them and in spite of their sins. In it he anticipates their future in his kingdom. By virtue of the patience with which he endures and sustains his fallen creatures he does not give up their future, but continually gives them new time and new future. 'Our God is a God who bears.'[22] It is true that we are used to think of a God who rules from above just as he likes, and whose will is for us human beings as inscrutable as fate. But a closer glance at the biblical testimonies shows us that the God of Israel and Jesus Christ is a bearing, patient, enduring and suffering God. His rule is not a rule that commands; it is a rule of love. His almighty power shows itself in his all-enduring patience. If we look at Israel's exodus history, which is what stands behind the first commandment, we perceive on the one hand his liberating power, which destroys the army of the Pharaoh, and on the other hand his sustaining power, which saves the people: 'You have seen what I did to the Egyptians, and how I bore you on eagles' wings' (Ex. 19.4). For this sustaining power of God, Scripture uses a feminine image—'Carry them in your bosom, as a nurse carries the sucking child' (Num. 11.12)—and a male one too: 'You have seen how the Lord your God bore you, as a man bears his son' (Deut. 1.31). The true revelation of the sustaining God is the suffering Christ on the cross. 'He has borne our sicknesses' (Isa 53.4) and has taken on himself the sins of the world, in order to heal and to redeem. 'He upholds the universe through his word of power' (Heb. 1.3). The God who so upholds and so bears the world is like the Greek *hypokeimenon*, the sustaining foundation of all things.

We read the signs of what God has created as reminders of God's good foundational conditions, as an expression of his sustaining energies, and as advance signs of his saving future.

The Sighs of the Divine Spirit in All Things and All People

I am assuming familiarity with the wonderful eighth chapter of the Epistle to the Romans and would recall: 1. the sighings and yearnings of creation for liberty in its sufferings from transience; 2. the yearning of human beings for the redemption of the body in the torments of death; and 3. the sighs of the divine Spirit, who intercedes for us.[23] On all three levels it is a matter of the torment and the hope of God's Spirit. The Spirit itself is the force of this universal hope. It both torments and encourages, for when freedom is near, the chains begin to chafe. What ferments and torments in believers is the Spirit of freedom, which fills body and soul. What makes all creation sigh and yearn is the indwelling Spirit of life. The divine Spirit itself, which fills the whole world, is seized by a driving force and torment, for it is beset by the birth pangs of the new creation. Paul interpreted the deathly torments of this transitory world as the birth pangs of the future world. The sufferings of this present time which run right through the world are the suffer-ings of an all-embracing divine dynamic.

To translate this world view of Paul's into our own language:

a) *The immanence of the transcendent divine Spirit* is the foundation and driving power for the *self-transcendence* of all open systems of matter and life, and of all human forms of life in history. If the infinite is to indwell the finite, it must, metaphorically speaking, contract itself; and yet the finite is still not able to comprehend the infinite in itself. It is drawn into the movement where it oversteps its own bounds. In this movement, the finite anticipates a future condition in which the infinite can come to rest in the finite and enduringly indwells it. 'God *in* creation' makes creation a world open to the future. That is the universal exodus of all created beings out of chaos and the destiny of death. The goal is the final and enduring cosmic Shekinah: and God will be 'all in all' (1 Cor. 15.28).

b) The immanence of the transcendent Spirit is also the foundation and driving power of the *evolution of life* into ever richer and more complex forms and syntheses. It is ancient wisdom: 'Lord, thou art a lover of life, and thy immortal Spirit is *in all things*' (Wis.11.26). The so-called self-organization of the universe is nothing other than the resonance of the universe as it responds to the immanence of the divine Spirit that drives it. Why else should life organize itself? Why else its torment of chaos and death, if there is not something present in all things which desires to endure and not pass away, which wills to love and not die? Why the struggle for survival if life does not promise more than it can give?

c) The immanence of the transcendent Spirit makes the sign language of nature and of our own bodies legible. In all things we see the many-faceted expression of the divine Creator. In everything that is, the eternal Being manifests itself. Everything living is a resonance responding to the living God. Through his creative Spirit, God is already present in all things. His presence is the presence of his coming. Consequently every *expression* of the divine is at the same time a *prefiguration* and *advance radiance* of the glory of God which will be manifested to everything.

d) The immanence of the transcendent divine Spirit transforms everything that exists into self-transcending movements. That fits in with the modern metaphysics of potentialities. That accords with the new cosmos-chaos theory and the dissipative, unbalanced systems of life. This insight also opens up new horizons for their interpretation. Not least, this theological concept offers an interpretative framework for a new *ecological* view of nature and culture. In a society of understanding, contradictions from which nature and we ourselves suffer can be resolved.

e) *God's Spirit in all things*: that makes the world in which we live a spiritual world. Our human spirituality must adapt itself to it. It will become the resonance of a *cosmic* spirituality. It will become a Pentecostal spirituality of the wakened senses and the attentive heart. It will be a spirituality not only of the soul but of the body too. Not least, in an *ecological* spirituality we shall rediscover the worship of the earth. That is the Sabbath which, according to biblical tradition, the earth is supposed to celebrate in the years of release, during which its fertility will be restored in a realistic way. The Sabbath of the earth will be an anticipation and a foretaste of 'the new earth' on which 'righteousness dwells'.[24]

17

The Theory of Evolution and Christian Theology: From 'the War of Nature' to Natural Cooperation and from 'the Struggle for Existence' to Mutual Recognition

When this subject is broached, many people immediately think of the conflict between the Darwinists and Christian fundamentalists about 'the origin of species' and the biblical doctrine of creation. This dispute is still going on in the United States today, but the dispute is purely ideological. Also on the ideological level is Teilhard de Chardin's brilliant attempt to coordinate the theory of evolution and the Christian teleology of history in the perspective of the Omega Point. In both these theological attempts to approach the theory of evolution, be it critically or affirmatively, what is lacking is discussion about the practical outcome of the theory in racist Darwinism and social Darwinism. We find no criticism of the deadly consequences of the theory of selection for the victims of evolution in the racist medicine of the Nazi dictatorship. The 'unfit' life of the disabled and of Jews and gypsies was destroyed in the name of the theory about 'the survival of the fittest' which in nature was necessary. Even if this racist mania has been surmounted, we are still living in a society of winners and losers, where 'the winner takes all'. A humane criticism and a theological assessment of Darwin must begin at a deeper level, and must call in question its hermeneutical frame of reference, scientifically, anthropologically and theologically.

Two questions:

1. Is it useful and appropriate to assume, like Darwin, that there is a permanent 'war of nature' and a continual 'struggle for existence' among human beings? Or is it better to begin with cooperation as the principle of natural evolution, and with mutual recognition as the principle for developing humanity?
2. Is it useful and appropriate to reduce human existence at its beginning to a 'collection of cells' or to biological 'preliminary stages' of an animal life? Or is it better to see the beginnings of human existence together with its future, and to comprehend it in the light of its potentiality?

We shall begin with Darwin:

Darwin's *Origin of Species* (1859), which sees all life on Earth linked together by way of a common genealogical tree, put the history of nature on a scientific foundation for the first time. The wealth of phenomena which Darwin brings together from the realm of nature is convincing. Out of simple forms of life, a growing variety of species develops by way of variations in the world of plants and animals. Starting from the fact that when the environmental conditions change, not only do ever-new species develop but old species also disappear, Darwin formulated the *principle of selection*. Only the species which have adapted best and most quickly survive, and go on to develop further: this is the survival of the fittest.

So far so good, where the description of the phenomena is concerned. But in 1871, in his book on *The Descent of Man*, Darwin drew up an interpretative frame of reference for the principle of selection, and this is not only based on the observation of natural phenomena, but is also influenced by the 'spirit of the age' in the imperial Great Britain of the nineteenth century.[1]

Inside England, the leading industrial nation, unregulated capitalism prevailed, while externally Great Britain was determined by the growing colonial empire which, as Cecil Rhodes put it, extended from Cairo to Calcutta via Cape Town. The more powerful classes and the victorious 'white race' dominated the world. The basis for the principle of natural selection was therefore supposed to be the fundamental and general 'war of nature', the struggle for existence of all against all. It is not merely the different species but even the individuals within a species, not merely the species but even the organisms themselves which fight against each other in the 'struggle for life', for survival. For human beings there is not only a 'war of nature', but a 'war with nature' too. The survivor reproduces itself. The loser is annihilated. The stronger must win. This is nature's will: evolution through selection. Of course Darwin also knew the natural phenomena of biological cooperation between organisms, species and their individuals; he even noted altruistic behaviour. But he saw these things as secondary phenomena which had developed in the interests of the struggle for existence.

In this essay:

1. We shall call in question the transference of natural selection to the artificial selection of the human race.

2. We shall take up today's neurobiological theory about the cooperation in nature and the coexistence of living things.

3. We shall consider the buildup of more complex systems of life on the basis of top-down causation. Among human beings this is the integration of the order of the body into the order of the person, and the integration of the personal community of human beings into the interpretative framework of the transcendence of values and of faith.

4. Finally, we shall evaluate the world in the development of evolution in the anteroom of its possibility—the world in its becoming, the future in its coming—in order to relate natural evolution and theological eschatology to each other.

Charles Darwin and 'Natural Selection as Affecting Civilized Nations'

In 1871, in his book *The Descent of Man*, Darwin, having described 'the advancement of man from a semi-human condition to that of the modern savage', goes on to ask about 'natural selection as affecting civilised nations' (158ff.). It is significant that here he appeals to three contemporary writers, W. R. Greg, A. R. Wallace and F. Galton, and bases his critical comments on what they have said.

> With savages, the weak in body or mind are soon eliminated; and those that survive commonly exhibit a vigorous state of health. We civilised men, on the other hand, do our utmost to check the process of elimination. (159)

Darwin is against smallpox vaccination since this also enables the weakest members of our species to survive and to 'propagate their kind', and he points to the wisdom of the breeders of domestic animals, who after all do not take the worst animals for breeding purposes.

Illogically enough, Darwin is against war waged between human beings with conscripted armies (thereby confuting his own fundamental assumption about the 'war of nature' which fosters evolution), his reason being that in war the best men die at the front, while 'the shorter and feebler ones, with poor constitutions are left at home, and consequently have a much better chance of marrying and propagating their kind' (160).

> Thus the reckless, degraded, and often vicious members of society tend to increase at a quicker rate than the provident and generally virtuous members. Or, as Mr Greg puts the case: 'The careless, squalid, unaspiring Irishman multiplies like rabbits: the frugal, foreseeing, self-respecting, ambitious Scot ... passes his best years in struggle and in celibacy, marries late,

and leaves few behind him. In the eternal "struggle for exist-ence", it would be the inferior and less favoured race that had prevailed—and prevailed by virtue not of its good qualities but of its faults.' (Greg, quoted by Darwin, 164)

In his 'General Summary and Conclusion' (675ff.) Darwin puts it in the following way:

Man scans with scrupulous care the character and pedigree of his horses, cattle, and dogs before he matches them; but when he comes to his own marriage he rarely, or never, takes any such care … Yet he might by selection do something not only for the bodily constitution and frame of his offspring, but for their intellectual and moral qualities… If the prudent avoid marriage, whilst the reckless marry, the inferior members tend to supplant the better members of society… There should be open competition for all men; and the most able should not be prevented by laws or customs from succeeding best and rearing the largest number of offspring. (688)

In an earlier passage he even praises Sparta:

In Sparta, also, a form of selection was followed, for it was enacted that all children should be examined shortly after birth; the well-formed and vigorous being preserved, the others left to perish. (47)

We may sum up critically by saying:
1. That the struggle for existence or nonexistence in the 'war of nature' which promotes the evolution of life through selection of the fittest is itself called in question by Darwin's rejection of wars in their modern form. War is always destructive, never productive. In wars both the vanquished and the victors are the losers.

2. The conclusion that extinct species such as the dinosaurs must be superseded by stronger species such as human beings is erroneous. The history of nature is more than a struggle between species.

3. At the same time, Darwin's own humane feeling must not be overlooked, for in addition to the passages quoted he also writes:

The aid which we feel impelled to give to the helpless is mainly an incidental result of the instinct of sympathy, which was originally acquired as part of the social instincts, but subsequently rendered ... more tender and more widely diffused. Nor could we check our sympathy, even at the urging of hard reason, without deterioration in the noblest part of our nature. (159; similarly 680ff.)

Possibilities of Artificial Selection: Eugenic Projects

In 1962 the renowned Ciba Conference took place in London. Its results were published by Robert Jungk and Hans Joseph Mundt under the title *Man and His Future.* The German title, translated, ran *Man, the Disputed Experiment.*[2] Is the human being an experiment on the part of nature, or a genetic experiment on its own part? In 1971 I met the most important supporters of the eugenic projects who spoke at that 1962 conference, this time at the international Hoffmann-LaRoche conference in Basel, at which I myself gave a lecture on 'Biomedical Progress and Human Values'. The futurologist Robert Jungk wrote a report on the conference which was published in 1972 under the title *The Challenge of Life.*[3]

The disputed ideas put forward at the Ciba Conference about a 'eugenic future for humanity' may be summed up as follows:

1. Natural selection endangers the future of humanity: the stupid multiply, the clever hold back. So in the civilized

nations humanity's genetic makeup deteriorates and in the industrial societies biological fertility diminishes, as can be shown to be the case in the United States. We therefore need an enhancement of the genetic constitutions of human beings in the advanced nations. It is not enough to use fiscal incentives to encourage the capable and educated to have more children, unless the incapable and uneducated are deterred from producing children. We must go over to artificial insemination in the interests of a selection of the better. From the eugenic point of view, AID (artificial insemination from a donor) is necessary, in order on the one hand to rule out hereditary diseases and on the other hand to further the fertility of the best genetic makeup.

2. For this, sperm banks should be set up with valuable material, that is, material 'with excellent heart, mental and physical capacity'. For this, similarly 'excellent' human ova should be stored. Nanotechnology makes the enhancement of human genetic material possible. 'Because of the general agreement about the supreme value of health, intelligence and humanity, the idealistic vanguard of human beings and their successors will initiate a healthy genetic advancement.' That was the prospect with which Herman Muller closed his lecture at the Ciba Conference. Earlier, he had asked: Which woman would not be proud to be the recipient of sperm from Darwin or Einstein? But he had not asked the women!

3. Joshua Lederberg, the Nobel Prize winner from Stanford University, wanted to regulate the size of the human brain by means of prenatal interventions. He promised that 50 percent more geniuses could be produced if the median IQ of the population was raised by 1.5 percent, and maintained that this was necessary because most of us do not consider the present world population to be intelligent enough to hold back the general annihilation of the world (315). But this is

an illusion. The sons of geniuses have seldom been geniuses themselves. Goethe's son was not a poet; Hegel's son was not a philosopher. Generally these people have become social misfits because of their fathers, since more was expected of them than they could live up to.

The participants in the Ciba Conference were convinced that eugenics of this kind was nothing other than the biological equivalent of the general moral education of the human race towards its betterment, and that it must be employed for the evolution of the human race.

One point that was discussed was: Which human beings have the right to have children? And what right to healthy children does the state have, if it has to look after those who are disabled? The general desire was to breed the qualities of 'health, intelligence and competence' and to eliminate hereditary diseases and transmitted disabilities. What remained unclear was what was meant by an 'improvement of the human genetic make-up'; for it is impossible to judge logically what is 'good' and what is 'better' on the basis of genetic concepts. Curiously enough, what was not discussed was whether a human being—let alone a healthy human being—could ever develop from a fatherless sperm and a motherless ovum. We do not have to do everything that it is possible to do, but only what has a point. 'Can does not imply ought.' It may perhaps one day be possible to clone a human being, but it would be totally pointless.

Sadly enough, the definition of 'embryo' always corresponds to the praxis of the use to be made of it. If embryos are merely animal 'preliminary stages' for the human being, they can be medically utilized; if they are 'developing human beings' their human dignity must be respected. Why is it apparently so difficult for scientists in this sector to see their isolated object in its wider contexts? If they talk only about collections of cells, embryos and foetuses, they are depriving their object of its own future and are seeing only its current state. Abstractions and isolations of this kind are necessary for the analysis that leads to precise results; but for an evaluation the part must be seen in relation to the whole, and its present state together with its future. *A fertilized ovum in its potentiality and with its future is a human being and nothing else.* Its destruction after it has been 'finished with' must be justified, for we were all once embryos ourselves.

In our society, the human being is viewed not merely as a product of its genes, or as a genetic construct; it is also seen as an accountable, determining subject of his or her life and as responsible for what he or she does and leaves undone. And this being so, genetic manipulation inescapably raises the question: Who undertakes the responsibility? Who is liable for the damage incurred by a fatherless semen or a motherless ovum? Who is answerable for embryos which have not been ideally produced, genetically speaking? Can children bring a case against their parents because they have failed to optimize them genetically? Even the laboratory cannot be viewed as a space outside the law. If 'freedom of research' collides with responsibility for life and its protection, the right to life must be given the preference. A scientific description of the human being as the product of his or her genes cannot displace or supersede public recognition of the human person as an accountable and responsible determining subject unless the freedom of the sciences itself is renounced in favour of an ideological genetic engineering.

The Neurobiological Thesis: 'At the Centre of Biology Is Mutual Relationship and Cooperation'

At the Hoffmann-LaRoche conference in Basel in 1971, I urged that 'the values inherent in the struggle for existence must be replaced by an ethic of peace in existence'.[4] This means that 'bio-medical progress must be integrated into a humane order which makes life worth living'. Scientific progress should not be hindered, but must rather be extended to increasingly complex system units. It is also important to integrate science into wider spiritual, social and political systems of communication and cooperation.

This 'ethic of peace in existence' which I called for in 1971 has been scientifically backed up today by neurobiology. I owe this recognition to the neurobiologist Joachim Bauer and the child neurologist Richard Michaelis.

The frame of reference for interpreting the evolution of life does not have to be the 'war of nature' and the 'struggle for existence'. On the contrary, the fundamental principle for the buildup of biological systems is cooperation. Even shortly after Darwin, this was already shown by the socialist and anarchist Pjotr Kropotkin in his book *Mutual Aid. A Factor of Evolution* (1902).[5] The famous naturalist Jakob von Uexküll also recognized that 'relationship' was a fundamental biological principle.[6] But it was only present-day neurobiology which was able to prove 'that we by nature co-operate', and that the development of more complex biosystems succeeds only through cooperation. We shall first look at this as it touches on the development of the humanity of human beings, and shall then come to the new functions which the whole assigns to its integrated parts.

From the neurobiological viewpoint, we human beings are aligned toward trust and social resonance, recognition and acceptance. The social tie is not a human weakness, nor is it merely a social instinct, as Darwin thought; it is the only element in which human life can develop.

In the Darwinian view of the human being, it is the fittest that prevail in the struggle for existence and drive evolution forward; and this viewpoint was further developed in the evolutionary biology of Edward Wilson (1975) and Richard Dawkins (1978).[7] According to this standpoint, the first true actors in evolution are not just living things but already genes, for the goal of all genes is to increase to the maximum degree, and to prevail in competition with other genes. 'The selfish gene' is the driving force of evolution. This is in line with the attitude to life prevalent in the modern competitive society. As evidence, I may cite an article by David Brooks in the *Herald Tribune* of 20 February 2007: 'From the content of our genes, the nature of our neurons and the lessons of evolutionary biology, it has become clear that nature is filled with competition and conflicts of interests. Humanity did not come before status contests, status contests came before humanity and are embedded deep in human relations.' He concludes from this that 'Rousseau was wrong and Hobbes right.' Consequently, since human nature is so aggressively aligned towards a struggle for power, we need a strong state, a harsh upbringing and, in our world view, what Steven Pinker calls a tragic vision. To crown his cynicism, Brooks maintains that 'Iraq has revealed what human beings do without a strong order-imposing state'. In saying this, is he intending to justify Sadam Hussein's dictatorship or the United States' intervention? At all events, his thesis is nothing less than the justification of dictatorship, a policy of violence, and the rights of the stronger, for which the 'egoistic' gene of sociobiology must be held responsible.

Present-day neurobiology has confuted this view of the human being, and hence also its transference to the interpretation of natural phenomena of life. It is not competition and the struggle for existence which drives forward the evolution of human life; it is mutual recognition and cooperation. 'The insight that the acceptance and recognition we receive from others is the most profound basis for all motivation has emerged during the last five to ten years, and is the result of a series of extensive investigations. In the course of these investigations it was discovered that the *motivation systems* switch off if there is no chance of social attention and appreciation, and they are activated if the contrary is the case—if recognition or love comes into play.'[8] That is in line with what everyone can discover for him or herself: social isolation and contempt are hurtful and lead to apathy and the breakdown of all motivation, in extreme cases even to suicide. On the other hand, recognition encourages the will to live and leads to undreamt of achievements. In early childhood the brain develops only by way of the love and attention of the mother, the parents and those close to it which the child experiences.[9] The human being is a relational being, as the discovery of the Spiegel nervous system shows. 'Intact social networks safeguard health and increase the expectation of life, whereas involuntary loneliness shortens life.' I need not go into that any further but would only add the following: where research into the gene is concerned, it is important not only to recognize the gene sequences (as research into the human genome has recently succeeded in doing) but also to see the functions of the gene in the human body as a whole. Who activates the gene? Who deactivates it? Genes are not components taken from a construction kit, where the relation of the individual components to each other is a random affair. They are integrated into the inner fabric of relationships in a human being. They also react in the outward fabric of relationships in which the living thing moves—that is to say, they react to the impressions of its sensory organs. If the gene is isolated from its inner and outer contexts, it can certainly well be recognized, but it can hardly be understood.

The Genesis of More Complex Forms of Life

The different biosystems or organisms do not merely cooperate with each other; they also integrate themselves in each other and form more complex forms of life. Without these processes life would not evolve. In the wake of these integrations new forms of organization develop.

It is generally said that 'the whole is more than the sum of its parts'. That is true. The whole is also more than the cooperation of separate parts with each other. The whole is a new principle for organizing the functions of the parts in relation to each other and on behalf of the whole. New organizational forms of this kind evidently arise from the aggregate conditions of the parts like a leap into a new quality. Because the whole displays a new quality, it is not just 'more than' the sum of the parts; it is also different. The function of the parts within the whole is perceived on the basis of top-down causation. How do the genes function in a human body, and how does the human body function in the life of a human person? Apparently the nerve cells and nerve networks in the brain determine the participation of the parts in the human being as a whole. They bring the genes into play, and suspend their influence. The brain contains both a person's physical and his historical memory. Through opamin and oxytozin it regulates the person's relationships, his ties and his trust.

That brings us to a brief observation of the open biosystems. Complex biosystems are *open systems*. Open biosystems are *communicative systems*, which develop in an ever richer exchange of energy and metabolism. Complex open biosystems are symbiotic forms of life. But the openness of biosystems also means the *scope of their possibilities*. The more complex a system, the more the possibilities which are open to it. Consequently open systems have various potentialities for change. Their future behaviour is not completely determined by their previous behaviour. Their future state is therefore different from their past one. They are involved in the process of their becoming, and they can be understood only if their possible future is understood too. Open systems *anticipate* their own future by realizing or excluding the potentialities of their present. Open systems are in a state of what is known as flowing balance, and are asymmetrical in regard to their time structure of past and their future. We can make no statements about 'closed systems', because all information needs a carrier in either matter or energy. But we know that if an open biosystem closes itself against communication, and against its own future, it dies.[10]

If we want to escape the reductionism of a specialist science, we have to absorb its results into *integrational* sciences, so as to arrive at a better understanding of the world we live in, and of ourselves. We integrate the bodies analysed by the specialist sciences, fitting them anthropologically into the social and historical orders of the person, and we integrate individuals sociologically into the communities in which we live; we integrate the special communities in which we live into the community of humanity, and ecologically fit humanity into the community of creation; and theologically we integrate the community of creation into the community of the triune God. This is not meant in the sense of a total world view, but it nevertheless indicates the perspectives in which we try to understand what we see.

The World in Its Becoming— The Future in Its Coming

Every theology of nature interprets the facts and signs of nature in the transcendent dimension, that is to say, 'before God'. The Christian theology of nature talks about 'the God of hope' and to the transcendent eschatological dimension adds the eschatological one. Does that mean changing or expanding Darwin's theory of evolution?

1. In the perspective of the Christian faith, human existence appears dynamically within the process of the history of God which is aligned towards the future: 'We are God's children now; it does not yet appear what we shall be, but we know that when he appears we shall be like him, for we shall see him as he is' (1 John 3.2). In the experience of this expectation, present human existence is understood as a bridge and a transition to a greater future. That would seem to be in line with the theory of evolution, which is orientated towards the future. But the difference is that this future does not *de*velop out of the potential of the past, but *ad*vances towards the present—that is to say it cannot be perceived with the category of evolution, but only with the category of the new.

2. If we look at the history of nature in the transcendent dimension 'before God', then every stage and every form of life are immediate to God, and their value lies not only in what proceeds from them but also in them themselves. That is true for

the dinosaurs and all the forms of life which preceded the human race. It is also true of embryos, foetuses and children. They are not just steps in the development of the human being. They also have their own value in themselves. Childhood is not just a preliminary stage on the way to adult life. It already has its own particular value in itself, and must be respected accordingly.

3. The concept of evolution is hardly applicable to human history, because human history was only seldom a history of development. Human history runs its course between the old and the new, an end and a beginning, catastrophes and fresh starts. In order to comprehend human history, we see the future in the expectation of the new, not in the perspective of an evolution out of what has been. The theory of evolution interprets the past, and tries to say why things had to happen as they did. It does not say what can come and, it may be, will come.

4. Between the God of evolution and the God of Christian faith there is contradiction: the general 'struggle for existence' knows only survivors and victims; but the God of the crucified Christ is the saviour of the victims and the judge of the survivors. Out of the victims in the history of nature and the victims of human history, God builds his coming kingdom of peace.

Notes

Preface

1   J. Moltmann, *In the End—the Beginning. The Life of Hope*, trans. Margaret Kohl, Minneapolis and London 2004, 53–78.

Chapter 1

1   For a definition of the terms cf. J. Moltmann, *The Coming of God. Christian Eschatology*, trans. Margaret Kohl, London and Minneapolis 1996, chap. 3 'The Kingdom of God, Historical Eschatology', 129–255.

2   It was in this linear sense that K. Koch interpreted Daniel 7; cf. his 'Spätisraelitisches Geschichtsdenken am Beispiel des Buches Daniel', *HZ* 193, 1961, 7–32. W. Pannenberg followed him with this universal-history interpretation in *Revelation as History*, trans. D. Granskou and E. Quinn, London, Sydney and New York 1969. To do this is to overlook the apocalyptic alternative, and the qualitative difference between the empire of the divine Son of Man and the chaotic empires of the world.

3   M. Delgado, *Die Metamorphosen des Messianismus in den iberischen Kulturen. Eine religionsgeschichtliche Studie*, Immensee 1994, 39–50. When Charles V said that in his empire 'the sun never sets', this was not a factual observation, but the claim of the Christian universal monarchy: one God in heaven—one emperor on earth—a universal empire. Cf. here now M. Delgado, K. Koch and E. Marsch (eds), *Europa, Tausendjähriges Reich und Neue Welt*, Fribourg and Stuttgart 2003.

4   E. L. Tuveson, *Redeemer Nation. The Idea of America's Millennial Role*, Chicago 1968; J. Moltmann, 'Die "Erlöser-Nation"—Religiöse Wurzeln

des US-amerikanischen Exzeptionalismus' in *Die Friedenswarte. Journal of International Peace and Organization*, vol. 73, 2/3, 2003, 161–171.

5   P. Althaus, *Die letzten Dinge. Lehrbuch der Eschatologie*, 7th ed., Gütersloh 1957, 18f.

6   F. D. E. Schleiermacher, *Der christliche Glaube nach den Grundsätzen des evangelischen Kirche . . . eingeleitet durch des Verfassers zwei Sendschreiben über seine Glaubenslehre*, Gotha 1889, 33: 'Are the knots of history to be unravelled in such a way: that Christianity goes along with barbarism and science with unbelief?' 'The Reformation . . . has conferred an eternal contract between the living Christian faith and scientific research, set free towards every side, working independently for itself, so that the one does not hinder the other and the other does not exclude the one' (65). (The *Sendschreiben* are not included in the English translation of *The Christian Faith* by H. R. Mackintosh and J. S. Stewart, based on the 2nd German edition, Edinburgh 1928, Philadelphia 1976.)

7   C. Cherry, *Hurrying towards Zion*, Bloomington, Ind., 1995.

8   235, 246. See *Jesus' Proclamation of the Kingdom of God*, trans. R. H. Hiers and D. L. Holland, London 1971 (quotation translated directly from the German). Typical of the surrender of apocalyptic eschatology is the liberal-Protestant restriction to Schleiermacher's tenet: 'In the midst of the finite to be one with the infinite, and to be eternal in a moment' (the final sentence of his second *Speech on Religion to Its Cultural Despisers*). For Schleiermacher this was mysticism, and the eschatological expectation was now to be absorbed in that: 'In every moment slumbers the possibility of being the eschatological moment. You must awaken it' (R. Bultmann, *History and Eschatology*. The Gifford Lectures for 1955, Edinburgh 1957, 154 [first published in English]). This brings to a standstill all eschatological alternatives to the state of culture as it exists at present. Anyone who confuses 'the eschatological moment' of 1 Cor. 15.32 with the historical 'kairos' of 2 Cor. 6.2, leaves world history empty handed.

9   R. Rothe, *Theologische Ethik*, I–V, Wittenberg 1867; E. Troeltsch, *Die Absolutheit des Christentums* (1902) [*The Absoluteness of Christianity*, trans. D. Reid, London 1972]; T. Rendtorff, *Theorie des Christentums. Historisch-theologische Studien zu seiner neuzeitlichen Verfassung*, Gütersloh 1972. On the further connection between the rebirth of millenarianism at the beginning of the modern era and the birth of that era out of secularized millenarianism, cf. J. Moltmann, *The Coming of God*, op. cit., 156–201.

10   G. Werth, *Verdun. Die Schlacht und der Mythos*, Bergisch-Gladbach 1982. In Verdun the aim was not victory, as it had been in Sedan in 1870; it was

'annihilation'. The idea of annihilation dominated German military thinking.

11   The title of the famous English translation, *The Decline of the West*, is an unduly innocuous rendering.

12   W. Härle, 'Der Aufruf der 93 Intellektuellen und Karl Barths Bruch mit der liberalen Theologie', ZThK 72, 1975, 207ff.

13   G. Besier, *Die protestantischen Kirchen Europas im Ersten Weltkrieg. Ein Quellen- und Arbeitsbuch*, Göttingen 1984, 78ff.

Chapter 2

1   See *Marcion. The Gospel of the Alien God*, trans. J. E. Steely and L. D. Bierman, Durham, N.C., 1990.

2   F. Schleiermacher, *The Christian Faith*, op. cit., § 12 (see above, n. 6). See also E. Hirsch, *Das Alte Testament und die Predigt des Evangeliums*, Tübingen 1936.

3   For a survey, with the particular Reformed standpoint, see A. A. van Ruler, *Die christliche Kirche und das Alte Testament*, Munich 1955. Most influential was G. von Rad's, *Old Testament Theology*, vol. 1 of which was published in 1958, vol. 2 in 1960 (Eng. trans. by D. M. G. Stalker, Edinburgh 1962–65).

4   J. Moltmann, *Theologie der Hoffnung*, first published in 1964 [*Theology of Hope*, trans. J. W. Leitch, London and New York, 1967].

5   See O. Weber, *Grundlagen der Dogmatik* I, Neukirchen 1955, 30. This principle has become the general presupposition of modern Protestant theology (E. Brunner, P. Tillich, E. Schlink, and others), so that now it must again be called in question to prevent theology from being restricted to the church.

6   In the spirit of Joachim of Fiore, F. W. J. Schelling wrote in 1841/2: 'Peter, Paul, John! This is the succession of the representatives of the three eras of Christian development. . . . Peter was the law-giver, the foundational legend, the stable factor. Paul broke out like a fire and is the Elijah, representing the principle of development, of movement, of liberty. John is the apostle of the future. . . . Peter is the apostle of the Father, Paul the apostle of the Son, John the apostle of the Spirit. . . . Peter is Christ's immediate successor, John is his successor only for the time when he will come.'

7   We need only compare Pius XII's encyclical *Mystici corporis Christi*

of 1943 with Vatican II's *Constitution on the Church* [*Lumen Gentium*] of 1965 (*Acta Apostolicae Sedis* 57, 1965, 5–75).

8   Hans Küng offers a comprehensive and balanced discussion of Catholic ecclesiology in 'Die Kirche' in *Ökumenische Forschungen*, ed. H. Küng and J. Ratzinger, 1967; see also M. Kehl, *Die Kirche. Eine katholische Ekklesiologie*, Würzburg 1992.

9   J. Moltmann, *The Church in the Power of the Spirit*, trans. Margaret Kohl, London 1977.

10   R. Weth, *'Barmen' als Herausforderung der Kirche. Beiträge zum Kirchenverständnis im Licht der Barmer Theologischen Erklärung*, Munich 1984; cf. also W. Huber, *Die Kirche*, Stuttgart 1977.

11   M. Luther, WA 41, 11. On this see O. Bayer, 'Theologie', HAST 1, Gütersloh 1994.

12   G. Eichholz, 'Was heißt Charismatische Gemeinde?', ThEx 77, 1957; E. Käsemann, 'Ministry and Community in the New Testament' in *Essays on New Testament Themes*, trans. W. J. Montague, London 1964, 63–94.

13   J. Moltmann, *The Spirit of Life*, trans. Margaret Kohl, London and Minneapolis 1992; M. Welker, *God the Spirit*, trans. J. F. Hoffmeyer, Minneapolis 1994. On the pneumatology of the Pentecostal movement, cf. D. Martin, *Tongues of Fire. The Explosion of Protestantism in Latin America*, Oxford and Cambridge 1990; H. Cox, *Fire from Heaven, The Rise of Pentecostal Spirituality and the Reshaping of Religion in the Twenty-first Century*, Reading, Mass., 1995.

14   J. Moltmann, *The Spirit of Life*, op. cit. 33. On this see now theologically S. Land, *Pentecostal Spirituality. A Passion for the Kingdom*, Sheffield 1993. F. Macchia, *Baptized in the Spirit. A Global Pentecostal Theology*, Grand Rapids 2006.

15   E. Moltmann-Wendel, *Rediscovering Friendship*, trans. J. Bowden, London 2000, Minneapolis 2001.

16   M. Volf, *Trinität und Gemeinschaft. Eine ökumenische Ekklesiologie*, Neukirchen and Mainz 1996 [ET: *After Our Likeness: The Church as the Image of the Trinity*, Grand Rapids and Cambridge 1998]; J. Moltmann, 'Der dreieinige Gott' in R. Weth (ed.), *Der lebendige Gott. Auf den Spuren neuerer trinitarischen Denkens*, Neukirchen 2005, 178–197, here chap. 3, 5.

Chapter 3

1   A. M. Goldberg, *Untersuchungen über die Vorstellung von der Schechina in der frühen rabbinischen Literatur*, Berlin 1969. B. Janowski, *Gottes Gegenwart in Israel*, Neukirchen 1993, 119–147, see chap. 3.2.

2   Theologically we probably entered into this anthropology of the modern, homeless human being too readily. See W. Pannenberg, *What Is man? Contemporary Anthropology in Theological Perspective*, trans. D. A. Priebe, Philadelphia 1970; J. Moltmann, *Man. Christian Anthropology in the Conflicts of the Present*, trans. J. Sturdy, London 1974.

3   J. G. Herder, *Über den Ursprung der Sprache* , 1770 [*On the Origin of Language*, trans. J. H. Moran and A. Code, New York 1967; the quotation is translated directly from the German].

Part Two

Ever since the *Theology of Hope* (1964; ET 1967), the resurrection of Christ and the Easter faith have been the foundation and starting point of my theology. Cf. *The Way of Jesus Christ. Christology in Messianic Dimensions*, trans. Margaret Kohl, London and San Francisco 1990, chap. 5, 213–273; *Jesus Christ for Today's World*, trans. Margaret Kohl, London and Minneapolis 1994, chap. 5, 71–87; 'Resurrection: the Ground, Power and Goal of our Hope', *Concilium* 1999/5, 81–89; 'The Resurrection of Nature: an Aspect of Cosmic Christology', *Concilium* 2006/5, 81–89. Together with Elisabeth Moltmann-Wendel, 'Mit allen Sinnen glauben. Überlegungen zur Auferstehung des Fleisches', *Stimmen der Zeit* 223, 11, 2005, 723–735.

Chapter 4

1   H.-J. Eckstein and M. Welker (eds), *Die Wirklichkeit der Auferstehung*, Neukirchen 2001; T. Peters, R. J. Russell and M. Welker (eds), *Resurrection. Theological and Scientific Assessments*, Grand Rapids 2002.

2   E. Bloch, *Das Prinzip Hoffnung*, Frankfurt 1959, 1313 [*The Principle of Hope*, trans. N. and S. Plaice and P. Knight, Cambridge, Mass., and Oxford 1986].

3   A. Schweitzer, *The Quest of the Historical Jesus,* trans. W. Montgomery, London 1910.

4   F. D. E. Schleiermacher, *The Christian Faith*, trans. from the 2nd German edition by H. R. Mackintosh and J. S. Stewart, Edinburgh 1928, Philadelphia 1976, §75.

5   That is why R. Bultmann began his *Theology of the New Testament* (trans. K. Grobel, London 1952) with the sentence: 'The message of Jesus is a presupposition for the theology of the New Testament rather than a part of that theology itself' (p. 3).

6   The Sonship of Jesus stamps the Christian doctrine of God in its doctrine of the Trinity. Cf. J. Moltmann, *The Trinity and the Kingdom of God. The Doctrine of God*, trans. Margaret Kohl, London and San Francisco 1981. That is therefore the irrelinquishable foundation of the specific Christian belief in God.

Chapter 5

1   D. H. Juel, *A Master of Surprise. Mark Interpreted*, Minneapolis 1994. For an exegetical discussion about the end of Mark, see R. Schwindt, 'Erschütterung statt Freude. Zum Schluss des Markusevangeliums', *Trierer Theologische Zeitschrift* 117, 1, 2008, 56–79.

2   H. Grass, *Ostergeschehen und Osterberichte*, Göttingen 1956.

3   Whereas 'raising' sees the activity as initiated solely by God, 'resurrection' talks about an activity on Jesus' part. Metaphorically the two processes belong together: the person who is raised must rise. The call to awaken mobilizes his powers. Without resurrection the raising does not attain its goal. Transferred into theological terms, this means: God the Father raises, Jesus the Son rises in the power of the Spirit.

4   W. Pannenberg rightly made this the foundation of his resurrection Christology in his *Jesus, God and Man*, trans. L. L. Wilkins and D. A. Priebe, London 1968.

5   W. Pannenberg, *Jesus God and Man*, op. cit., 95–96. See here M. Welker 'Die Wirklichkeit der Auferstehung' in H.-J.Eckstein and M. Welker (eds), *Die Wirklichkeit der Auferstehung*, op. cit., 316f.

6   Here I am following S. M. Schneiders, 'Touching the Risen Jesus: Mary Magdalena and Thomas the Twin in John 20' in *The Catholic Theological Society of America. Proceedings of the Sixtieth Annual Convention, St. Louis, Missouri, June 9–12, 2005*, vol. 60, 13–35.

7   Christian Knorr von Rosenroth, 'Morgenglanz der Ewigkeit'.

8   In his morning hymn 'Christ, Whose Glory Fills the Skies.'

9   For more detail see J. Moltmann, *The Source of Life. The Holy Spirit and the Theology of Life*, London and Minneapolis 1997, 18–30.

10   M. Welker offers an illuminating analogy here: He asks: 'Who was my mother?' and answers: 'The little girl on the yellowing photograph, the young woman with me in her arms, the anxious wife, the frail old lady. . . . She is all this, and more' (*Die Wirklichkeit der Auferstehung*, op. cit., 32, n. 2). Identity lies in the simultaneity and the diachronic sum of a whole life.

11   That was Ernst Käsemann's 'new question' about the historical Jesus. See 'The Problem of the Historical Jesus' in his *Essays on New Testament Themes*, trans. W. J. Montague, London 1964, 15–47.

12   'Shattering the doors of Hades, Lord,
Thou hast through thy death
destroyed the kingdom and rule of death.
Yea, thou hast drawn the human race
out of destruction,
conferring upon the whole cosmos
life and immortality,
thou who art great in mercy'
(translated from E. Benz, H. Thurn and C. Floros (eds), *Das Buch der Heiligen Gesänge der Ostkirche*, Hamburg 1962, 121).

13   For example, 'Hell Today Is Vanquished' (Venantius Fortunatus: 'Welcome, Happy Morning!') or 'Christ Has Burst the Gates of Hell'(Charles Wesley, 'Love's Redeeming Work Is Done').

14   Thus in the Credo Aquileiensis. See G. Pressacco, *Marco 'Christianus et Medicus'*, Marsilio 1996.

Chapter 6

1   E. Moltmann-Wendel and J. Moltmann, 'Mit alle Sinnen glauben: Auferstehung des Fleisches' in *Leidenschaft für Gott. Worauf es uns ankommt*, Freiburg 2006, 22–43.

2   E. Moltmann-Wendel, ibid., 26.

3   For more detail see J. Moltmann, *In the End—The Beginning. The Life of Hope*, trans. Margaret Kohl, Minneapolis and London 2004.

4   M. Luther, WA 37, 151. See here J. Moltmann, *The Coming of God*, trans. Margaret Kohl, London and Minneapolis 1996, 101–104.

5   Augustine, *Confessions* XI. See here M. Grabmann, *Die Grundgedanken des Hl. Augustinus über Seele und Gott*, Darmstadt 1957.

6   Boethius, *Philosophiae consolationis (The Consolations of Philosophy)* Book V, 1 , See here E. Jüngel, 'Die Ewigkeit des ewigen Lebens' in *Ganz werden. Theologische Erörterungen* V, Tübingen 2003, 345–353.

7   H. Arendt, *On Revolution*, New York and London 1963.

Chapter 7

1   I owe this pointer to M. Kahl, foreword to P. C. Sicouly, *Schöpfung und Neuschöpfung. 'Neuschöpfung' als theologische Kategorie im Werk Jürgen Moltmanns*, Paderborn 2007, 14.

2   K. Marx, *Die Frühschriften*, ed. S. Landshut, Stuttgart 1953, 330. It was from him that J. Habermas took his talk about the 'resurrection of nature' in *Glauben und Wissen*, Frankfurt 2001, 23.

3   E. Bloch, *Das Prinzip Hoffnung*, Frankfurt 1959, chap. 17: 'Die Welt, worin utopische Phantasie ihr Korrelat hat', 224–258 [ET *The Principle of Hope*, trans. N. and S. Plaice and P. Knight, Cambridge, Mass., and Oxford 1986]; idem., *Das Materialismusproblem. Seine Geschichte und Substanz*, Frankfurt 1972.

4   K. Marx, *Frühschriften*, op. cit., 237. See also p. 235: 'This communism is … the true solution of the conflict between the human being and nature … It is the solved riddle of history and knows itself to be that solution.'

5   D. Bonhoeffer, *Dein Reich komme. Das Gebet der Gemeinde um das Reich Gottes auf Erden* (1932), Hamburg 1958, 12.

Chapter 8

1   J. Bauer, *Warum ich fühle, was du fühlst. Intuitive Kommunikation und das Geheimnis der Spiegelneurone*, Hamburg 2005, 109–112: 'Die

Folgen fehlender Spiegelung: Biologische Zerstörung durch soziale Isolation.'

2   Hans Jonas has pointed this out; see *The Imperative of Responsibility*, trans. H. Jonas with D. Herr, Chicago 1984

3   N. O. Brown, *Life against Death,* New York 1959, from which I have taken the title of this section. I should like to point to the book's psychoanalytical viewpoint on the resurrection of the body. Cf. also his book *Love's Body*, New York 1966.

4   L. Ragaz, *Der Kampf um das Reich Gottes in Blumhardt, Vater und Sohn—und weiter*, Zurich and Munich 1922, 60.

Chapter 9

1   In the remains of Bonhoeffer's library there were four books by Blumhardt. At that time all the younger theologians knew Leonhard Ragaz's book about the Blumhardts (see n. 4 above). Cf. J. Moltmann, 'Dietrich Bonhoeffer und Christoph Blumhardt', CuS 60, 2007, 2–3, 11–17. Cf. also L. Rassmussen, 'Bonhoeffer's Song of Songs and Christianity as Earth's Faith' in C. Gremmels and W. Huber, *Religion in Erbe*, Gütersloh 2002, 186–193.

2   L. Ragaz, op. cit., 60.

3   J. Harder (ed.), *Christoph Blumhardt. Ansprachen, Predigten, Reden, Briefe, 1865–1917*, Neukirchen Band 2, 1978, 295.

4   The German words *Hinterweltler* and *Hinterweltertum* (not general usage) seem originally to have been coinages by Nietzsche, meaning the attempt to find out what is behind this world.

5   D. Bonhoeffer, 'Dein Reich komme. Das Gebet der Gemeinde um Gottes Reich auf Erden', Hamburg 1957, 8, 9.

6   L. Ragaz, op. cit., 57.

7   D. Bonhoeffer, *Letters and Papers from Prison*, trans. R. H. Fuller et al., enlarged edition, London 1971, 285f. (letter of 5 May 1944).

8   L. Ragaz, op. cit., 57.

9   *Letters and Papers from Prison*, op. cit., 286 (letter of 5 May 1944).

10 D. Bonhoeffer, 'Dein Reich komme', op. cit., 12, 13.

11 D. Bonhoeffer, *Letters and Papers from Prison*, op. cit, 336f. (letter of 27 June 1944).

12 Ibid , 415 (trans. altered). See also R. A. von Bismarck and U. Kabitz (eds), *Brautbriefe Zelle 92*, Munich 1992, 38 [*Letters from Cell 92*, trans. J. Brownjohn, London 1994] For a new theological evaluation of the earth, cf. J. Moltmann, 'Die Erde und die Menschen. Zum theologischen Verständnis der Gaja-Hypothese'. EvTh 53, 5, 420–438.

Chapter 10

1 'Monotheismus', *Historisches Wörterbuch der Philosophie* VI, 143–146.

2 M. de Ferdinandy, *Tschingis Khan,. Steppenvölker erobern Eurasien*, Hamburg 1958, 153.

3 Aristotle, *Metaphysics*, Book XII. Cf. here E. Peterson, 'Monotheismus als politisches Problem' (1935) in *Theologische Traktate*, Munich 1951, 45–148.

4 For more detail see J. Moltmann, '"I believe in God the Father" Patriarchal or non-Patriarchal Talk of God', in *History and the Triune God*, trans. J. Bowden, London 1991, 1–18.

5 Lactantius, *De ira Dei*; see *Works*, trans. W. Fletcher, Ante-Nicene Christian Library, Edinburgh 1886.

6 J. Assmann, *Moses the Egyptian*, Cambridge, Mass., and London 1997.

7 See here B. Janowski, 'Der barmherzige Richter. Zur Einheit von Gerechtigkeit und Barmherzigkeit im Gottesbild des Alten Orient und des Alten Testaments' in R. Scoralick (ed.), *Das Drama der Barmherzigkeit Gottes*, Stuttgart 2000, 58–64.

8 B. Janowski, *Gottes Gegenwart in Israel. Beiträge zur Theologie des Alten Testaments*, Neukirchen 1993. Cf. also here C. Markschies, 'Jüdische Mittlergestalten und die christliche Trinitätslehre' in M. Welker and M. Volf (eds), *Der lebendige Gott als Trinität. Festschrift für J. Moltmann*, Gütersloh 2006, 199–214.

9 A. J. Heschel, *The Prophets*, New York 1951, and F. Rosenzweig, *Der Stern der Erlösung* III, Heidelberg 1954, 192–193 [*The Star of Redemption*, trans. W. W. Hallo, London 1971].

10 For more detail see J. Moltmann, *The Trinity and the Kingdom of God. The Doctrine of God*, trans. Margaret Kohl, London and San Francisco 1981; idem., *Experiences in Theology. Ways and Forms of Christian Theology*, trans. Margaret Kohl, London and Minneapolis 2000, 303ff.

11 W. H. Vanstone, *Love's Endeavour—Love's Expense. The Response of Being to the Love of God*, London 1977, 120.

12 W. Schrage, 'Unterwegs zur Einigkeit und Einheit Gottes. Zum "Monotheismus" des Paulus und seiner alttestamentlich-jüdischen Tradition', EvTh 61, 2001, 3, 190–203.

13 S. Raeder, *Der Islam und das Christentum. Eine historische und theologische Einführung*, Neukirchen 2001.

14 However, in Judaism and in Islam holy countries and places are reverenced as well as the Holy Book. There is really only one religion which is in the strict sense a 'religion of the Book', and that is Protestantism, with its *sola scriptura*.

15 J. Moltmann, 'Die Sehnsucht nach dem Ende der Welt. Was den apokalyptischen Terrorismus mit der neuen Weltordnung verbindet', DIE ZEIT, 27 December 2001, 39.

16 We are not given an answer to this question even in the collection edited by J. Manemann: *Monotheismus. Jahrbuch Politische Theologie* , vol. 4, Münster 2001.

Chapter 11

1 This essay is the outcome of an advanced seminar which I held together with Professor Bernd Janowski in Tübingen in the summer semester of 2003. I presented it in London on 20 November 2003 in the St. Johns Wood Street Synagogue in London as the Lily Montague Lecture.

2 Ernst Bloch, *Das Prinzip Hoffnung*, Frankfurt 1959 (*The Principle of Hope*, trans. N. and S. Plaice, Cambridge, Mass., and Oxford 1986).

3 Franz Rosenzweig, *Der Stern der Erlösung* , 3rd ed., Heidelberg 1954 (*The Star of Redemption*, trans. W. W. Hallo, London 1971).

4 Cf. the following: J. Assmann, *Ägypten. Theologie und Frömmigkeit einer frühen Hochkultur*, Stuttgart, Berlin and Cologne 1984; 25–67, here 50ff.; H. Gese, 'Der Johannesprolog' in idem., *Zur biblischen Theologie*, Tübingen 1989,

152–201, here 185ff. (*Essays on Biblical Theology*, trans. K. Crim, Minneapolis 1981); B. Janowski, "'Ich will in euerer Mitte wohnen." Struktur und Genese der nachexilischen Schekina-Theologie' (1987) in idem., *Gottes Gegenwart in Israel. Beiträge zur Theologie des Alten Testaments,* Neukirchen-Vluyn 1993, 119–147; K. Scholtissek, *In ihm sein und bleiben. Die Sprache der Immanenz in den johanneischen Schriften*, Freiburg, Basel and Vienna 2000, 75–93.

5   Cf. H. Ernst, *Die Schekhina in rabbinischen Gleichnissen*, Bern 1994; A. M. Goldberg, *Untersuchungen über die Vorstellung von der Shekhinah in der frühen rabbinischen Literatur—Talmud und Midrasch*, Berlin 1969; idem., *Ich komme und wohne in deiner Mitte. Eine rabbinische Homilie zu Sacharja 2,14 (PesR 35),* Frankfurt 1977; P. Kuhn, *Gottes Selbsterniedrigung in der Theologie der Rabbinen*, Munich 1968.

6   E. Wiesel, 'Der Mitleidende' in R. Walter (ed.), *Die hundert Namen Gottes*, Freiburg 1985, 70–74.

7   Cf. A. Heschel, *The Prophets*, New York 1962, 221–231.

8   Cf. E. Bloch, *Das Prinzip Hoffnung*, op. cit., 17 (*The Principle of Hope*).

9   Cf. G. Scholem, *Von der mystischen Gestalt der Gottheit. Studien zu Grundbegriffen der Kabbala*, Frankfurt 1977, 148–149 (*On the Mystical Shape of the Godhead: Basic Concepts in the Kabbalah,* trans. J. Neugroschel, revised J. Chipman, New York 1991).

10   Ibid., 148.

11   Ibid., 149.

12   Cf. J. Maier (ed.), *Die Kabbala*, Munich 1995, 52.

13   F. Rosenzweig, *Der Stern der Erlösung* III/3, op. cit., 192–194: 'Die Irrfahrt der Schechina', here 192 (*The Star of Redemption*).

14   Ibid., 58.

15   E. Bloch, *Geist der Utopie*, 2nd ed., Berlin 1923, 365 (*Spirit of Utopia*, trans. A. Nassar, Stanford, Calif., 2000).

16   J. Jonas, *Zwischen Nichts und Ewigkeit. Zur Lehre vom Menschen,* Göttingen 1963, 55–62, here 55f. Cf. also H. Jonas and F. Stern, *Reflexionen finsterer Zeit*, Tübingen 1984, 61–86.

17   Ibid., 58.

18   Ibid., 60.

19   Ibid., 62.

20   S. Kierkegaard, *Eine literarische Anzeige. Anhang: Reflexionen über Christentum und Naturwissenschaft* in *Gesammelte Werke, 17. Abteilung* , trans. into German by E. Hirsch, Düsseldorf 1954, 124. See here also J. Moltmann, *Science and Wisdom*, trans. Margaret Kohl, Minneapolis and London 2003, 54–67.

21   Cf. O. Hofius, *Der Christushymnus Philipper 2,6–11*, 2nd ed. Tübingen 1991.

22   Cf. J. Moltmann, *Experiences in Theology. Ways and Forms of Christian Theology*, trans. Margaret Kohl, London and Minneapolis 2000, 321ff.; also J. Moltmann, 'Gott und Raum' in J. Moltmann and C. Rivuzumwami (eds), *Wo ist Gott? Gottesträume—Lebensträume*, Neukirchen-Vluyn 2003, 29–41; cf. also chap. 14.2 below.

23   Cf. K. Scholtissek, *In ihm sein und bleiben. Die Sprache der Immanenz in den johanneischen Schriften* (HBS 21), Freiburg 2000, 75–83.

24   Cf. K. Barth, *Church Dogmatics* II/2, § 33: The Election of Jesus Christ.

25   Cf. J. Moltmann, *The Crucified God*, trans. R. A. Wilson and J. Bowden, London 1974.

Chapter 13

1   The present text is an outline deriving from the advanced seminar held by Bernd Janowski and myself in January 2005, under the title 'Is God a Punitive Judge?'

2   In general: J. Assmann, B. Janowski and M. Welker, *Gerechtigkeit. Richten und Retten in der abendländischen Tradition und ihren altorientalischen Ursprüngen*, Munich 1998; R. Scoralick (ed.), *Das Drama der Barmherzigkeit Gottes. Studien zur biblischen Gotteslehre und ihrer Wirkungsgeschichte im Judentum und Christentum*, Stuttgart 2000; B. Janowski, *Die rettende Gerechtigkeit. Beiträge zur Theologie des Alten Testaments* II, Neukirchen 1999. In particular: M. Arneth, *'Sonne der Gerechtigkeit'. Studien zur Solarisierung der Jahwe-Religion im Licht von Psalm 72*, BZAR 1, Wiesbaden 2000.

3   B. Janowski, 'Zur Einheit von Gerechtigkeit und Barmherzigkeit im Gottesbild des Alten Orients und des Alten Testaments' in *Der Gott des Lebens. Beiträge zur Theologie des Alten Testaments* III, Neukirchen 2003, 75–133.

4   G. von Rad, *Old Testament Theology* II, trans. D. M. G. Stalker, Edinburgh and London 1965, 112ff.

5   J. Assmann, *Tod und Jenseits im Alten Ägypten*, Munich 2000/2003; E. Hornung (ed.), *Das Totenbuch der Ägypter*, Zurich and Munich 1979; A. Champdor, *Das ägyptische Totenbuch,* Munich and Zurich 1980.

6   R. Stock, *Annihilatio Mundi. Johann Gerhards Eschatologie der Welt*, Munich 1971; H. Schmid, *Dogmatik der evangelisch-lutherischen Kirche*, Gütersloh 1893, op. cit., 407: 'The Last Judgment will be followed by the complete end of the world. Except for angels and human beings, everything belonging to this world will be burnt with fire and will be dissolved into nothingness. So what must be expected is not a transformation of the world but a complete cessation of its substances.' For a contrary view cf. J. Moltman, *The Coming of God. Christian Eschatology,* trans. Margaret Kohl, London and Minneapolis 1996, 267–272.

7   *The Mystery of Salvation; A Report by the Doctrine Commission of the General Synod of the Church of England*, London 1995, 198.

8   W. Kreck has emphatically drawn attention to this in *Die Zukunft des Gekommenen. Grundprobleme der Eschatologie*, Munich 1966, 121–123.

9   Christoph Blumhardt Jr., in L. Ragaz, *Der Kampf um das Reich Gottes in Blumhardt, Vater und Sohn—und weiter,* Zurich and Munich 1922, 57.

10   M. Volf, 'The Final Reconciliation. Reflections on the Social Dimension of the Eschatological Transition', *Modern Theology* 16 (2000), 91–113; idem., *The End of Memory? Mistreatment, Memory, Reconciliation,* Grand Rapids, Mich., 2006.

11   C. Blumhardt in J. Harder (ed.), *Blumhardt. Ansprachen, Predigten, Reden, Briefe: 1865–1917*, vol. II, Neukirchen 1978, 184.

12   L. Ragaz, *Der Kampf um das Reich Gottes*, op. cit., 153.

13   In J. Harder (ed.), op. cit., 131. Cf. here F. Groth, *Die 'Wiederbringung aller Dinge' im württembergischen Pietismus, Theologiegeschichtliche Studien zum eschatologischen Heilsuniversalismus württembergischer Pietisten des 18. Jahrhunderts*, Göttingen 1984.

14   P. C. Sicouly, *Schöpfung und Neuschöpfung. 'Neuschöpfung' als theologische Kategorie im Werk Jürgen Moltmanns*, Paderborn 2007. For the systematic discussion about universal salvation, cf. C. Janowski, *Allerlösung. Annäherung an eine entdualisierte Eschatologie*, NBST 23/1 and 23/2, Neukirchen 2000.

15   H. U. von Balthasar, *Dare We Hope 'That all Men be saved'? With a short discourse on Hell*, San Franciso 1988; N. J. Ansell, *The Annihilation of Hell. Universal Salvation and the Redemption of Time in the Eschatology of Jürgen Moltmann*, Toronto 2005. Christ's destruction of hell is one of the themes in the Easter hymns, for example: 'Christ hath burst the gates of hell' (in C. Wesley, 'Christ the Lord Is Risen Today); 'Hell today is vanquished' (in Venantius Fortunatus, 'Welcome, Happy Morning') ; 'He brake the age-bound chains of hell' (in the Latin hymn 'The Strife Is O'er'). This is in line with Luther's free rendering of 1 Cor. 15.55: 'Hell, where is thy victory!'—which is also given as an alternative reading in the King James Bible. The Greek word used in the text is *thanatos*.

16   A. Grund, 'Die Propheten als Künder des Gerichts' in R. Heß and M. Leiner (eds*)*, *Alles in Allem. Eschatologische Anstöße. Festschrift für Christine Janowski*, Neukirchen 2006, 167–181.

17   H. Lindsay, *The Late Great Planet Earth*, New York 1970.

18   On Carl Schmitt's apocalyptic, cf. H. Meier, *Die Lehre Carl Schmitts. Vier Kapitel zur Unterscheidung Politischer Theologie und Politischer Philosophie*, Stuttgart 1994.

19   Cf. here now G. Müller-Fahrenholz, *America's Battle for God*, Grand Rapids, Mich., 2006.

20   C. Blumhardt cited in J. Harder (ed.), op. cit., 2, 133.

21   G. Etzelmüller, *. . . zu richten die Lebenden und die Toten'. Zur Rede vom Jüngsten Gericht im Anschluß an Karl Barth*, Neukirchen 2001.

22   Cf. G. Pressacco, *Marco, Christianus et Medicus*, Marsilio 1996; idem., *Musical Traces of Markan Tradition in the Mediterranean Area*, Orbis Musicae, Tel Aviv 1993.

23   W. Hryniewicz, *Nadzieja zbawjenia dla wszystkich. Od eschatologii leku do eschatologii nadziei*, Warsaw 1989; see also his essays 'Hoffnung der Heiligen. Das Zeugnis Isaaks des Syrers' and 'Schönheit und Heil. Über die Eschatologie der Ikone'. *Ostkirchliche Studien* 45, April 1996/1, 21–41; No. 49, September 2000/2–3, 145–161. See further Przemyslaw Kantyka (ed.), *Instaurare Omnia*

in Christo. About Salvation, Theology, Dialogue and Hope. Festschrift for Waclaw Hryniewicz OMI, Lublin 2006.

Chapter 14

1   M. Schmaus, *Die psychologische Trinitätslehre des Hl. Augustinus*, Münster 1927. According to the psychological doctrine of the Trinity, the divine Trinity consists of God as the subject (the Father) of understanding (the Son, Logos) and will (the Spirit).

2   K. Barth, *Die christliche Dogmatik im Entwurf*, Munich 1931, chap. 2: Die Offenbarung Gottes, 311–514.

3   K. Rahner, 'Der Dreifaltige Gott als transzendenter Urgrund der Heilsgeschichte', *Mysterium Salutis* II, Einsiedeln 1967, 317–401

4   W. Pannenberg, 'Der eine Gott als der wahrhaft Unendliche und die Trinitätslehre' in *Denkwürdiges Geheimnis. Festschrift für E. Jüngel*, Tübingen 2004, 426: 'The attempt to deduce the Trinity from the unity of God must count as a failure, even in the form of a deduction from the concept of the divine Spirit.'

5   This new trinitarian thinking already begins with Karl Barth in the new approach of his trinitarian doctrine in the doctrine of reconciliation. Cf. *Church Dogmatics* IV/1–IV/4, trans. G. W. Bromiley, Edinburgh 1956–1969. E. Jüngel took this up in *God's Being Is in Becoming: The Trinitarian Being of God in the Theology of Karl Barth, a Paraphrase*, 2nd Eng. edition, trans. J. Webster, Edinburgh 2001. For an excellent presentation of the new trinitarian thinking, see S. J. Grenz, *Rediscovering the Triune God. The Trinity in Contemporary Theology*, Minneapolis 2004. He establishes that after Karl Barth and Karl Rahner, there were three stages: 1. Jürgen Moltmann, Wolfhart Pannenberg and Robert Jenson. 2. Leonardo Boff, John Zizioulas and Catherine LaCugna. 3. Elizabeth Johnson. From the wealth of more recent work on the doctrine of the Trinity, I may mention: S. J. Grenz, *The Social God and the Relational Self*, Louisville and London 2001; C. E. Gunton, *The One, the Three and the Many: God, Creation and the Culture of Modernity*, Cambridge 1992; D. S. Cunningham, *These Three Are One. The Practice of Trinitarian Theology*, Oxford 1998; R. Jenson, *The Triune Identity. God according to the Gospel*, Philadelphia 1982; T. Peters, *God as Trinity. Relationality and Temporality in Divine Life*, Louisville 1993; P. S. Fiddes, *Participating in God: A Pastoral Doctrine of the Trinity*, London 2000; C. Schwöbel (ed.), *Trinitarian Theology Today: Essays on Divine Being and Act*, Edinburgh 1995; G. Buxton, *The Trinity, Creation and*

Pastoral Ministry. Imagining the Perichoretic God, Carlisle 2005. Books belonging to the beginning of the 'new trinitarian thinking' are: J. Moltmann, *The Trinity and the Kingdom,* trans. Margaret Kohl, London and San Francsico 1981; W. Pannenberg, *Systematic Theology,* vol. 1, trans. G. W. Bromiley, Grand Rapids, Mich., 1991; G. Greshake, *Der dreieinige Gott. Eine trinitarische Theologie,* Freiburg 1997; L. Boff, *Trinity and Society,* London, 1988; J. Ziziouslas, *Being as Communion. Studies in Personhood and the Church,* Crestwood 1985; C. Mowry LaCugna, *God for Us. The Trinity and the Christian Faith,* San Franciso 1991; E. Johnson, *She Who Is. The Mystery of God in Feminist Theology Discourse,* New York 1992; M. Volf, *Trinität und Gemeinschaft,* Mainz and Neukirchen-Vluyn 1996 [ET: *After Our Likeness: The Church as the Image of the Trinity,* Grand Rapids and Cambridge 1998].

6   O. Weber, *Grundlagen der Dogmatik* II, Neukirchen 1962, 11, pointed emphatically to the one Name.

7   See K. Hasumi, 'Jürgen Moltmanns Theologie und das Nichts' in J. Moltmann and C. Rivuzumwami (eds), *Wo ist Gott? Gottesräume— Lebensräume,* Neukirchen 2002, 124: 'Die Theologie des Namens'.

8   Thus G. Greshake, *Der dreieine Gott. Eine trinitarische Theologie,* Freiburg 1997.

9   I. Dalferth and E. Jüngel, 'Person und Gottebenbildlichkeit' in *Christlicher Glaube in moderner Gesellschaft,* vol. 24, Freiburg 1981, 83.

10   B. Janowski, *Gottes Gegenwart in Israel. Beiträge zur Theologie des Alten Testaments,* Neukirchen 1993, esp. 119–147.

11   F. Rosenzweig, *Der Stern der Erlösung* III, 3rd ed., Heidelberg 1954, 3, 192 (*The Star of Redemption,* trans. W. W. Hallo, London 1971).

12   C. Sorč, 'Die perichoretischen Beziehungen im Leben der Trinität und der Gemeinschaft der Menschen', EvTh. 58, 1998, 100–118; idem., *Entwürfe einer perichoretischen Theologie,* Münster 2004.

13   A. Deneffe, 'Perichoresis, circumincessio, circuminsessio', *Zeitschrift für katholische Theologie* 47, 1923, 497–532; C. A. Disandro, 'Historia semantica de perikhoresis', *Studia Patristica* XV, 1984, 442–447.

14   H. Denzinger, *Echiridion Symbolorum,* 26th ed., Freiburg 1947, 704.

15   I differ here from W. Pannenberg, *Systematic Theology* I, trans. G. W. Bromiley, Grand Rapids, Mich., 1991, 325. Cf. K. Koschorke (ed.), *J.*

Moltmann, Wege zu einer trinitarischen Eschatologie. Festakt anlässlich des 75. Geburtstag von W. Pannenberg, Munich 2004, 11–22.

16   The first to describe the trinitarian perichoresis as 'an image of dancing together' was Patricia Wilson-Kastner, *Faith, Feminism and the Christ*, Philadelphia 1981, 127: 'Because feminism identifies interrelatedness and mutuality—equal, respectful, and nurturing relations—as the basis of the world as it really is and as it ought to be, we can find no better understanding and image of the divine than that of the perfect and open relationship of love.'

17   Gregory of Nyssa thought particularly about the relation between movement and rest in God. See D. Munteanu, 'Die Heilige Dreieinigkeit als heimatlicher Raum unserer ewigen Vollendung' in M. Welker and M. Volf (eds), *Der lebendige Gott als Trinität. Festschrift für J. Moltmann*, Gütersloh 2006, 257–278.

18   For the inception of the new spatial thinking in theology and ecology, cf. S. Bergmann's informative summing up, 'Theology in Its Spatial Turn: Space, Place and Built Environments Challenging and Changing the Images of God', *Religion Compass* 1 (2007) 10.111/j.1749–8171.2007.00025x.

19   M. Volf, *Trinität und Gemeinschaft. Eine ökumensche Ekklesiologie*, Mainz and Neukirchen 1996, 199–203.

20   J. Moltmann, *The Trinity and the Kingdom*, trans. Margaret Kohl, London and San Francisco 1981, 94–96.

21   G. Greshake, op. cit., 552–553, goes into C. J. Jung's construction in detail.

22   J. Moltmann, '"I believe in God the Father." Patriarchal or Non-Patriarchal Talk of God' in *History and the Triune God*, trans. J. Bowden, London 1991, 1–18.

23   '"The Fellowship of the Holy Spirit." On Trinitarian Pneumatology'. *History and the Triune God*, op. cit., 57–69.

24   J. Moltmann, *The Source of Life*, trans. Margaret Kohl, London and Minneapolis 1997, 22–25.

25   This is rightly, but one-sidedly, stressed by B. Nitsche, 'Die Analogie zwischen dem trinitarischen Gottesbild und der communialen Struktur von Kirche' in *Communio—Ideal oder Zerrbild von Kommunikation*, QD 176, Freiburg 1999, 81–114, esp. 86 , following Vatican II's Decree on

Ecumenism *Unitatis redintegratio*, 2. Cf. here also M. Kehl, *Die Kirche. Eine katholische Ekklesiologie*, Würzburg 1992; B. J. Hilberath, 'Kirche als communio. Beschwörungsformel oder Projektbeschreibung?' ThQ 174, 1994, 45–65. From the Protestant side cf. M. Volf, *Trinität und Gemeinschaft*, op. cit., 224–230.

26 See, for example, Vatican II's Dogmatic Constitution on the Church *Lumen Gentium*, 4.

27 Geevarghese Mar Osthathios, *Theology of a Classless Society*, London 1979; idem., *Sharing God and a Sharing World*, Thiruvalla 1995.

28 M. D. Meeks, *God the Economist. The Doctrine of God and Political Economy*, Minneapolis 1989.

29 L. Boff, *Die dreieinige Gott*, Düsseldorf 1987, 173–179. Cf. here T. R. Thompson, *Imitatio Trinitatis. The Trinity as Social Model in the Theologies of Jürgen Moltmann and Leonardo Boff*, ThD diss., Princeton 1996.

30 For more detail here see M. Volf, '"The Trinity Is Our Social Program". The Doctrine of the Trinity and the Shape of Social Engagement', *Modern Theology* 14, 1998, 412ff.

31 G. Freudenthal, *Atom und Individuum im Zeitalter Newtons*, Frankfurt 1982, convincingly shows the inward connection between the atomization of nature and the individualization of the human being in the first modern age that followed Descartes and Newton.

32 H. J. Iwand, *Die Gegenwart des Kommenden*, Siegen 1955.

33 R. Bultmann, *History and Eschatology* (the Gifford Lectures 1955, Edinburgh 1957; first printed in English), especially its final sentences: 'In every moment slumbers the possibility of being the eschatological moment. You must awaken it.'

34 Max Jammer, *Concepts of Space*, Cambridge, Mass., 1954, Oxford 1955, 28.

35 For the fruitfulness of spatial thinking in theology I may point to D. Staniloae, *Orthodoxe Dogmatik* I, Gütersloh 1985, 182ff., and to M. L. Frettlöh, 'Der trinitarische Gott als Raum der Welt. Zur Bedeutung des rabbinischen Gottesnamen maqom für eine topologische Lehre von der immanenten Trinität', in R. Weth (ed), *Der lebendige Gott. Auf den Spuren neuerer trinitarischen Denkens*, Neukirchen-Vluyn 2005, 197–232.

Chapter 15

1   George Herbert (1593–1633), 'The Elixir.' I am indebted to Margaret Kohl for this reference.

Chapter 16

1   J. von Uexküll, *The Theory of Meaning*, trans. B. Stone and H. Weiner, Amsterdam 1982.

2   Ibid., German edition, 161.

3   Jürgen Moltmann, *Science and Wisdom*, trans. Margaret Kohl, London and Minneapolis 2003, 141–157.

4   Jürgen Moltmann, *God in Creation. An Ecological Doctrine of Creation* (The Gifford Lectures 1985–85), trans. Margaret Kohl, London and San Francisco 1985, 244–275.

5   J. von Uexküll, op. cit, German edition 158.

6   P. G. Heltzel, 'Interpreting the Book of Nature in the Protestant Tradition', *The Journal of Faith and Science Exchange*, 2000, 223–239; Guiseppe Tanzella-Nitti, 'The Two Books Prior to the Scientific Revolution', *Annales theologici* 18, 2004, 51–83; H. M. Nobis, 'Buch der Natur' in *Hist W. Ph.*, vol. 1, Basel und Stuttgart 1971, 958–959. I am here following J. Reiter's excellent article 'Bild und Sprache der Gentechnik. Zur Hermeneutik naturwissenschaftlicher Rede und Argumentation' in K. Hilpert und D. Mieth (eds), *Kriterien biomedizinischer Ethik. Theologische Beiträge zum gesellschaftlichen Diskurs*, qd 217, Freiburg 2006, 337–353.

7   On the relationship: revealed theology—theology of nature—natural theology, cf. J. Moltmann, *Experiences in Theology. Ways and Forms of Christian Theology*, trans. Margaret Kohl, London and Minneapolis 2000, I.6: Natural Theology, 64–83.

8   This theory is discussed in detail in H. Blumenberg, *Die Lesbarkeit der Welt*, Frankfurt 1983.

9   L. E. Kay, *Who Wrote the Book of Life? A History of the Genetic Code*, Stanford, Calif., 2000; C. Schwarke, *Die Kultur der Gene. Eine theologische Hermeneutik der Gentechnik*, Stuttgart 2000; J. Reiter, 'Bild und Sprache'. op. cit., 348–351.

10   On the code metaphor, see J. Reiter, 'Bild und Sprache', op. cit., 344–346.

11   For the concept of metaphor in general cf. E. Jüngel and P. Ricoeur, *Metapher. Zur Hermeneutik religiöser Sprache,* EvTh special number, Munich 1974.

12   Thus Max Scheler, *Die Stellung des Menschen im Kosmos,* Munich 1949, 44, 90 (*Man's Place in Nature,* trans. H. Meyerhof, New York 1961).

13   Rupert Sheldrake, *The Presence of the Past,* London 1988, to which I am indebted. I should also like to point to Ilya Prigogine and Isabella Stengers, *Order out of Chaos: Man's New Dialogue with Nature,* London 1984 (based on the authors' *La nouvelle alliance*). For insights into the various connections between science and religion I am indebted to John Polkinghorne, *Exploring Reality. The Intertwining of Science and Religion,* London 2005.

14   Carl Friedrich von Weizsäcker, *Die Geschichte der Natur,* Göttingen 1957.

15   Gernot Böhme, *Für eine ökologische Naturästhetik,* Frankfurt 1989, esp. 121–140: Sprechende Natur. Die Signaturenlehre bei Paracelsus und Jakob Böhme.

16   G. Wehr, *Jakob Böhme,* Hamburg 1971, 93–96.

17   Thomas and Brigitte Görritz, *Der kreative Kosmos. Geist und Materie aus der Quanteninformation,* Elsevier, Spektrum Akademischer Verlag 2007.

18   Jürgen Moltmann, *The Church in the Power of the Spirit,* trans. Margaret Kohl, London 1977, chap. 2.3: The church under the spell of 'the signs of the times', 37–50.

19   Rudolf Bultmann, *Theologie des Neuen Testament,* Tübingen 1953, 5 (*Theology of the New Testament,* trans. K. Grobel, London and New York 1951–55).

20   J. Moltmann, *The Church in the Power of the Spirit,* op. cit., 242–260.

21   Michael Welker, *Schöpfung und Wirklichkeit,* Neukirchen 1995, 64ff. (*Creation and Reality,* trans. J. F. Hoffmeyer, Minneapolis 1999).

22   Cf. Dietrich Bonhoeffer, *Discipleship. Works,* vol. 4, ed. J. D. Godsey and G. B. Kelly, Minneapolis 2001, 90.

23   Ernst Käsemann, 'The Cry for Liberty in the Worship of the Church' in *Perspectives on Paul,* trans. Margaret Kohl, London 1971, 122–137.

24   For more detail cf. J. Moltmann, *God for a Secular Society*, trans. Margaret Kohl, London and Minneapolis 1997, 'The Destruction and Liberation of the Earth: Ecological Theology', 92–116.

Chapter 17

1   The text used in the present essay is Charles Darwin, *The Descent of Man, and Selection in Relation to Sex*, Penguin Books, 2004. For the general discussion see G. Altner (ed.), *Der Darwinismus. Die Geschichte einer Theorie*, Darmstadt 1981; T. Gondermann, *'Evolution und Rasse.' Theoretischer und institutioneller Wandel in der viktorianischen Anthropologie*, Bielefeld 2007: R. Weikart, *From Darwin to Hitler. Evolutionary Ethics, Eugenics and Racism in Germany*, New York 2005. For the theological discussion cf. M. K. Cunningham (ed.), *God and Evolution*, London 2007; J. B. Cobb Jr. (ed.), *Back to Darwin. A Richer Account of Evolution*, Grand Rapids, Mich., 2006.

2   R. Jungk and H. J. Mundt, *Man and his Future*, London 1963; in German, *Das umstrittene Experiment Mensch* ('The Disputed Experiment Man'), Munich 1966.

3   R. Jungk, *The Challenge of Life, Hoffmann LaRoche Basel* 1972. My own lecture, 'Ethics and Biomedical Progress', was published in *The Future of Creation*, trans. Margaret Kohl, London 1979, 131–148.

4   See J. Bauer, *Prinzip Menschlichkeit. Warum wir von Natur aus kooperieren*, Hamburg 2006, to which I am indebted for stimulating the present chapter, and also for material.

5   Kropotkin published this in London during his exile. In 1920, at the time of the Munich soviet republic (*Räterepublik*), Gustav Landauer published the book in German under the title *Gegenseitige Hilfe in der Tier-und Menschenwelt* ('Mutual Aid in the Animal and Human World').

6   J. von Uexküll, *Theoretical Biology*, trans. D. L. Mackinnon, London and New York 1926.

7   E. O. Wilson, *Sociobiology. The New Synthesis*, Cambridge, Mass., and London 1975; R. Dawkins, *The Selfish Gene*, Oxford 1976.

8   J. Bauer, *Prinzip Menschlichkeit*, op. cit., 35.

9   R. Michaelis, *Die ersten fünf Jahre im Leben eines Kindes*, Munich 2006.

10   E. von Weizsäcker (ed.), *Offene Systeme I, Beiträge zur Zeitstruktur von Information, Entropie und Evolution*, Stuttgart 1974; J. Moltmann, 'Creation as an Open System' in *The Future of Creation*, op. cit., 115–130.

Index

249